LIBRARY OF RELIGIOUS BIOGRAPHY

Edited by Mark A. Noll, Nathan O. Hatch,
and Allen C. Guelzo

The LIBRARY OF RELIGIOUS BIOGRAPHY is a series of original biographies on important religious figures throughout American and British history.

The authors are well-known historians, each a recognized authority in the period of religious history in which his or her subject lived and worked. Grounded in solid research of both published and archival sources, these volumes link the lives of their subjects — not always thought of as "religious" persons — to the broader cultural contexts and religious issues that surrounded them. Each volume includes a bibliographical essay and an index to serve the needs of students, teachers, and researchers.

Marked by careful scholarship yet free of footnotes and academic jargon, the books in this series are well-written narratives meant to be *read* and *enjoyed* as well as studied.

LIBRARY OF RELIGIOUS BIOGRAPHY

The Puritan as Yankee

A Life of Horace Bushnell

Robert Bruce Mullin

William B. Eerdmans Publishing Company
Grand Rapids, Michigan / Cambridge, U.K.

Wm. B. Eerdmans Publishing Co.
255 Jefferson Ave. S.E., Grand Rapids, Michigan 49503 /
P.O. Box 163, Cambridge CB3 9PU U.K.

Printed in the United States of America

07 06 05 04 03 02   7 6 5 4 3 2 1

Library of Congress Cataloging-in-Publication Data

Mullin, Robert Bruce.
    The Puritan as Yankee: a life of Horace Bushnell / Robert Bruce Mullin.
        p.   cm.   — (Library of religious biography)
    Includes bibliographical references (p.   ) and index.
    ISBN 0-8028-4252-6 (alk. paper)
        1. Bushnell, Horace, 1802-1876.   2. Congregational churches —
    United States — Clergy — Biography.   3. Theologians — United States —
    Biography.   4. Sociology, Christian — United States — History — 19th century.
    I. Title.   II. Series.

    BX7260.B9 M79   2002
    285.8'092 — dc21
    [B]
                                                                          2002067928

www.eerdmans.com

To Elizabeth,

who has grown

as this book has grown

Contents

Foreword

HORACE BUSHNELL is one of those figures more often talked about than read in American theology. The title he has been given, more or less accurately, is the "father of American liberal Christianity," and he has been treated as a signpost character, marking the end of the old Puritan hegemony and the beginning of Protestant modernism. With Bushnell, New England (and America, for those for whom New England's intellectual history *is* the intellectual history of America) sets aside its stern, impassioned stress on biblical literalness and embarks on a perilous voyage into linguistic uncertainty, inoffensive pluralism, and the secularized morality of the Social Gospel. Certainly there is an element of truth in all this. But as Robert Bruce Mullin is determined to show in this new biography of Bushnell, it is at best a half-truth. Although Bushnell faces in one direction toward Kant and Schliermacher, he turns another, very possessive face toward the New England Calvinist past.

That past is one scarred by the most fundamental conflict of New England's religious experience — the "Puritan dilemma" of desiring a purified church, disciplined to include only the elect, which manages to be at the same time a church-in-society that embraces and directs the life of all members of a community. No one could have successfully pulled this off in England, where maintaining the church-in-society was the only state priority and where calls for purifying the church were treated as politically subversive. But the Puritan colonists of the New England settlements believed that Massachusetts Bay offered them an entirely new context in which to work. The English state was three thousand miles away, and there need be no conflict between the pure church and the church-in-society in New England because there the elect would be both the congregation and the community.

They had not counted on the potential waywardness of their own progeny. The second generation grew up with Calvinist purity taken for granted, and pined for something else. Their attention turned to making this-worldly fortunes in trading rum, slaves, timber, iron, and other goods, and they ducked the daunting tests of church membership invented years before by their greying and worried elders. By the mid-1700s, New England churches had, by and large, decided that it was better to worry about community influence than congregational purity, and so New England Calvinists invented a series of self-deceiving devices that allowed them to pretend to purity while practically lowering the bar of church membership to anyone but the village idiot. These devices included *preparationism* (whereby one gradually "prepared" oneself to be truly converted), the Half-Way Covenant (which allowed those who had been baptized to have their own children baptized, whether or not they ever actually qualified for church membership), and finally open communion (where no one at least better than a pirate or pimp might be excluded from the Lord's Supper).

The resort to these devices disturbed the genuinely pure, and their uneasiness erupted in the 1740s in the Great Awakening. The Awakening was a revival of religious fervor whose secondary purpose (after converting its subjects) was to point an accusing finger at the official New England church establishment for tolerating for so long the watering down of purity. The revivals demonstrated that the struggle of identifying the elect could be, in fact, no struggle at all, since the burning flash of immediate conversion that was the trademark of the revivals eliminated any guesswork. Hence there was no longer any excuse for tolerating impurity. And if this cost the churches members (and even more, cost it control and influence in society), then that was the price purity had always had to pay in an impure world.

It was now the turn of the establishment to be disturbed, not only at the loss of public status such a retreat into purity demanded, but also at the prospect of having to make decisions about the purity of its members, which it was not nearly so confident as the revivalists that it could make. The New England churches fractured along three lines — the *Unitarians,* who had not only rejected purism but also had been drifting for some time into the genteel and undemanding "natural religion" of the English Enlightenment; the revivalists, or *New Lights,* whose intellectual fountainhead was Jonathan Edwards and his followers, who became known as the "New Divinity"; and, occupying a broad spectrum in the middle, the *Old Calvinists.* The Old Calvinists are probably the least well understood of the three, since the revivalists saw anyone to their right as all cut from the same cloth, while the Unitarians viewed the Old Calvinists as mindless traditionalists, lacking both the crude originality of the Edwardseans and their own good Beacon Street breeding.

It is always more interesting to read history through the eyes of the extremists, but it is this amiable failing that has put our understanding of Horace Bushnell so horribly off the mark. The Old Calvinists may have lacked color, but not convictions. Many of them, like Experience Mayhew, were sympathetic to the revivalists; others, like Moses Hemmenway and Moses Mather, were as committed as Edwards to personal holiness but believed that holiness was a virtue that required time, patience, and a decent sense of church and community order to inculcate properly. It was exactly this influence that decisively shaped Bushnell when in 1831, as a twenty-nine-year-old law student, he abandoned legal studies to enter the Theological Department at Yale and study under the doyen of Old Calvinism, Nathaniel William Taylor.

Bushnell had little to say about Taylor in later years, apart from the cryptic comment that Taylor was the man who had taught him how to think for himself. But it is certain that Bushnell learned from Taylor his profound respect for the idea of a church-in-society, a "holy republic" in which the ministry would help guide the affairs of community as well as church. Bushnell also learned from Taylor a suspicion of the precise and sharp-edged theological vocabulary of the New Divinity radicals and a willingness to employ linguistic relativism against the Unitarians.

Bushnell was ordained as pastor of the North Church in Hartford,

Connecticut, in 1833, a congregation founded as an Old Calvinist split-off from the Edwardsean-minded First Congregational Church of Hartford. And Bushnell's first uses of his new ideas, in the immediately controversial *Discourses on Christian Nurture* (1847), would be to offer a strikingly conservative defense of Old Calvinism. The general purpose of *Christian Nurture* was to discuss the principles and structure of family government, especially with reference to children. In so doing, Bushnell took Edwardsean revivalism as an object for criticism almost at once, since he looked upon revivals as a serious and threatening distraction to family government, an erratic and extravagant fireworks show. If membership in families had no spiritual significance, then neither did membership in the church, and Christianity was thereby reduced to being merely an association of consenting adults.

But Bushnell was also operating from a much more romanticized version of the church-in-society than Taylor. The best example of this is his use of the term *organic*. By *organic*, Bushnell meant something very close to what Coleridge had meant by *reason* — a sense of wholeness or connectedness based on intuition and being rather than relationships achieved as acts of will based on language, positive law, or discursive logic. What the antics of the revivalists were predicated upon was the principle of individualism; Bushnell believed that genuine Christian nurture could be recovered only by insisting on the principle of organicism.

All of this, predictably, aroused the ire of the Edwardsean loyalists. Bushnell was attacked on the floor of the Massachusetts General Association, and the publisher of the *Discourses* was intimidated into withdrawing the book from publication, despite Bushnell's plea that he "had done nothing more than to revive, in a modern way, the lost orthodoxy of the church." Surprisingly, at least one major Calvinist theologian defended Bushnell on just those grounds. In the October 1847 issue of the *Biblical Repertory and Princeton Review,* Charles Hodge (who himself had broken several lances with revivalism in New England theology) saluted Bushnell and his "organicism" as allies in the defense of Old School Presbyterianism.

Yet even Hodge recognized a certain ambiguity in Bushnell. Much as Bushnell protested that by *organic* he did not mean merely natural, or that by *nurture* he never meant to suggest that there was no supernatural change of heart required for salvation, the fact was that

Bushnell's organicism made Christian nurture sound like no more than the growth (in Hodge's words) "of a cultivated intellect, or of a majestic tree." Hodge also cannily detected that Bushnell did not seem to be overly careful in how he used theological language. "What he calls supernaturalism is something very different from what is commonly understood by that term." Whatever Bushnell had in common with the Old Calvinists, Hodge still found that Bushnell had "resolved the whole matter into organic laws, explaining away both depravity and grace, and presented the whole subject in a naturalistic attitude," a kind of ecclesiastical sociology.

What wounded Bushnell about such criticism was that his intentions, if not his results, were profoundly conservative. As with many of his contemporaries in Europe — Hengstenberg, Tholuck, Newman — Bushnell's dismissal of propositional language in favor of Kantian notions of spiritual intuition was directed at the easygoing rationalism of the Enlightenment, not at orthodoxy. If he criticized much that passed for orthodox theology, it was only because it seemed to him to have sold itself to the Enlightenment. He was, in that sense, the last of a breed rather than the beginning of a new wave in American theology. He was also the last rather than the first in several other categories. He was, for instance, the last major theological voice to be heard in America from the parsonage, the last to speak from the standpoint of a serving minister and not (as most of his critics did) from an academic desk. He was also the last significant holdout in the professionalization of knowledge in America (he turned down two college presidencies), and his obsession with organicism was his protest against the rampant individualism of American democracy and its loss of connection with the rhythms of rural and natural life.

That his organicism was really intended to be a conservative force often proved embarrassing for Bushnell's later liberal admirers. In 1858 Bushnell published *Nature and the Supernatural*, which he considered his finest statement of organic principles. But in it, and in several subsequent articles, he savagely criticized evolutionary models of development, and in a March 1868 article on "Science and Religion" he attacked Darwin for reducing nature to a mechanical system of cause and effect. Similarly, in one of his least-known works, *Women's Suffrage: The Reform against Nature* (1869), he broke with many of his reform-minded friends to oppose granting the vote to women. In both

cases, Bushnell feared that mechanism and individualism were gnaw-
ing at the vitals of an organic notion of life. Bushnell loved the com-
pleteness of a divine order and longed for a web of connection and relationship imbedded by creation in every living thing, and he could
not abide the idea of a world in which there was either no order at all,
or an order imposed by voluntary, atomistic decisions.

Which is why Robert Bruce Mullin has written such a perceptive
biography of Bushnell. I first met Bruce Mullin on the pages of *Episco-
pal Vision/American Reality: High Church Theology and Social Thought in
Evangelical America* (1986), the book on nineteenth-century Episcopal
High Churchmanship that emerged from Mullin's dissertation at Yale.
Mullin was one of the last graduate students of the late Sydney
Ahlstrom, whose affection for people outside the liberal mainstream of
American religion showed up in quixotic ways in his summa of American church history, *A Religious History of the American People* (1973),
and in his wonderful and mysteriously neglected anthology, *Theology
in America: The Major Protestant Voices from Puritanism to Neo-Orthodoxy*
(1967). As an Episcopalian, Mullin absorbed some of Ahlstrom's curi-
osity for the reactionary bypaths of American religion and applied
them to John Henry Hobart and the High Church party's resolutely
anti-liberal, anti-democratic, anti-commercial, and anti–Puritan-
Protestant-revivalistic-individualistic high churchmanship.

The interest this held for Mullin (now a member of the faculty at
Hobart's favorite preserve, the Episcopal Church's General Theological
Seminary) would seem to be light-years removed from the white,
clapboarded universe of Horace Bushnell. To the contrary, no one could
be more able than Bruce Mullin to capture the fundamentally conservative core of Bushnell's thinking. For Bushnell (with allowances for the
differences in theological dialect between the Hudson River valley and
the Connecticut) suffered from the same suspicion of democracy, the
same anxiety to anchor the relentless drift of American society to an orthodox past, and the same willingness to use tradition as the bridge by
which to cross blindfolded from the past to the present as did Hobart.
Bushnell thus stands with one foot in the past and the other in the New
England future. He did not cause that future, but he was, in ways that
would surprise him, the occasion and the license for it.

ALLEN C. GUELZO

THE PURITAN AS YANKEE

Introduction

U NDERTAKING a biographical study is always a risky endeavor. Students approach their long-dead central character with a bucketful of assumptions and presuppositions, but as with any person-to-person encounter, the subjects all too often have surprises of their own. They will not stand there and be sketched in the author's own image. The immense reality of the subject forces students to jettison some of their most cherished presuppositions and begin to see the subjects in their own terms.

The following study of the pastor-theologian Horace Bushnell is the product of such an encounter. For students of American religious history Bushnell is (or has been) one of the most familiar of figures. He has usually been recognized as the father of American theological liberalism, the great champion of Christian education, and the paradigmatic figure of nineteenth-century American Protestantism. Indeed, he is often seen as parallel to another famous New England pastor-theologian, Jonathan Edwards. According to the standard account, both typified and shaped their given centuries — Edwards the eighteenth and Bushnell the nineteenth. Edwards responded to the challenges of the Enlightenment and forged the "New England Theology," a creative reinterpretation of traditional Calvinism. Bushnell, responding to a world shaped by Romanticism, a new middle-class culture, and a bevy of new intellectual questions, laid the groundwork for a post-Calvinistic liberal American theology.

For these reasons he has been one of the most written about figures of the nineteenth-century religious landscape. Scores of monographs, articles, and dissertations have been penned concerning his life and ideas. The popularity of Bushnell as a subject may in part stem from the breadth of his interests. Ranging far beyond narrow theological questions, he offered opinions on race, language, the Civil War, immigration, city planning, and many other topics. Whatever a researcher's interest might be, one can usually find a quotation from him to make a point. He has generally been recognized as the great American theologian of the nineteenth century, and accordingly in surveys of this period's theology he often appears as the token American. He has also been viewed as the key to understanding the great theological and religious shift that many American Protestants underwent in the decades following the Civil War. His *Christian Nurture* has been seen as almost prophetic of the gradual abandonment of a conversion-oriented piety in favor of a Christian-education model. *Nature and the Supernatural* has been pictured as a visionary response to the crisis of religion and science that followed the publication of Charles Darwin's *On the Origin of Species*. And his famous oration "The Age of Homespun" has been seen as a moving account of the old world of rural New England as it prepared to enter the new.

Like all common pictures there is truth in this portrait. But its weakness is that it does not take the person of Bushnell seriously. It is more concerned with how the man paved the way for a new generation than with the man himself. The more one encounters the person of Horace Bushnell the clearer it becomes that he does not easily fit into this picture. There is a stubborn independence that fights against any easy caricature. And this flinty character forces one back to the great writings upon which his fame rests, at which point one discovers that here too there is discord between perception and actuality. A perusal of the early editions of *Christian Nurture*, for example, shows far more interest in New England ecclesiastical controversies than in the idea of Christian motherhood. A close reading of *Nature and the Supernatural* likewise uncovers not a merging of nature and supernature into some pantheistic porridge but rather a spirited defense of modern miracles and glossolalia. Indeed, one even discovers crucial discontinuities between the idyllic picture etched in "The Age of Homespun" and what we know about Bushnell's own youth.

The following is a new life of Horace Bushnell and it hopes to do justice to these discords. At the same time, however, it rests on the earlier studies. No biographer can hope to avoid the influence of Bushnell's first two biographers, his daughter Mary Cheney and his student Theodore T. Munger. Cheney not only included in her biography the majority of her father's existing correspondence — a fact of great importance since the originals are now lost — she also shaped the classic narrative of her father's life, including his rural roots, his crisis of faith, his challenge to the religious authorities of the time, his prosecution and perseverance, and, finally, his late honors. The picture that emerges from her pages is that of a great New England patriarch. Munger provided the first (and still best) interpretation of Bushnell's thought. For Munger, Bushnell is the one who liberates the New England theological tradition. "He was a theologian," Munger explained, "as Copernicus was an astronomer"; he set the course for the new understanding. But each picture contains a key weakness. Cheney, in painting her father as a New England patriarch, softens the sharp edges of the picture. Few would realize after reading *The Life and Letters of Horace Bushnell* that he was a first-class controversialist who could cut down an opponent with glee. Munger views his subject from the next generation, showing how Bushnell laid the groundwork for the new theology, but is less interested in those ideas of Bushnell that were not taken up by his successors.

I try to see Bushnell as a figure of his time. He was both a product of and a force behind the northern American society (particularly that of New England) of the middle of the nineteenth century, or the years between 1830 and 1865. It is true, as many have written, that these were years that saw an old traditional society shifting and a new order taking its place. But for those who lived during these years the complete breakup of the old order was by no means certain. Like every generation, they were far more in tune with the immediate past than they were with the coming future. A person of Bushnell's age — that is, an individual born near the turn of the century — could remember that well into his teens Connecticut had been governed by the standing order that bound together a religious and social vision. She would

3

have been aware that in her youth the religious world of New England was still united, and that the orthodox-Unitarian split was a recent occurrence. Even when people of the time sensed change, they knew not what the future would bring. A sensitive observer in the early 1830s would have been aware that the homogeneity of Connecticut society was giving way, but he would have had no inkling of what that society would be like by the end of the century. Likewise, although Bushnell's generation had experienced changes, it would have been unclear whether or not those changes would be permanent. Was the traditional order of the society really dead or could it be revived? Was the sundering of the religious world of New England irreversible? This generation lived their lives in a recognized tension between the old and the new, and they had no certain knowledge as to which would prevail. It was to such a generation that Horace Bushnell ministered, and it was to this set of questions that he addressed his labors.

It is the thesis of this study that Horace Bushnell was a bold innovator, reconceptualizing in his writing and orations almost everything that crossed his path, and a great tinkerer, always interested in improving that which he found before him. It is also the thesis here, however, that these innovations were all motivated by a profoundly conservative desire to preserve the values and confidences of the world of his youth. He was both a Yankee and a Puritan: a Yankee in his love of innovation, a Puritan in his abiding trust in the values he first learned as a child in Connecticut. He reflected the paradox that the historian Richard Hofstadter used to describe Woodrow Wilson: "even as a reformer, he held up for approval not so much the novel aspects of his work as its value in sustaining the continuity of tradition."

The portrait of Bushnell offered here is the "public" Bushnell. It does not focus on him as a devoted husband or loving father, nor does it concentrate upon his role as a faithful pastor to his flock, although all of these were parts of his life. Rather, the focus here is on the Bushnell who wrestled long and hard with a series of challenges that confronted his generation. How was religion to be grounded? How was it best communicated? How could a people maintain their virtue in a changing world? What was distinctive about America as a religious people and as a political experiment? To each of these questions Bushnell directed his energy, and his labors lie at the heart of this study. These might be intellectual questions, but they are in no way abstruse intellectual questions. They cut to the very heart of what it meant to live, work, and pray in this new American context. Furthermore, they were not simply Bushnell's questions; they were also the questions of his generation.

In the following narrative I have attempted to recast the standard picture of Bushnell, locating the social purpose of his many innovations, and trying to interpret him as a figure of his age. My narrative differs from earlier ones in four distinct ways. The first is that I have placed much more emphasis on the importance of Bushnell's European travels of 1845-46. Much of my emphasis flows from a careful reading of his unpublished travel journal for this trip. Bushnell's handwriting was terrible, and many passages are virtually indecipherable. This barrier caused most earlier students to avoid his manuscript journal and to rely on the printed excerpts found in Cheney's biography. But his European sojourn, I will suggest, had a crucial effect on his later career and offers enticing hints of the origins of some of his most arresting ideas.

Second, I have linked for the sake of common analysis the writings of one of Bushnell's most productive periods, those composed between his return from England in 1846 and the publication of *God in Christ* early in 1849. These include two of his most famous books (*God in Christ* and *Christian Nurture*) as well as two of his most famous essays ("Christian Comprehensiveness" and "Barbarism the First Danger"). These works have often been treated separately, but when grouped together they reveal a concern of great importance for Bushnell: a desire to restore the lost religious unity of the children of the Puritans. Although treating very different topics, each contributes to his agenda of overcoming the division that had occurred between the orthodox (the term used to refer to the Trinitarian evangelicals) and the Unitarians.

Third, I have attempted to shape the narrative in light of the tremendous renascence of American religious historiography that has emerged over the past forty years. It is now possible to contextualize religious discussions of the period to a far more nuanced degree than was possible in the late 1950s when Barbara Cross penned her still influential *Horace Bushnell: Minister to a Changing America*. In particular, our knowledge of the intricacies of Protestant evangelical thought has freed us of a number of stereotypes. This has allowed for a fresh examination of the great controversy over *God in Christ*. The standard account of this episode was forged by Bushnell's later liberal defenders and failed to take seriously the arguments of his critics. This approach has in turn obscured some of the more important aspects of the controversy, including its repercussions in England. I have attempted to offer a new evaluation of the "Bushnell controversy" in chapter seven.

Finally, I have both elevated and reinterpreted the significance and meaning of Bushnell's *Nature and the Supernatural,* going so far as to suggest that it is Bushnell's greatest and most original work. According to the interpretation I offer, the book is primarily concerned with defending the idea of divine personal activity in the world, the idea that God was truly involved in the world. Bushnell's interest in God's willful activity and his fascination with the miraculous — particularly with modern miracles — set him apart from his successors. The significance of the volume is that it reflects still another paradox: that Bushnell can equally be seen as a proto-liberal and a proto-Pentecostal.

The Horace Bushnell that emerges from these pages differs in one final way from the usual picture. He is not presented as the great nineteenth-century American theologian. He was far too impetuous and impatient to write theology in any traditional sense. As Frank Hugh Foster, a historian of the New England theology, observed over a century ago, "he neither carefully criticized the positions of his opponents, scrupulously refuted them, nor elaborately defended his own." Bushnell was far more a preacher than a theologian in any technical sense, but what he lacked as a technical theologian he made up for as a religious genius. His most moving and insightful passages are not his discussions of doctrine but his reflections on how one might believe or on what anchors religious belief in a world of change. If there is one unifying theme in his many-faceted life and career it was this concern for religious belief. In this sense he bears interesting parallels with his English contemporary, the great John Henry Newman. Although they were different in so many ways — Newman the Anglican turned Roman Catholic and Bushnell the proud Puritan suspicious of Canterbury and Rome — there is in both of them that recognition that belief could no longer be assumed. The old world where the God of Christianity was anchored in the landscape like the proverbial whitewashed church on the proverbial New England village green was dead. One now had to be far more purposeful, and indeed bolder, in anchoring religious faith. Both men saw the world of the nineteenth century as a world in which true religious vitality was but a shadow of its earlier strength, and both believed that creative thought and action were needed to make it real again. This awareness gave to Newman and Bushnell a sense of innovation yet also a deep conservatism.

It was this concern for religious reality that led Bushnell to find value in both Friedrich Schleiermacher and Charles Finney. It made him interested in both family nurture and speaking in tongues. Ultimately it connected for him many things that we, living in a later age, no longer seem able to connect. But here too he was a man of his age. If some decisions and divisions were not yet seen to be irreversible, other decisions and divisions were not yet imagined.

At the time of the hundredth anniversary of his birth (1902), most of his works were carefully republished. He was held up as one of the morning stars of New England liberalism and, throughout the early twentieth century, was invoked as one who could help men and women of the time better understand their own age. Now, at the time of the two-hundredth anniversary of his birth, this study is offered not to cast light on our own age, but rather his.

*   *   *

This study had its origins twenty years ago in a quick comment made to me by the late Hans Frei, one of the great theological figures of the latter twentieth century. When I told him I was reading Horace Bushnell, he paused and said, "I have been trying to make sense of Bushnell for twenty-five years, and I still find him confusing." If a professional theologian like Frei could not understand Bushnell's theology, I reasoned, then perhaps he was not the great American theologian as I had theretofore assumed. What was he, then, and what was the source of his influence?

In attempting to answer this question I have along the way incurred many debts. Conversations with William Adler, Richard W. Bailey, Randall Balmer, Russell Richey, David Hall, George Marsden, Daniel W. Howe, Richard Bushman, Brooks Holifield, Conrad Cherry, Donald Scott, Mark Massa, Harry Stout, Mark Noll, Cynthia Miller, and Donald Dayton have helped clarify my ideas. Grant Wacker has not only been a good friend and better critic but has read the entire manuscript and offered his insights. Parts of this study were presented at three scholarly colloquiums: the Southeastern Colloquium on American Religion in Durham, North Carolina, the Columbia University Seminar in American Religion, and the Columbia University Seminar in Religion, and the criticisms offered in these venues have improved this work.

Since this work is so much based upon printed sources, it could not have been accomplished without the help of numerous libraries. The staffs of the libraries of Duke University, Duke Divinity School, the University of North Carolina–Chapel Hill, North Carolina State University, Harvard University, Columbia University, and Yale University, as well as the New York Public Library, the New York Historical Society, the Connecticut Historical Society, the British Library, the Bodlein Library, and the Dr. Williams Library, were uniformly helpful. Special mention must be made of the libraries of three institutions: Union Theological Seminary (and in particular Seth Kasten), Yale Divinity School (and in particular Martha Smalley and Paul Stuehrenberg), and the General Theological Seminary (and in particular David Green). I will always be in the debt of the kindness and consideration of these three institutions.

I wish to express appreciation to the University Seminars at Columbia University for help in publication. Material in this work was presented at the University Seminar of Religion and the University Seminar on Religion in America.

Part of chapter eight has appeared in different form in an essay published first in *Church History.* I am grateful for permission to use this material.

I wish to thank the Department of Philosophy and Religion at North Carolina State University (and in particular former head Tom Regan) for a sabbatical leave that allowed me to begin this project, and one from the General Theological Seminary that allowed me to complete it. I am also indebted to support offered by the Conant Fund of the Episcopal Church during my second sabbatical that allowed me to obtain crucial resources.

I also must thank the faculty, students, and staff of General Theological Seminary for providing such a warm and supportive environment for doing scholarship. Writing in a residential community in which so many people have taken an interest in the project has been an enriching experience that I have treasured.

Finally, as always I must thank my wife (Viola) and daughter (Elizabeth) for their patience and support. In the course of this book they have experienced many changes, but, like Bushnell, I hope that the organic connections of family have only become stronger.

1 Taking the Measure of a Man

IN 1851 an embattled New England pastor, with storms of theological controversy threatening his ministry, was invited to speak at the centennial celebration of the county of Litchfield, from whence he hailed. The people of Litchfield, which lay in the far northwestern corner of Connecticut, chose the pastor not only because of his roots there but, in all probability, because of his reputation as a powerful orator. The pastor's address was entitled "The Age of Homespun." In it he quickly passed through biblical images of spinning — in particular Lemuel's praise (in the book of Proverbs) of his wife who "layeth her hands to the spindle" — and came to the theme of his talk. He urged his hearers to recall a world that was quickly vanishing, remembering the Litchfield of their youth as a "Puritan Arcadia" inhabited by hard-working and self-sufficient men and women; a people who were "not in trade, whose life center[ed] in the family, homebred in their manners, primitive and simple in their character, inflexible in their piety, hospitable without show, intelligent without refinement."

The speaker touched on many aspects of the life of this Puritan Arcadia but lingered on two scenes. The first was an evening gathering. After working all day on their farms the citizenry would gather in the farmhouse of some neighbor to tell stories, sing, and enjoy each other's company. "They are serious and gay by turns," he remembered; "the young folks go on with some play while the fathers and mothers are discussing some hard point of theology in the minister's last sermon." Then, after snacking on the simple fare of apples (carefully dried over the fireplace), hickory nuts, doughnuts, and cider, they end the evening with prayer. The world of homespun, he reminded his listeners, was a community "in the sacred retreats of natural feeling, truth and piety."

The second scene he lingered on was the meetinghouse. There, in common dress, the people gather. The building is simple, and seating is based not on wealth (as it is in 1851) but in deference to age. The worship shows no signs of affectation or mannerism; it is as plain and as direct as the physical setting. The people have come to hear the preacher. The congregation "appear like men who have a digestion for strong meat, and have no conception that trifles more delicate can be of any account to feed the system. Nothing is dull that has the matter in it, nothing long that has not exhausted the matter." The laws of God were to be followed, particularly those concerning keeping the Sabbath. There was iron in the wills of the citizens of this Puritan Arcadia.

This book is a study of that embattled minister, Horace Bushnell, perhaps the most famous preacher-theologian of nineteenth-century America. He was a man with a wide array of interests: language theory, political thought, and urban planning, to name but a few. He was a great public figure in his era, with wide influence. But I have chosen to begin not with Bushnell the public figure, but with the Bushnell of Litchfield. An understanding of the world of Litchfield and Connecticut is necessary if one is to understand Bushnell, for he would reflect many of the hopes, ideas, prejudices, and presuppositions of his native state.

PURITANS AND YANKEES

From the perspective of the twenty-first century it is hard to recapture the world of old Connecticut. Connecticut was a Puritan commonwealth unlike others. Its distinctiveness rested in large part on two documents: the Charter of 1662, which ordered the political life of the colony, and the Saybrook Platform of 1708, which ordered the church.

Both church and government worked together for a common goal. As one seventeenth-century cleric explained, "God hath designed the Civil Government of his People to concenter with Ecclesiastical Administrations: and (though by different Mediums) they are both levelled at the same end; the maintaining of Piety and promoting of a Covenant walk with him."

The charter was a deceptively simple document. It provided for the establishment of a governor, deputy governor, and a General Assembly consisting of an upper house (of magistrates or the "Council") and a lower house (of deputies). All were to be elected by the inhabitants of the colony. The Assembly in turn was given the authority "from tyme to tyme to Make, Ordaine, and Establish All manner of wholesome and reasonable lawes . . . not contrary to this Realme of England." The charter's defenders lauded it for its combination of democratic freedom and stability. "Connecticut is a singular phenomenon in the political hemisphere," wrote one proud native son; "such a degree of freedom was never before united with such a degree of stability." There were some aspects of the charter that reflected this concern for order. Nominations for the Assembly were made in September, but elections were not held until the following April, seven months later. Elections had nothing to do with the passions of the moment, in other words; voting took place only after a thorough and sober examination of the candidates, particularly their character. As one explained, "In a community so small and so intelligent as that of Connecticut, it is impossible that within this time their character should be unknown." The act of voting was also public. The voter handed a slip of paper to the selectman when his candidate's name was called. Both practices were inclined to favor incumbents, who were valued for their experience and insights, so officeholders were rarely rejected by the voters. It was not without reason that Connecticut became known as "the land of steady habits."

The charter also explicitly recognized the importance of religion. Indeed, the express purpose of the political structure set forth in its pages was to ensure that the inhabitants might be "religiously, peaceably, and civilly Governed." Likewise, the end of the colony was to be the "knowledge and obedience of the onely true God and Saviour of Mankind." Twenty-three years earlier the community had dedicated the new colony to God, and the charter continued to see this as the duty of the governors. The Congregational Church was established by law and ecclesiastical societies were given the right to levy assessments in support of the church. Although religious dissent was legalized in 1708, the requirement that even nonconformists had to continue to support the established church was doggedly maintained. After 1727 members of the Church of England were no longer required to attend the established Congregational Church or to pay the church rate to the established church, but were allowed instead to have it directed to their own communion. Gradually other churches were granted similar (or alternative) exceptions, and in 1789 the legislature passed a general toleration act. This freed all dissenters who could present a certificate of membership in some religious society recognized by law from paying the Congregationalist tithe. But for a decade and a half after the birth of Horace Bushnell the Congregational Church was established by law and was a key part of the standing order (the careful interrelationship of magistrates, Congregational clergy, and prominent citizens) of Connecticut. The established church in turn helped buttress the society. On Election Day its ministers dutifully reminded voters of their religious responsibility, and throughout the year they helped shape the education of the colony and participated in public events such as the opening of the General Court.

But the religious responsibility of the governors did not end with establishing a church. By law, the governor was required to be a member of the established church. Furthermore, the legal code of the colony was written to insure godliness and true religion. Laws protected the Sabbath and morality and assailed vice. In the seventeenth century the head of a household who failed to catechize his family and servants ran the risk of being called before the grand jury. As late as the beginning of the nineteenth century adultery was still punished by whipping and branding the letter "A" on the guilty parties' foreheads; the penalty for exhibiting a theatrical performance was a fine of fifty dollars, and the penalty for either men or women cross-dressing was a fine of seventeen dollars.

The combination of all of this was to make the citizenry of Connecticut a remarkably sober community. Its native sons boasted of the lack of crime in the region, and visitors viewing public gatherings, such as the inauguration of a governor, had been known to ask, "where are your rabble?" Connecticut under the charter was a society of order and sobriety, a fact which assured the success and well-being of the body-politic. "The inhabitants of Connecticut," wrote one leader, "are the only people within my knowledge, to understand the nature of elected government."

The charter organized the governance of the colony of Connecticut, but it was a charter and not a constitution. It was merely a limited document that structured the system of government. It did not establish a series of checks and balances in order to assure freedom. Freedom and liberty rested rather on the virtue of the people and the responsibility of the legislators. While other colonies at the end of the eighteenth century abandoned their colonial charters for new and more elaborate constitutions, the citizenry of Connecticut would have none of it. As one commentator wrote, in Connecticut one found a citizenry "so devoted to good order and stable government, as to invest their public functionaries with all the power of government unencumbered by that train of scrupulous and useless provisions which embarrass many modern American constitutions." Constitutions smacked of modern and suspect political theories. Connecticut residents might sufficiently mistrust non–New Englanders to support a constitution for the new nation, but they would have none for themselves. It would not be until 1818 that the colonial charter would be abandoned and a new constitution put in its place. If defenders of the standing order were wary of constitutions, they were even more suspect of Bills of Rights. The standing order emphasized duty and responsibility; language of inalienable rights and human freedom sounded foreign and threatening, and one had to be careful not to accept such language too quickly. The Connecticut legislature finally ratified the Bill of Rights only in 1939!

The established Congregational Church was part of the standing order, but what distinguished Connecticut Congregationalism from that of its neighbors was the Saybrook Platform. Church leaders in the opening years of the eighteenth century had sensed a waning of piety among the laity and took action to reverse this trend by tightening both the doctrine and the order of their church through the Platform. The Platform recognized the authority of the Westminster Confession of Faith as modified by the Savoy Conference of 1658 and included a statement on church order, but its most important element was its tightening of church discipline. A series of consociations of churches were established throughout the colony. These were usually coterminous with the county boundaries but were occasionally smaller. The consociations were standing councils of both clergy and laity who exercised discipline. Individual congregations were urged to make use of the consociations "upon all occasions ecclesiasticall" such as questions of ordination, installation of clergy, and clerical dismissals. Clergy also gathered in "associations," and these groups were concerned with consultation and licensing of ministers. The Saybrook Platform nudged Connecticut Congregationalism in the direction of Presbyterianism, in which clergy of a given area rather than the individual congregations themselves would have control over ordination and discipline. Fellow pastors could now sit in judgment on their own brothers. There was never a unanimity about what the ultimate power of the consociations and associations was. What would happen if a congregation rejected the decision of the consociation? Just as the Charter of 1662 emphasized duty and discipline over rights and privileges in the realm of the government, the Saybrook Platform emphasized these same virtues in the church.

The Saybrook Platform would have one further effect on the Congregational Church of Connecticut. Through its influence Connecticut Congregationalists gradually moved from the orbit of their fellow Congregationalists in Massachusetts (who had rejected a similar platform) toward the world of the Presbyterians of the Middle Colonies. The Plan of Union of 1801 between Connecticut Congregationalists and the Presbyterians can be seen as an offspring of the Saybrook Platform.

The Charter of 1662 would govern the political world of Connecticut until 1818; the Saybrook Platform would adjudicate the ecclesiastical order until the second half of the nineteenth century. Both reflected the virtues of order and stability that were deeply embedded in the citizens of the Nutmeg State. From the time of Thomas Hooker (the founder of the colony) in the seventeenth century the importance of law abidance as both a civic and religious virtue had been stressed. Wherever the citizens of Connecticut moved, they brought with them this heritage of order and stability. Neat New England–style villages would pepper the Northern states of the union, each with its village green with church and courthouse testifying to the colonial heritage.

This was a heritage of which Bushnell was intensely proud. He enjoyed waxing eloquent about the memory of the Puritans and vigorously defended them against any vilification. Much of the life and ca-reer of Horace Bushnell can be seen as an attempt to rescue and re-establish that sense of order. He recalled being sent, while still a child, on a Saturday afternoon to fetch some apples, only to be refused by the farmer who explained that Horace would not be able to get them home before sundown, and would then be guilty of violating the Sabbath by laboring on it. It was a much older Bushnell who decried the profana-tion of the Sabbath in gold-rush California, commenting that Sunday "is a day that corrupts more virtues, ruins more character, than all the six days together!" He was also fearful of any collapse of order and of the role of the "rabble." One of his early published works was entitled "Barbarism the First Danger," and in it he warned of the fate of com-munities untouched by true religion.

But Connecticut society was never simply about Puritanism. There was another element in the Nutmegger's character that can be called the Yankee. The Connecticut Yankee made famous in the Mark Twain novel was not an invention, but a reality. The people of Con-necticut were tinkerers; they were inventors. They had to be. One needed ingenuity to get the most out of their rock-filled fields, and they were always inventing some new technique or gadget to make their tasks a little easier. One foreign visitor, Michel Chevalier, ob-served that there was hardly an artisan in the state who could not claim credit for inventing a tool or machine. They were not particu-larly interested in theory, either; it was the results that mattered. The Yankee tinkerer was typically not a trained expert — indeed, where could one get such a training? — but an individual who followed his own sense and instincts and applied his ingenuity directly to the task at hand. Yankees were known for their stubborn independence, and foreigners noted one other quality in the Yankee character: a spirit of innovation. "There is not a man of much consideration who has not his scheme for a railroad, a project for a village or town, or who has not *in petto* . . . some grand speculation." Yankees on the frontier were always scheming, always striving, always moving. The true Yankee "is de-voured with a passion for locomotion, he cannot stay in one place; he must come and go, he must stretch his limbs and keep his muscles in play."

Bushnell was not merely a Puritan, he was also a Yankee. Some-times the inherited traits are obvious to see. As a boy he was always inventing things. He reconstructed his father's engine for carding wool, devised a lure for catching fish that needed no bait, and fiddled with the sail of his boat to get the maximum power from the wind. But sometimes the sense of ingenuity and stubborn independence surfaced in other ways. One friend told a story of a camping trip he took with an elderly Bushnell in New York State. Despite his guide's assurance to the contrary, Bushnell became convinced that there had to be a shorter path between their camp and their fishing spot. To prove the guide wrong he struck out on his own. Along the way he became stuck in an oozy maze of tamarack swamp and so exerted himself that his lungs began to hemorrhage. His friend feared for his safety. But Bushnell would not turn back. Eventually he reached the fishing spot and declared triumphantly that he had indeed proved that his way was shorter!

At first sight the sober and well-ordered Puritan, living in his land of steady habits, and the innovative and stubbornly independent Yankee, always scheming to improve himself and the world, seem worlds apart. But both groups reflect aspects of the Connecticut heritage and both shed light on Horace Bushnell. He was both a Puritan and a Yankee — a Yankee tinkerer who tinkered with the Puritan tradition in order to refashion it for a rapidly changing world.

LITCHFIELD AND NEW PRESTON

It was into one of the epicenters of this Connecticut culture that Horace Bushnell was born on the fourteenth of April in 1802. There had been Bushnells in Connecticut since 1639 but they were comparative newcomers to the town of Litchfield (in Litchfield County). In the far northwest corner of the state, the town had only been founded in 1720, but by the turn of the century it had become a prosperous and distinguished place of over four thousand inhabitants. Its minister described the town accordingly: "a delightful village on a fruitful hill, richly endowed with schools, both professional and scientific, with its venerable governors and judges, with its learned lawyers, and senators, and representatives . . . and with a population enlightened and respectable, Litchfield was now in its glory." During the Revolution it had increased in prosperity and importance, both because it was safe from

British attack and because it stood on the key supply road between Boston and West Point. It was also an educational center and boasted both the first female academy in the nation and the first law school. These too brought prosperity and distinction to the town. The prosperity of the time also allowed the citizens of Litchfield to spruce up their city. Some had begun a tree planting campaign to make the village more elegant. This, to be sure, puzzled some older residents. "We have worked so hard in our day and just finished getting the woods cleared," one man complained, "and now they are bringing the trees back again." But the refinement of Litchfield was not limited to foliage. The presence of a law school and a female academy meant that there was a constant swirl of cotillions and other events.

And then there was the church. The meetinghouse of the established Congregational Church was a center of authority in Litchfield. Litchfield County was one of the most religiously homogenous areas of Connecticut, and many of its ministers were busy stirring up the piety of their flocks through great works of revival. We have a description of the building itself from a contemporary of Bushnell's: "To my childish eyes," one woman reminisced, "our old meeting-house was an awe inspiring thing. To me it seemed fashioned very nearly on the model of Noah's Ark and Solomon's temple, as set forth in the pictures in my Scripture Catechism — pictures which I did not doubt were authentic copies." Like other meetinghouses of the period the central feature was a pulpit with a sounding board above it. "How magnificent to my eye, seemed the turnip-like canopy that hung over the minister's head, hooked by a long iron rod to the wall above! And how apprehensively did I consider the question of what should become of the preacher if it should fall!"

It was into this little world that Horace was born. But he did not quite fit. There was the question of religion. In this center of the standing order neither of his parents were members of the established church. His mother, Dotha Bishop Bushnell, had been reared in the Episcopal Church — the ancient *bête noire* of the standing order — with its emphasis upon sacraments, liturgy, and episcopacy rather than upon preaching. His father, Ensign Bushnell, was drawn to the new Methodists. The elder Bushnell's family had left the established church for Methodism perhaps as early as 1789. They had been attracted by the Methodist preachers' emphasis on human freedom and their rejection of predestination. Although Horace's parents would both eventually join the established church, they were outsiders. There was also the question of location. In 1805 the Bushnells moved from Litchfield to the rural village of New Preston fourteen miles away. There the senior Bushnell combined farming with manufacturing. He constructed a mill for finishing domestic cloth and a carding machine to which neighbors could bring their wool. New Preston offered a better supply of waterpower than Litchfield, and the hills surrounding Lake Waramaug were beautiful. Still, New Preston was a far less refined place than Litchfield, and the elements of high culture were lacking. The Bushnells did what they could. Horace remembered going into the nearby woods to dig up shade trees to replant in front of their house to beautify the scene. Nonetheless, New Preston would always be a far cry from Litchfield.

Horace's parents differed not only in their religion but also in their temperaments and in their influence on their son. Ensign Bushnell, who served as a justice of the peace along with his farming and manufacturing, seems to have been a solid, phlegmatic, but not overly intelligent individual. A childhood acquaintance of Horace remembers that the senior Bushnell often had to consult his teenage son to clarify difficult questions that came before him as a justice of the peace. In addition, he was quite strict. One of the very few stories Horace Bushnell recounted about his father described a serious "flogging" he had received from his father which always reminded him of the judgment of God. Almost nothing else is recorded about Ensign Bushnell. Perhaps, however, the "wiry patriarch of homespun" that Horace Bushnell later described was modeled after Ensign, and if so we have a fuller picture that softens some of the ruggedness surrounding the elder Bushnell. Here, "the man who is heard threshing in his barn of a winter evening by the light of a lantern . . . will be seen driving his team next day, the coldest day of the year, to a distant wood-lot to draw a load of wood for a present to his minister." Likewise, the trip of the sturdy farmer to Hartford or Bridgeport "to exchange the little surplus of his year's production . . . and taking his boy along to show him the great world" may also have been an autobiographical glimpse of the senior Bushnell.

Of far more influence was Horace's mother. A simple woman, with only a common school education, she did not cut an imposing figure in the eyes of the world. But in the domain of her household she shone. Feeding and clothing her six children, boarding the hired farm hands, helping out at the mill, she did much to provide for her children and her household. She may have been the model of the women of homespun, who "made coats every year like Hannah for their children's bodies, and lined their memory with catechism." And, indeed, Dotha Bushnell also oversaw the education of her children. But what Horace remembered most about her was her character, particularly her sense of discretion and judgment. "She was . . . the only person I have known," he later remarked, "in the close intimacy of years who never did an inconsiderate, imprudent, or any way excessive thing that required to be afterwards mended." She took great interest in her oldest son, encouraging him in his education. He in turn was devoted to her. In childhood he was her constant companion. It was also his mother who snatched him from a fast-rushing stream when he had fallen off a footbridge. She caught the young toddler by his hair, pulling him to safety moments before he might have drowned. If Horace Bushnell remembered his father for enforcing the judgment of God, it was the mother he remembered as his savior.

Education for the Bushnell children continued in local schools. The emphasis on learning was still another part of the Puritan tradition on which Bushnell would later wax nostalgic. He recalled for his hearers the days in which the schoolteacher "boarded round" with the different families of the village, and described how the status of a pupil was measured by the quality of wood he or she provided for the common stove. He christened these local schools "primitive universities of homespun, where your mind was born." The teacher who inspired these words was a man named Perry Averill, who taught the five-year-old Horace in 1808. Although only under his tutelage for a year, Bushnell always remembered Averill as opening his eyes to a wider world. "My enthusiasm," he wrote, "my delight in my teacher I do not forget, and never lost the benefit of it." Yet by contemporary accounts he was not a stellar student. One man recalled that ideas seemed to flow rapidly from him, and he uttered them fluently, "[b]ut I used to think that he lacked the power to concentrate upon any subject for more than a moment." Although he learned his lessons quickly, his vigor and impatience stood between him and greater learning. "He would rather play than study," remembers another. After attending different local schools in 1818 he entered the New Preston Academy, but his father's machines were more attractive to him than was higher learning.

Still another part of his education was music — a touchy subject among the citizens of New England, whose forebears had protested the elaborate music of the Church of England, with its fancy organs and professional choirs. In the meetinghouses first built in the New World organs were absent and singing was reduced to the metrical psalms. Some preachers continued to condemn music as being perverting; the Methodist evangelist Lorenzo Dow condemned schools of music as "Schools of Babylon" that strove to "divert the mind and touch the passions." But in practice there was far more openness. The great Congregationalist evangelist Lyman Beecher went to singing school outside of New Haven, where he was instructed in Andrew Law's *Select Harmony,* and singing schools flourished in New England beginning in the early eighteenth century. But Bushnell was self-taught in music. His mother provided him with a book of music, and, by carefully comparing the notes, intervals, and times on the page of music with the song his mother sang to him, he taught himself to read music.

The result was that the Bushnell household was "filled with hymns and glees and such like humorous and sentimental pleasures." But the power of music for Horace was greater than that of mere pleasure. It had, to begin with, a social dimension. In his recollection of the earlier age Bushnell described young persons coming together in the evening "round some village queen of song, and chasing away the time in ballads and glees." Music, Bushnell believed, quite literally harmonized a group, uniting it and ordering it, and giving it a common shape. Music was the opposite of the cacophony of Babel. In song there was a unity that could never be achieved in merely spoken word. Furthermore, music had a profoundly religious dimension. Bushnell spoke of "evening schools of sacred music, in which the music is not so much sacred as preparing to be." Music was a means for the soul to reach out, to touch a depth of feeling that prose could never reach. Music had a power that mere words did not when it came to religion. Throughout his later career Bushnell would continue to be attracted to music, to reflect upon the relationship between music and religion, and to further reflect on what that relationship implied about the meaning of religion.

When we turn, however, to the subject of religion we discover dissonance between the idyllic picture Bushnell paints in "The Age of Homespun" and his own youthful experience in the church. The preaching of the age was doctrinal, logical, and long. Sermons reflected a strict Calvinism, and sermon lengths were measured in hours, not minutes. In his 1851 address Bushnell speaks of how the faces of listeners "glowed" when a visiting preacher, "some one of the chief apostles, a Day, a Smith, a Bellamy, has come to lead them up to some higher pinnacle of thought, or pile upon their sturdy minds some heavier weight of argument." Yet there is little mention by Bushnell of his own experience of the meetinghouse. While Bushnell years later spoke fondly of his teacher of but one year, the name of his childhood minister, Samuel Whittlesey, is never even mentioned. The student of Bushnell can only speculate about his ecclesiastical nurturing. We know that he was baptized in the Episcopal Church of his mother, and we know that upon moving to New Preston he and his family attended the established Congregational Church. The minister at the time was Jeremiah Day, father of the famous president of Yale College, and a follower of the New Divinity school of theology (to be discussed in the next chapter); but although Bushnell refers to the presidential son in his recollections, he does not mention the reverend father. Day died within a year of Horace's move to New Preston. His successor, Whittlesey, who served to 1817, was a Yale College graduate who separated from his congregation because of money questions, but other than that we know little about him.

We know a bit more about his final New Preston minister, Charles Boardman, who served there from 1818 to 1830. His sermon at the dedication of the new meetinghouse in 1823 revealed two things about his theology. The first was that he was a passionate advocate of revivalism. He noted that in the past God had replenished the church "during gradual progress," but "he *now* accomplishes his object with a noticeable uniformity *through the medium of powerful revivals of religion.*" Second, he believed that the great spirit of revivalism suggested that the world stood at the dawn of the coming of the Kingdom of God. The great imposition of God's favor "is an indication of the approach of that day, when the great and universal revival of religion, promised in the word of God, shall come." As we will see, Bushnell would eventually reject the first teaching, but he always had a sympathy with the latter.

Both Bushnell's parents were uncomfortable with the strict Calvinism that marked the New Divinity clergy. Bushnell recalled that after some services his father would harshly criticize the "tough predestinationism" "or rather the over-total depravity of the sermon." His mother as well seemed to be unmoved by the Calvinistic doctrine that was the stuff of much preaching. As a youth Horace shared some of his family's attitudes, but he went further. When he was seventeen, and completely untrained in theology, he decided to solve some of the problems he saw in Calvinism, writing a small theological treatise while tending his father's carding machine. He examined the famous predestinarian passages in the ninth chapter of Paul's letter to the Romans and proceeded to correct the logical errors of the apostle. As he explained, "where Paul 'wishes himself accursed from Christ for his brethren,' he must have been mistaken in himself, and could not, consistently with his character as an apostle, have felt such a willingness." He then proceeded to address the questions of election, predestination, and the sovereignty of God. Theology was like his father's carding machine: with a little bit of tinkering it could always be improved.

It was not the meetinghouse that appeared to be the locus of the young Horace's religious reflections but rather the home and the world of nature. As a younger brother described it, the Bushnells' was "a household where religion was no occasional and nominal thing, no irksome restraint nor unwelcome visitor, but a constant atmosphere, a commanding but genial presence." Much of this was due to Dotha Bishop Bushnell. As Horace Bushnell later reflected in an autobiographical fragment, "My mother's loving instinct was from God, and God was in love first to me therefore." The figure of the pious mother is of course a regular occurrence in religious biographies, particularly those of the nineteenth century, but the religiosity of Dotha Bushnell stands out. What her children remembered of her was neither doctrine nor religious sensibility but rather her character. Her patience, dedication, and wisdom were the marks of religion that clung to the minds of the Bushnell children. One of Horace's younger brothers recalled that although they dutifully learned the Westminster Catechism, doctrine was not at the center of their religious life. But then again neither was religious affection. The Scriptures were seen to be above the theological formulas of the Westminster divines, and the facts and principles of the Christian faith and their role in the shaping of character were seen as more important than the emotional aspects of religion. Religion in the Bushnell household was a plain and practical thing and bore few parallels with Bushnell's picture of sturdy farmers feeding on a diet of rigorous theology — "Free-will, fixed fate, foreknowledge absolute, trinity, redemption, special grace, eternity — give them anything high enough, and the tough muscle of their inward man will be climbing sturdily into it."

The other place where the young Horace found his religion was in nature. An avid outdoorsman and an excellent fisherman, he, like many lads his age, felt at home in nature. Acquaintances recalled that he seemed more at home in the hills surrounding New Preston than anywhere else. But he found more than sport and exercise in those hills. He drew a religious sense out of nature, finding there, as he later explained, "not . . . fear, nor . . . a sense of wrong, but a sense of the divine beauty and majesty." His boyhood memories record no instance of ever praying in church, but do recall incidences where the power of nature led him to prayer. There was a favorite boulder in a pasture behind his home where he often prayed at the beginning of day. He also once recalled being moved to pray in the shadow of a haystack on his way back from church. Nature was a powerful medium of the divine aura.

Bushnell's openness to the spiritual power of nature has intrigued many over the years. Some have seen in it echoes of the old Puritan idea of physical nature being an image or shadow of the divine. The great Jonathan Edwards in a famous passage in his *Personal Narrative* spoke of how God's excellency, "his wisdom, his purity and love, seemed to appear in every thing; in the sun, moon, and stars; in the clouds, and blue sky; in the grass, flowers, trees; in the water and all nature." Others have seen in Bushnell's openness to the spiritual power of nature a sensibility in keeping with the great Romantic poets and philosophers of the early nineteenth century. For the Romantics, nature was the great vessel of the universal spirit, and to commune with nature was to place oneself in connection with the fundamental power of the universe. It was in this context that Ralph Waldo Emerson would later urge his readers to allow the spirit of nature to flow within their souls until they became a "transparent eyeball." Only then could they experience the liberating power of nature.

There are reasons to believe, however, that Bushnell's relation to nature was more complex. His daughter noted that he did not simply commune with nature but labored to classify and organize it as well. "It was not only the picture which filled his eye and kindled his imagination, but the recesses of nature. . . . It was his habit to survey by his eye the lines of the hills and valleys and to print thus upon his mind a map of the surfaces." He took great interest in figuring out the most efficient path a road or railroad might take. There was always a touch of the practical Yankee in Bushnell's approach to nature. Nature was inspiring, but a nature with roads through it was even better. Roads helped domesticate nature and were the mark of civilization, and domesticated nature was to be preferred over wild nature.

Bushnell's daughter tells another story of his childhood that should make us pause before lumping him in with the Romantics. One Sunday he and some companions decided to skip the services at the meetinghouse and instead to take an outing to a nearby mountain known as the "Pinnacle." There they were caught in a ferocious thunderstorm, and the frightened boys had to seek refuge under a projecting rock to wait out the storm. The frightened and humbled Horace saw the storm as a judgment on their Sabbath-breaking, and he sorrowfully repented his transgression. Behind Bushnell's universe was not some universal spirit, but a personal God, a God who could and would execute a "flogging" just as surely as his own father might. The realm of nature was not simply where one experienced God in the splendor of creation, but where one could also experience him at times in a far more direct and dramatic way.

As we will see, by focusing religion on character and the facts and principles of the Christian faith, and by anchoring it in the home and in nature, Bushnell's religious sensibilities would eventually become out of step with those of his contemporaries. It is true that his distinctive approach to religion did not seem to affect his sense of propriety or morality, and his boyhood friends agreed that he was a lad of irreproachable morals and free from vice. But he did wrestle with the question of religious assurance: how did one know that he or she was truly a Christian? In his mother's old Episcopal tradition the answer would have been simple enough: in the sacrament of baptism the child was regenerated and incorporated into the church, and the Christian life entailed continuing in the life of the church. But in the sixteenth century the Puritans had claimed that this was not enough, that there must be something more. True Christians must show evidence of an inner spiritual transformation; only then could they truly be members of the church. The exact nature of this transformation was always a matter of debate, but its reality had been assumed for centuries. In the Litchfield of Bushnell's youth such a transformation was seen as necessary for church membership. And for all the piety and character of the Bushnell household, and for all of the presence of God Horace found in the hills of New Preston, he had undergone no such experience. How one knew one was a Christian was a question to which he would return again and again, and it was an issue that would inspire some of his most controversial theology. But at this point in his life he assumed that the answer to the question was the same as his neighbors': it was to come through the experience of conversion. It was not until he was nineteen years old that he sensed he had achieved such an experience. In March of 1821 he wrote, "Lord here I am a sinner. Take me. Take all that I have and shall have. . . . I am ready to do anything or be anything for thee." In December of that year he joined the Congregational Church at New Preston, one of forty-one members.

Bushnell's early experience there gave him a new enthusiasm for work in the church, and he eagerly volunteered to lead religious meetings. The church records suggest that he was not particularly successful, since in 1822 only one person joined the church. His experience may also have influenced a more important decision — to travel to New Haven and study at Yale College. His mother had dedicated him to the Christian ministry, yet earlier Bushnell had seemed more interested in his father's carding machines than in pursuing higher education. Perhaps the reconciliation of his ecclesiastical status made him more open to attending Yale. Or, perhaps, there were more mundane reasons; by the beginning of the 1820s it was becoming clear that his father's carding machines were giving way to much more mechanized forms of production. The age of homespun was passing away.

To attend Yale, however, required a more sophisticated level of learning than Bushnell had experienced in the schools of New Preston. He would be tested in Latin, Greek, arithmetic, English grammar, and geology. His parents took in as a boarder a young lawyer recently graduated from Yale to help tutor Horace, and an area minister was also enlisted for assistance. But with stubborn Yankee independence

Bushnell bore the brunt of the labor by himself, struggling to acquire the learning he had earlier taken so lightly. The Yankee side of his character revealed itself once again when the time for the entrance examination approached. Normally a young scholar cramming to catch up in his studies would use every available hour to his advantage. But not Bushnell. He became convinced that the routine of study was harming his health, so in the summer of 1823 he traveled to New Haven and sat for the exam two months early. Despite the disadvantage at which he put himself, he passed the examination and was admitted to the college. He then returned to his family's farm and happily labored there for the rest of the summer, building a stone dam for his father's mill for relaxation.

Stone masonry was a regular feature of Connecticut life. Since the plows were made of wood, no farming could begin until the field had been gleaned of its stones, which were then used for stone walls, a common sight throughout the countryside. In part these walls reflected the strong Puritan sense of order and solidity. They clearly delineated the separate fields, ordering the countryside, anchoring the village, and contributing to its neat and tidy appearance. But masonry was the work of the Yankee. The mason was not a professional. He followed no pre-devised plan, as one might in building with brick. The Connecticut farmer used his wits and instincts in building his walls. To turn a pile of rocks into a solid wall required imagining how a jumble of irregular stones might best fit together. Bushnell always loved to build in stone. Just as he was gifted in sizing up the lay of the land, he had a knack for sensing the shape of the stones and enjoyed putting them together through ingenuity and imagination.

As Horace Bushnell left for New Haven he was leaving the age of homespun as well as a world that was inhabited exclusively by Puritans and Yankees. But he would take with him many of the values and prejudices of his upbringing, and he would always be in some ways a Connecticut stonemason, using his imagination and wit to put the various pieces together. But now his medium would be ideas and beliefs.

2 Jerusalem and the World

FOR a loyal citizen of Connecticut to visit New Haven was no mean thing. One man recalled that for a pious Congregationalist in the early nineteenth century, journeying to New Haven was like going up to Jerusalem. It was a "holy place containing Yale College of which Dr. Dwight was president." The city's charm lay in its artful combination of physical beauty and Puritan order. It occupied a large plain, originally divided into nine squares of sixty rods each, but by the nineteenth century subdivided by additional streets. The center of the city was the Green. Originally just an open square, by the 1820s it was adorned by an external railing, fine gravel walks, and rows of fine elms. The trees were a distinctive part of the ambiance. Beginning at the end of the eighteenth century James Hillhouse planted elms along the streets of the city, and these trees would eventually earn for the town its nickname of the Elm City. All in all it was a place that combined "rural freshness and city elegance."

But the association with Jerusalem was not because of the city's beauty and charm. Like the Jerusalem of old, New Haven was a center of government, learning, and religion. Gracing the Green was the old colonial statehouse of 1763 (that was soon to be replaced by the far more impressive structure, designed by Ithiel Town), which proudly attested that the city served (along with Hartford) as a co-capital of the state. New Haven had also been the home of Yale College for over a century. In 1823 the college's six principal buildings all looked on the Green. Yale was in a period of advance. Younger professors like Benjamin Silliman were gaining for it a reputation in the sciences, and its "Mineralogical Cabinet" with its collection of minerals (including a piece of the recently fallen meteor) was one of the great jewels of New England. But it was in the area of religion that Yale's influence had been most striking. For decades Timothy Dwight, so often referred to as "Pope" of Connecticut, had used Yale College as his Vatican. As president he had striven to root out any hints of infidelity and had left his mark on a generation of students. He had died by the time Bushnell journeyed to Yale, but his successor, Jeremiah Day, was not only another Congregationalist minister but the son of Bushnell's first New Preston pastor as well. As if the link between Yale and the religious life of Connecticut was not already strong enough, in 1822 a theological department (the forerunner of the college's Divinity School) was established to better train candidates for the ministry. The new professorship of didactic theology was occupied by Nathaniel William Taylor, student of Dwight and pastor of the old Center Church that proudly adorned the center of the New Haven Green. It was thus easy for the pious Congregationalist to feel that in entering New Haven he or she was approaching Jerusalem.

But all was not what it seemed. If Center Church occupied the middle of the city Green, a symbol of the old standing order, it was now flanked by two other religious buildings that reminded the people that no one had a monopoly on the religious options of the citizens of Connecticut. To the right stood a second Congregational Church, a product of the theological debates that had swirled within Congregationalism over the past eighty years. To the left stood Trinity Church, which testified that Episcopalians would also now compete for the hearts and minds of the people.

THE SUNDERING OF NEW ENGLAND

It was in 1630, years before any of those churches on the Green were built, that John Winthrop, aboard the *Arbella*, gave New England its

29

most prized epithet. New England, he challenged, was to be a "city on a hill" for all to see. Any idea of a united New England being a city on a hill, however, received a mortal blow with the religious excitements of the 1740s now known as the Great Awakening. The original settlers of New England had envisioned a "Holy Commonwealth," an idea that rested on both social and individual sanctity. On the social level, life was seen as being dedicated to the glorification of God. Clergy and magistrates, citizens and inhabitants, all were to mold their actions in accordance with God's will. The Westminster Catechism asked, "What is man's chief end?" and the famous response followed, "Man's chief end is to glorify God." This was the responsibility, or calling, of everyone and it gave purpose to all endeavors or labors. The role of the clergy was to instruct the faithful, whether in their duties in voting or their responsibilities in trade, and in order to train learned clergy Harvard College was established in 1636 and Yale College in 1701. But if social sanctity was communal in nature, there was also a crucial individual element of piety. The Puritans were followers of John Calvin and the Reformed tradition, and as good Calvinists they knew the world was inhabited by saints, or those chosen to move toward glory, and the reprobate, or those chosen for condemnation. This election had occurred before anyone's birth, so one could not affect one's own status but only discover it. How to determine one's status became a great Puritan theme, and their answer was to turn within. If one could identify elements of saving grace within one's inner life, this could give hope that one was chosen for salvation. True Christianity rested upon this experience — baptism and even loyal church attendance were not enough. As one divine explained, "now the Word and the Sacraments barely considered cannot work upon the spirit unless the Lord work a new frame inwardly by the infusion of Grace." This was the reason why church membership rested upon the recitation of a conversion narrative.

All worked well when these two forces of social and individual sanctity pulled together, but what happened when they pulled apart? What happened when only a small proportion of the congregation was able to claim membership in the church? By the end of the seventeenth century, a series of compromises was worked out allowing the unconverted partial or "halfway" church membership in which they could continue to have their children baptized. It was not a perfect solution, but it did allow the church to remain the center of the community. A precarious peace was maintained between the two centers of the Puritan vision.

The Great Awakening challenged any notion of such compromises. In preachers and theologians like George Whitefield and Jonathan Edwards the transformed heart took center stage, becoming associated with public preaching and often with the display of great emotion. When Whitefield preached, scores and sometimes hundreds of people would respond. The emotionalism let loose by this new preaching, however, was troubling. It seemed as if a power had been released that overcame reason and propriety. One person committed suicide as a result of the power of Edwards's preaching. Others committed similarly disturbing acts. In one infamous occurrence in New London, Connecticut, wigs, cloaks, and even books were set aflame at the urging of a passionate revivalist. Looking back, Ezra Stiles, Dwight's predecessor as president of Yale and no fan of the revivals, referred to it as a time when "multitudes were seriously, soberly, and solemnly out of their wits."

One practical reason conservatives worried over the religious excitement sweeping the land was that it was tearing apart the religious fabric of the society. Among the Awakening's devotees, any minister or church that did not proclaim and manifest the converting power of the Spirit was suspect. Itinerant ministers warned of the "dangers of an unconverted ministry" and urged true believers to separate from such persons and institutions. The second Congregational church on the New Haven Green testified to the power of this call for separation, with some members becoming Strict Congregationalists and others Baptists. Later, Methodist itinerants appeared (such as the ones who won over the Bushnell family). There were theological divisions within the Separatist ranks, but they agreed on one point: the new wine of the evangelical revivalism could not be contained within the old wineskins of the standing order.

While this was happening the established church was suffering losses from another direction as well. In 1722 the colony was shocked when Timothy Cutler, the rector of Yale College, and other tutors and former tutors announced that they were renouncing their ministries and seeking membership in the Church of England. The "Yale Apostates," as they were pejoratively known, were ordained as Anglicans and served as missionaries to their former Congregational brethren. The upstart Episcopal Church increasingly presented itself as an oasis of peace amid the turbulence of the Awakening. As one missionary observed, "The Church has . . . gained by these commotions, which no men of sense of either denomination have at all given in to." Large groups of conservative Congregationalists, reacting to what they called "insufferable enthusiastick whims and extemporaneous jargon," sought the order and dignity of the Episcopal Church. Episcopalians were condemned as immoral for their less rigorous membership requirements and charged with Tory disloyalty, but they continued to grow and were a very visible alternative to the standing order.

While some fell under the spell of the emotionally charged preaching of the evangelists and joined the Separatist movement, and others left the established church for the Episcopal Church, still another theological debate was beginning, one which would have far-reaching effects. In eastern New England a number of clergy and laity recoiled against the emotional tenor of the Awakening. They began to combine some of the more liberal religious understandings coming out of Restoration England — such as a new and softer image of God and a growing respect for the power of human reason — with their inherited faith.

Key divisions emerged between the traditionalists and those in this new liberal movement on a bevy of questions. First arose the issue of the degree to which original sin hindered natural virtue and the extent to which human beings were culpable for the sin of Adam. Then arose the question of the freedom of the will: Does the human will have moral freedom? Can it choose the good, or is it locked into always choosing evil until enlightened by supernatural grace? Then came the question of justification: was the spiritual transformation (that all affirmed) an external, supernatural act of God in which the pious soul was passive, or was it a process in which human participation played an important role? Finally, there arose the question, who was the Christ and what had he accomplished? For those in the liberal movement, the image of God as an autocratic king exacting retribution from his son to pay the debt of human sin could not be tolerated. They pictured Jesus as the embodiment of divine love, the teacher of righteousness, the manifestation of true virtue. He came into the world not to pay a debt but to show humanity the way of truth, a truth that lay at the heart of the heavenly Father. The traditional speculative doctrines concerning Christ had, the liberals felt, led the church down a blind alley. For over a millennium the reasoning had been that if Christ had to pay for Adam's sin and open the gates of heaven then he had to be both fully God and fully human. If he were fully divine then God must be a Trinity in which the Father and the Son shared a divine nature with the Spirit. Thus, the liberal critic concluded, the simple appeal of Jesus to a heavenly Father had been lost and replaced by a Trinitarian metaphysic.

The above narrative chronicles the emergence of Unitarianism from the soil of Puritan New England. What had begun as a tendency became a movement, and by the end of the first decade of the nineteenth century Harvard College and much of eastern New England were devotees of the new liberal faith. Its message was a picture of God as a loving, ethical parent, and an emphasis on the free and morally responsible core of human nature.

By the early nineteenth century, then, there existed two distinct New England religious cultures: a liberal or Unitarian world emphasizing reason, culture, and morality, and an "orthodox" or evangelical world emphasizing Calvinism and conversion. For those in the latter camp, their first task was containment. The alarm needed to be rung to awaken the pious of New England, and institutions needed to arise and combat the threat. Jedidiah Morse — author of the first comprehensive geography of North America and father of the painter and inventor Samuel F. B. Morse — saw the decision by Harvard College to replace both its president and professor of divinity with liberals as a sign of the "loss" of that institution to the Unitarian side. In response he helped organize Andover Theological Seminary in 1808 to be the "West Point of Orthodoxy." Over a decade earlier Timothy Dwight had begun stirring the fires of revival at Yale College to purge all adolescent skepticism from the student body, and by the second decade of the new century it too was a center of opposition to the message of eastern Massachusetts.

The period between 1810 and 1830 saw a great battle throughout New England where congregation after congregation was fought over by the orthodox and liberals. The latter were on the whole triumphant in eastern New England; the Massachusetts court decision in the Dedham Case of 1820, which ruled that the ownership of property and the right to call a minister belonged to the religious society (containing all citizens of the township whether converted or not) rather than simply to (converted) church members, allowed many churches to embrace the new liberal faith. But the story was different elsewhere. In both western Massachusetts and Connecticut the Unitarian threat was beaten back. The more developed polity of Connecticut Congregationalism, with its consociations and clerical associations, allowed for a more rigorous defense, and ultimately only one Connecticut Congregational church went over to the Unitarians. At the time, however, the outcome was never certain. Lyman Beecher, one of the leaders of the Second Great Awakening in New England, fretted that "the Unitarians are gaining. . . . They have sowed tares while men slept, and grafted heretical churches on orthodox stumps, and this is still their favorite plan. Everywhere, when the minister dies, some society's committee will be cut and dried, ready to call in a Cambridge student, split the Church, get a majority of the society, and take house, funds, and all." As passionately as their mid-twentieth-century descendents would fear Communist infiltration of their institutions, men like Beecher worried about the Unitarian menace and called for its defeat.

Though the anti-Unitarian forces prevailed throughout most of Massachusetts and Connecticut, they were not helped by the fact that they were no longer united. The result of the theological divisions had been the ultimate collapse of the standing order, despite attempts by Timothy Dwight and others to save it. By the second decade of the nineteenth century even conservative Episcopalians, frustrated by the second-class standing accorded their church, supported the campaign for a new state constitution and the disestablishment of the Congregational Church. Finally in the new Connecticut constitution of 1818, the special status of the Congregational Church in the state was formally abandoned. Jerusalem in this sense was no more. Those who had remained in the Congregational Church were themselves split into two main groups, each with its own opinion of how best to answer the charges of the Unitarians against the Calvinist faith.

One group of divines was known as the New Divinity Movement. Inspired by Edwards, men like Joseph Bellamy, Samuel Hopkins, and Nathaniel Emmons strove to answer Edwards's critics. Perhaps the most important of the "farmer metaphysicians" (as their critics dubbed them) was Hopkins, one of Edwards's students, who authored the first system of Calvinistic thought indigenous to America. Priding himself on being a "Consistent Calvinist," Hopkins pushed the concept of the sovereignty of God to its limit. God did not merely permit sin; he willed it (albeit because of the good it would eventually produce). Hopkins also recast the notion of regeneration in a similarly consistent way. If regeneration was a divine action then a sinner who used the means of grace simply to gain salvation was more loathsome in God's eyes than an unawakened sinner. Such individuals were hypocrites, using God's gifts in a profane way. There could be no compromise on the question of church membership, so all compromises (like the old "half-way" covenant) were to be rejected.

But Hopkins did respond to critics by significantly modifying the understanding of the saving work of Christ. In place of the traditional language of God demanding satisfaction or retribution for the sin of Adam, and of Christ's death paying this debt, Hopkins set forth a different schema. God, he suggested, was more a benevolent moral governor than a vengeful deity. The death of Christ served not to pay a debt but to restore the moral order of the universe. When law has been broken, the penalty must be enacted, or else justice is not served. Christ's sacrifice was for this sake, to restore order and maintain justice. God's action was, in Hopkins's words, "doing that which is both right and just both with respect to himself, his law and government, and all the subjects of his kingdom." The "moral governor" theory of the atonement became one of the hallmarks of early-nineteenth-century New England theology.

New Divinity theology undergirded much of the evangelical response to Unitarianism, particularly in western Massachusetts. It was represented in the theological faculty at Andover where, along with representatives of the older Calvinist tradition, followers of the movement helped shape the theological outlook of a generation of ministers. Its proponents drew from their theology support for revivalism, missionary endeavors, and moral reform. But it was not the only theological voice in the province. From Yale College (and after 1822 from what would become Yale Divinity School) came a different rendering of the Calvinistic theological system.

The great Yale theologian of the age was Nathaniel William Taylor. His theological method was referred to at the time as "logic and tears," and those two words reflected Taylor's understanding of human nature. All humans, Taylor believed, possessed a "common sense" that enabled them to recognize the truth when it was clearly presented. Logic, accordingly, was the means by which one approached the study of theology. If the theologian could clarify his concepts through right definitions, his case would fall into place. But humans also possessed a moral sense, through which the individual could intuitively know the right. "Tears" or affectation could be used to appeal to this moral sense.

Through logic and tears Taylor boldly took up two of the great concerns of the nineteenth century. The first was the question of the origin of sin. The New Divinity writers had continued to hold that if God were sovereign he must be in some sense the author of sin. Unitarian critics took great glee in taunting their orthodox opponents on this point. It was one of the leading topics in a series of pamphlets between the Andover professor Leonard Woods and the Unitarian Henry Ware. Woods had admitted that the doctrine of election or predestination did fly against both human reason and moral sense, and that it could lead to the charge that God was the author of sin; nonetheless, since the doctrine was scriptural it had to be defended. Taylor believed that the New Divinity position was untenable and icily noted that Woods had put the course of orthodoxy back fifty years in his dispute with Ware. Humans, Taylor argued, were the authors of their own sin. They sinned freely and willfully. But what did one then make of the doctrine of original sin? Sin was universal, Taylor claimed; all persons sinned as soon as they could. In this sense one could speak of original sin. But no one sinned out of necessity. Human beings had a "power to the contrary" when it came to sin. They were responsible for their own sins because they freely committed them. Taylor's associate, Lyman Beecher, attempted to prove to Unitarian skeptics that the belief in infant damnation was not a Calvinist doctrine, but an insidious corollary of a Catholic, exalted view of baptism.

Taking up his second issue, Taylor used his theology to buttress a theology of revivalism. A preacher could address his flock as morally responsible agents, Taylor argued, and individuals could and should repent. They had the common sense to recognize the truth and they had the moral sense to intuit the good. Accordingly the preacher could let the sinner know that "he can go to hell only as a self-destroyer. . . . Let us if we can, make this conviction take hold on his spirit, and ring in his conscience like the note of the second death." It was the recognition of this that gave to New England ministers — particularly those trained at Yale — their power. On this point Lyman Beecher contrasted the success of New England preachers with those of old England. Both held the same Calvinist doctrine, but the fruit they produced was different. "Look at the revivals that are filling our land with salvation. They do not prevail in England. In this country they are combined almost exclusively to the New England manner of exhibiting the truth." In contrast to their English compatriots who could tell sinners only to "pray and wait," New England clergy could tell them to "repent and believe."

Taylor's boldness was controversial. His *Concio ad Clerum* of 1828 caused a firestorm. Andover was shocked, and opponents, under a man by the name of Bennett Tyler, organized a new theological seminary (later to become the Hartford Theological Seminary) in East Windsor, Connecticut, in response to the suspect teachings at Yale. In this action Tyler had the support of many of the leaders at Andover. But Yale continued to be a center for theology, and its graduates carried Taylor's theology far and wide. Thus by 1823 there were three distinct centers in the theological world of New England: Cambridge and Harvard as a center for Unitarianism, Andover, and Yale. Leaders at each claimed that they were the spiritual heirs of the Puritans.

YALE

It was into this world that Horace Bushnell entered as he journeyed from New Preston to New Haven in September of 1823. At twenty-one he was much older than most of his classmates. Furthermore, with his suit of homespun and strong physique formed by years of hard labor his appearance was very different from that of the sons of more gentrified parents. It is little wonder that he later admitted he had few if any intimate friends among his classmates.

Like the other students Bushnell faced the formidable Yale curriculum, in which Classics still occupied a central place. Livy and Horace as well as Greek were covered in the freshman year, while by the junior year Cicero and Tacitus were required reading. The other staple of the curriculum was mathematics; geometry, trigonometry, logarithms, and conic sections were all studied. The last subject was notoriously difficult, and in Bushnell's class there occurred an event known as the "Conic Section Rebellion." The students were led to believe that they would not be responsible for the corollaries to the formulas, yet at examination time discovered that they were. Rebellion resulted. Bushnell and thirty-seven of his classmates (out of a class of eighty-seven) refused to recite for the faculty. Unamused, the faculty voted to suspend the rebellious students and to send them home to their equally unsympathetic parents. The combination of professorial and parental displeasure was enough to break the strike, and eventually the recalcitrant students dutifully swore, "We, the undersigned, having been led into a course of opposition to the government of Yale College, do acknowledge our fault in this resistance, and promise, on being restored to our standing in the class, to yield a faithful obedience to the laws."

It was not until their senior year that Yale students studied materials that are now usually associated with collegiate education. Psychology was represented in Dugald Stewart's *Elements of the Philosophy of the Human Mind* and Thomas Brown's *Lectures on the Philosophy of the Human Mind;* theology was treated through William Paley's *Natural Theology* and *View of the Evidences of Christianity;* and political economy was also studied. All of these works reflected the reason and spirit of the British Enlightenment. Stewart and Brown were representatives of the Scottish Common Sense tradition, and Paley reflected the empirical and evidentialist tradition in English theology.

Bushnell spoke little of his college experience, but we might intuit that it was not an easy time for him. Nineteenth-century education stressed recitation and memorization rather than creativity, and those were not the directions in which Bushnell's mind worked. His handwriting also reveals something about his mind-set. When he wrote for himself (as he did in his journal) his handwriting was so singular that it is extraordinarily difficult to decipher, yet at Yale he was required to write in the set style of the time. He did so, but it must have seemed unnaturally stifling. Likewise, when he wrote for himself the ideas flowed so quickly that it seems as if his pen had difficulty keeping up. Often he would skip words just to keep pace with his mind's speed. This was not a character trait that made the study of either Greek or mathematics particularly easy. As one classmate later reminisced, "he was all energy, both on the playground and in the division room." Many aspects of his personality had to be reined in to master the Yale curriculum.

He did take great delight in music at Yale, as he had throughout his childhood. He joined the college choir that sang in chapel, and in his junior year he helped organize a Beethoven Society to further an interest in fine music, and in particular in sacred music, among the students. It was to that same society twenty-five years later that he returned and spoke on the topic of "Religious Music." The address put into words some of Bushnell's love of music. The power of sound, he explained, was in its association with feeling, emotion, and affection. Music did not work through the intellect but directly through the "sounding board of the heart." Furthermore, music connected the world. All that existed — wood, shell, horn, copper — had tone, given by God. And through this music, Bushnell believed, we are led back to God:

> [W]e have an argument for God . . . from the fact that a grand harmonic, soul-interpreting law of music pervades all the objects of the material creation. . . . It is as if God had made the world around us to be a grand organ of music, so that our feelings might have play in it as our understanding has in the light of the sun and the outward color and forms of things.

But even in his appreciation for music, the Puritan lurked. The use of music in Christian worship was particularly appropriate, he noted, but it must flow from a pure heart. Music merely as a science or artistic construct had no power, but when it came from the heart it soared. "When the soul is simple and God is templed in the inmost recesses of its feelings, then there is a quality in the voice and the touch, that reveals and communicates the inspired joy of the heart."

On one aspect of his life at Yale Bushnell did comment, and that was religion. Although it had long ceased to be an institution dedicated exclusively to preparing men for the ministry, Yale took religion very seriously in the 1820s. Morning and evening prayers were held daily in the chapel, and all students were required to attend. Four absences led to a warning; two warnings led to a letter to one's parents; and three warnings resulted in suspension. On Sundays there were

39

two additional services, with a doctrinal sermon preached in the morning and an address on "practical character" given in the later service. Although non-Congregationalists could be excused from these Sunday services in order to attend their own churches, only the handful of Episcopal students chose to do so. In addition to this schedule a prayer and conference meeting preceded the Sunday evening service, and each class commonly held a weekly prayer meeting whose purpose was "to keep alive and augment the flame of religion in the hearts of those who participated in it."

Bushnell seems to have received no warnings, and his classmates recalled him to be punctual in attending chapel, but his time in New Haven was a time of religious uncertainty. The more he became accustomed to the ways of the larger world, the weaker his religion became. He later recalled, "My figure in college was not as good as it should have been, especially at first, got better and came out well; but my religious character went down." Although he was a member of the church at Yale, he was not the model of piety. Another classmate recounted, "Though he came to college a church member, he never had, through the whole four years, nor for two years after, anything positively or distinctly Christian about him."

Here we stumble upon one of the puzzling aspects of Bushnell: his religious life never fit neatly into the accepted pattern. In theory, the sinner, awakened to his terrible plight by the power of the Spirit, should confess and receive the saving grace of God. This experience of conversion would give him confidence in God's favor and serve as a badge for entrance into full church membership. As Bushnell's last New Preston minister, Charles Boardman, explained, "The peace . . . of the reconciliation of the heart to God [is] produced by the renewing influence of the Holy Spirit and the tranquility of the soul connected with that reconciliation." Evidently, Bushnell's experience in New Preston had been sufficient to convince Boardman and others of the acceptability of his spiritual state. But his conversion was not according to form. Normally God used the vessel of the church and particularly the tool of preaching to accomplish this great work. Furthermore, Boardman insisted, as we saw earlier, that God "now accomplished this object with a noticeable uniformity, *through the medium of powerful revivals of religion.*" Bushnell had found his heart affected not in a church revival, but in his own private sphere. Was this a true conversion after all?

Bushnell's religious struggles while at Yale have been variously explained. In the latter nineteenth century it was suggested that the doubt flowed from the intricacies of the doctrine and theology he encountered at Yale, which overshadowed his naturally religious nature. One of his friends commented, "My impression is that his consuming love of study and his high ambition, aided by a growing spirit of doubt and difficulty as to religious doctrine, was the secret here." From this perspective theology damaged the religious spirit. In contrast, twentieth-century writers have preferred to emphasize the social nature of the religious crisis and tie it to the difficulties of transporting a religious faith that bore so many marks of a homespun nature, family, and environment into a much more sophisticated world. Did his childhood faith have any more place in a city like New Haven than his handmade clothing? There is probably truth in both interpretations. In any event, Bushnell was one of those persons who recognized the fragility of religious belief and how easily it could fall apart. A constant concern in his later ministry was how one grounded religious belief, and many of his most sensitive works would return to this theme.

In the biography of Bushnell written by his daughter, she recalls an incident that sheds light on his religious outlook. One evening while a student at Yale, after a period of hard study, Bushnell had what could be called an out-of-body experience. He felt as if his body were rising and floating in the air. Grasping his bed for reassurance, he had no sense of feeling in his hands. "He began to believe he was dead and that this was his voyage to the world of the spirits," his daughter wrote. The state lasted for an hour or two, and then gradually subsided. According to Bushnell's daughter, his mental poise sometimes became disturbed, particularly in times of physical stress. However one chooses to interpret the cause and nature of such an experience, Bushnell was keenly interested in such experiences throughout his life and saw in them glimpses of the greater spiritual world. Deep within his hardheaded Yankee nature, there was a touch of the mystic.

In September of 1827, in the Center Church on the New Haven Green, Bushnell's college experience came to an end with the reception of his degree. In recognition of his academic achievements he was given the honor of making one of the commencement orations. He chose as his theme "Some Defects in Modern Oratory."

Graduation meant finding a profession. Like many young college graduates (including Ralph Waldo Emerson and Henry David Thoreau) Bushnell tried his hand at school teaching and accepted a position in Norwich, Connecticut. The observation made by one of Thoreau's biographers, "College having prepared him for no occupation, he turned to school teaching," was perhaps true in Bushnell's case as well, and certainly his success was only little better than Thoreau's. He later admitted that he liked to do anything better than to teach school. But if the "petty vexations of a pedagogue" (to use his phrase) were unappealing to him, he enjoyed the wider social life his occupation allowed him.

In the winter of 1828 a new opportunity beckoned. His commencement oration had caught the eye of persons of influence, and in February he was invited to come to New York City and join the staff of the *Journal of Commerce* as an associate editor. The newspaper had been founded a year earlier by Arthur Tappan, an extremely devout Congregationalist businessman who desired a business gazette that would not allow advertisements for the theater, liquor, or other offensive trades. The journal, which combined religious and commercial news, was edited by William Maxwell (who also served as the head of a Presbyterian seminary in Richmond, Virginia) and distributed free of charge. It was a disaster. In short order the paper devoured nearly thirty thousand dollars of Tappan's money. Tappan then turned the paper over to his brother Lewis, who seems to have been the one who hired Bushnell. It was Bushnell's responsibility to gather the foreign news fresh from the packet boats in the harbor and to prepare the paper for its morning issue. He also wrote many of its editorials.

The hundred-dollars-a-month salary seemed like a princely sum, helping repay his college debts and even allowing him to put away a bit of savings. And the appeal of New York City was not merely professional. Even a strict believer like Lewis Tappan could enjoy *some* of the delights of the city, and often Bushnell tagged along. But ultimately journalism was no more his profession than school teaching had been. When the paper was sold to David Hale in late autumn, Bushnell turned down an opportunity to stay on. He later said that he found journalism a "terrible life." In 1829 he left New York and returned to New Haven with the intention of studying law. His stint as a journalist made the tuition of seventy-five dollars that Yale charged its law students no insuperable barrier.

Formal legal study in America was in its infancy in the early nineteenth century. Most young men apprenticed themselves to a practicing attorney and read law in that way; Yale had started its law faculty only in 1824. The restless Bushnell had planned to spend a minimum of time in formal study, and after six months he decided to leave Yale once again and accept a position with a law firm in Ohio. His goal was then to enter into a career in politics among the multitude of transplanted New Englanders there. While still a law student he had been offered the position of tutor at Yale College by President Day. A tutor had the responsibility of hearing the young students' recitations of their lessons — a task that seemed as unattractive to Bushnell as school teaching had been — and he immediately rejected the idea. Before he could officially reject the position, however, he made a visit home and, as he later recalled, "As I was going out of the door, putting the wafer in my letter, I encountered my mother and told her what I was doing. Remonstrating now very gently but seriously, she told me she could not think I was doing my duty." She urged him to reconsider and to accept the appointment. No nineteenth-century son could reject such an appeal from a pious mother, and particularly not this son. It is impossible to say whether Dotha Bushnell hoped that if her son stayed at Yale and accepted the job of tutor the path would remain open for him to enter the ministry, but the decision was to be a momentous one.

Bushnell proved successful as a tutor, being far more adept working with young men than he had been with boys. His athletic prowess undoubtedly impressed the students, and the force of his personality and his enthusiasm for ideas were equally appealing. He is also remembered for the improvements he made to the tutorial system. When Bushnell started his work as a tutor, each class was broken into groups, with each tutor responsible for the recitations of his group in Greek, Latin, and mathematics. As a result of Bushnell's suggestion each tutor became responsible for hearing recitations in a single subject. This made the lot of the tutor easier and thus more attractive. One problem remained for Bushnell, however. A tutor was responsible not only for his students' intellectual development but for their religious development as well. Tutors also took turns leading the public prayers in chapel. Public prayers were perhaps the least attractive aspect of his appointment, but Bushnell did not shirk his responsibility. He dutifully took his turn, and it was recalled that his performance, if "not free-hearted," was not "dry."

"ALL OF THIS WOE"

The year 1831 found Bushnell finished with his law studies and ready for admission to the bar. But here again events changed his plans. Since the days of Timothy Dwight revivals had often taken place among the students of the college. In each year from 1820 to 1824 the fire of revival had touched the campus, but the revival of 1831 was perhaps the most intense. It began in the fall of 1830, was in full swing by November, and by early January had spread to include almost everyone on campus. Over one hundred students joined the college church and seventy-four made public professions of faith. The revival transformed the college. Faculty members reported that not a single student needed disciplining for moral lapses during the entire year.

It was during this season of revival that Bushnell again considered the question of his own religious state. He fretted that some of his students were using his own doubts to stem the tide of the revival. "I must get out of all of this woe," he confessed to a fellow tutor. "Here am I, what I am, and these young men hanging to me in their indifference amidst this universal earnestness on every side." To his fellow tutors he confessed,

> O men! What should I do with arrant doubts I have been nursing for years? When the preacher touches the Trinity and when logic shatters it all to pieces, I am all at the four winds. But I am glad I have a heart as well as a head. My heart wants the Father; my heart wants the Son; my heart wants the Holy Ghost — and one just as much as the other. My heart says the Bible has a Trinity for me, and I mean to hold by my heart. I am glad a man can do it when there is no other moving, and so I answer my own question — what shall I do? But that is all I can do yet.

Like Bushnell's earlier religious experience, this was an atypical conversion. Doubt was not destroyed. There is no "knockout" here; faith only wins on points. It is the will and desire to believe and not the experience of some blinding work of grace that is the driving force. Furthermore, the context of the conversion is suggestive. Faith became a duty. When his doubts seemed to be harming others it became no longer morally defensible to hold them. Throughout his ministry he would posit different models of Christian initiation, and entrance into the religious life became a recurring theme in his sermons. But always initiation was a means to an end; the Christian life was the end, initiation was only the how. And as before, character was more important to Bushnell than doctrine. There is the touch of the Yankee tinkerer here. A model of conversion that did not work was as useless as a mill that failed to grind. There would always be room for improvement. By adjusting the typical shape of the conversion experience, Bushnell was able to resolve his spiritual crisis.

We have, however, one more indirect insight into this experience. Near the end of his days he came across a work of Johann Wolfgang von Goethe, *Wilhelm Meister,* and was particularly struck by a section of it entitled "The Confessions of a Fair Saint." Writing to his wife, he confessed, "I never read a Christian experience that so beautifully tallied with my own." In this story a young girl comes of age, and like Bushnell has a crisis with her childhood faith. "In the course of four hectic years I had forgotten [God] completely," she admits. But in trying to find her way back she finds doctrine blocking her way. "How I wish that in those days . . . I had been without formal doctrine." The religion of her youth had taught that any change of heart had to begin with a deep dread of sin, move to an awareness of punishment, and only then perceive God's graciousness. But for her God was always somehow present; "He let Himself be found, and did not reproach me about sins of the past." Yet still she lacked true faith. She described her crisis in the following way:

> "Now Almighty One, grant me faith!" I once implored when under the greatest emotional pressure. . . . At this point I was in the position that we have to be in, if God is to pay heed to our prayers, and one in which we seldom are. [It was like the pressure] which draws our soul to an absent lover, an approach that is presumably much more fundamental and truthful than we assume. In this way my soul drew near to Him Who had died on the cross, and in that moment I knew what *faith* was.

45

Bushnell's "conversion" also brought him to his profession. He now felt free to accede to his mother's desires and begin preparing for the ministry. In the autumn of 1831 he entered the Theological School of Yale. The faculty (in addition to Taylor) consisted of Eleazor T. Fitch in homiletics, Chauncy Goodrich in rhetoric, and Josiah Willard Gibbs in the sacred languages. Bushnell was one of twenty students who entered that fall, all of whom were New Englanders or transplanted New Englanders. At the school the students learned Taylor's theology in full. As a proponent of one prominent version of the Common Sense tradition Taylor presented truth as a hard and solid thing. Truths were as solid as bricks and, like bricks, could be carefully assembled into a system. A theologian was something like a good bricklayer, who built up his system piece by piece. And like a good bricklayer, order, logic, and regularity were the marks of a skilled craftsman.

Bushnell, however, was constitutionally more at home with stone walls than with bricks, and preferred imagination and insight to logic and regularity. His own experience with religious faith and doubt made him suspect that religious truth was not anything like solid brick. There was always something tentative about it. But while he often chafed at Taylor's mechanical assumptions, he did value his emphasis upon human freedom and responsibility and, in all probability, appreciated his emphasis on intellectual honesty. "Follow the truth," Taylor told his students, "if it carries you over Niagara." On other occasions he would remind them, "Do not be afraid of investigation and argument — there is no poker in the truth." Bushnell proceeded to practice this preaching. One of his earliest theological writings is an 1832 untitled discourse usually referred to as "Natural Science and Moral Philosophy." The work is aimed against unnamed "philosophers" who attempted to organize scientifically the moral world in a way analogous to the methods used by students of physical nature. He may have had in mind here Taylor, but more likely his target was William Paley, particularly Paley's *Moral Philosophy* (which was still used at Yale), in which Paley had linked morality to prudence and self-interest.

Bushnell began by observing that the scientific method begins with the study of facts, moves from them to the discovery of natural law, and culminates in the setting forth of first principles. There was a natural tendency to use the same method in the construction of moral philosophy and create a moral science that could make sense of the human mind. All attempts, however, broke down in practice. "Nature's man is soon observed to do things which the philosopher could never have dreamed of." Human nature could not be reduced to regularity.

The problem involved the issue of sin. Sin was a topic which New England writers had spent much effort analyzing, but Bushnell suggested a new tack. He started with a psychological observation: If a right action is one that is in conformity with the constituted properties of the agent, a wrong action is always self-contradictory. It subtly rebels against the true nature. The individual has the power or capacity to sin, but is not fitted to do so. It is like buttoning a shirt incorrectly: the buttons will connect, but the wearer is immediately conscious that the shirt does not fit correctly. Bushnell agreed with the prudentialists that there were certain elements in the human makeup that assisted humans in choosing the right: a sense of duty, recognition that duty and happiness are one, and a sense of self-regard. So why did humans continue to sin? A "philosopher" must argue that humans sin out of a misunderstanding of happiness or self-regard, but Bushnell went to great lengths to show how this could not be. The "philosopher," he argued, cannot explain sin. "We are brought again to the conclusion . . . that if a man becomes a sinner, he must come in spite of opposing principles in his nature, which formally affirm the certainty of his rectitude." The presence of these principles also proved that humans were not created to sin. Like his teacher Taylor, Bushnell placed the responsibility of sin firmly in humanity's lap. Sin was tied to human choice. To answer why we choose sin he turned to the apostle Paul, and paraphrasing the famous passage from the seventh chapter of the Letter to the Romans explained, "I do not understand my own conduct, for that which I will to do I do not practice but that which I hate I do." Paul stressed the reality of sin, not its explicability. "If Paul had taken a different view of sin . . . as the proper working of first principles in the agent, he would have done the cause of his master a very questionable service." Sin, Bushnell concluded, was a reality that must be addressed. Any philosophy must be true to the facts of human existence, but philosophy could not deal with sin. Religion could succeed where philosophy failed, showing human beings not only that they were sinners, but at the same time that they were more. "When man . . . rises to a steady contemplation of the spiritual, he feels himself to be no longer a clod but a particle of the divine nature. . . . Religion elevates itself to a divine and heavenly reality — why God should care for him as a Father he now understands."

This early essay reveals elements of Bushnell's theological method that would reappear regularly in his later writings. There is, for example, a touch of the practical Yankee, uninterested in theory and unconcerned with conforming to the niceties of the New England theological tradition. Bushnell's only desire was to figure out from the facts what was the issue at hand, and then to try to solve it. He was trying, as one biographer put it, "to hew out a new and short cut through the woods." There is also more than a touch of Nathaniel William Taylor here. Bushnell concluded "Natural Science and Moral Philosophy" by noting that the answer to the question of how all persons became sinners was simply, "we became such by sinning" — an answer that could be taken almost verbatim from Taylor's *Concio ad Clerum*. It is also worth noting the very traditional message here. Bushnell not only favors the apostle Paul rather than the "philosophers" but also chooses a Pauline passage that was dear to the hearts of seventeenth-century Puritans. Earlier Puritans had also appealed to this passage to emphasize the stubborn persistence of sin and its power over unaided reason. Finally, there is a quasi-mystical element in Bushnell's reference to the believer being a "particle of the divine nature." This too would find a place in his later writings. On the manuscript an older Bushnell scribbled, "Boy's work. Much of it false, though a truth tis hereabout." Perhaps the older man was being a bit too harsh.

In addition to Taylor, there were two other individuals who perhaps influenced Bushnell as he studied for the ministry, and shaped important elements of his later thought. One was his professor of sacred language, Josiah Willard Gibbs, a noted philologist. During these years Gibbs was working on a theory of language that would influence Bushnell greatly. A human being, he argued, inhabited two worlds, *"the world of sense,* in which he is surrounded by physical objects, which operate on his senses variously, and awaken the corresponding sensations and perceptions, and *the world of intellect* in which he rises above the physical world, and becomes aware of objects, operations, and relations, which do not strike the external senses." To speak about the world of intellect necessitated a borrowing from the language of sense. Gibbs would explain (in an article published in 1838) that abstract nouns had their roots in the physical world. They were "faded metaphors," in which the literal or physical sense of the word had been lost. Bushnell would modify and make use of these ideas, and credit them to Gibbs, in his own later writings on language. Whether he learned them in their unpublished form while still a student is impossible to say.

The other individual was Samuel Taylor Coleridge. Poet, literary critic, and religious philosopher, Coleridge voiced many of the themes that would distinguish the nineteenth century from its immediate predecessor. If the eighteenth century was enamored of the machine — imaging nature as a great watch and God as the supreme watchmaker — Coleridge saw the world as vital and ultimately spiritual. In writings such as his *Aids to Reflection* he set forth three important themes that would reverberate throughout the century. The first was the distinction between reason and understanding. The understanding was the logical and empirical way of knowing; it was the adding-up-the-sums or counting-the-noses way of knowledge, and was useful for the accountant or the apothecary. But reason was that intuitive or creative path to knowledge; in his words, "Reason is the power of Universal or necessary Convictions, the Source and Substance of Truths above Sense, and having their evidence in themselves." Its venue was not empiricism but the flash of insight. True religious knowledge for Coleridge lay in the realm of the reason, so that no accumulation of evidence or logical construct could ever reach the essence of religious knowledge. A second theme was the interplay between the natural and the spiritual. Just as understanding and reason operated in tandem so too did the natural and the supernatural. Because Coleridge saw the spiritual or supernatural as always lying behind the natural, he rejected any attempt to divide them into separate spheres. Finally, Coleridge emphasized that the essence of religion was not doctrine but life. When religion found itself reduced to a speculative system it became "a bare Skeleton of Truth, without life or interest, alike inaccessible and unintelligible to the majority of Christians."

Coleridge's writings would make their mark in America, particularly with James Marsh's 1829 edition of the *Aids to Reflection*. But the date and degree of Coleridge's influence on Bushnell continue to be disputed questions. Bushnell claimed that he discovered the writings of Coleridge while at Yale, possibly even before his "conversion" of

1831, and toward the end of his life he was emphatic about the poet's influence on him. He was "more indebted to Coleridge than to any [other] extra-scriptural author," he claimed. Since many of Coleridge's themes can be seen in Bushnell's writings, it would be easy to classify Bushnell as an early and enthusiastic disciple of the man. But perhaps one should take neither the date nor the indebtedness at face value. Despite the suggestion that he discovered Coleridge before 1831, there are few distinctly Coleridgean themes in his 1832 essay, particularly in contrast to writing that he produced a few years later. In addition, the *Aids to Reflection* was a famously enigmatic book; the observation one American made upon reading another of Coleridge's writings — "It is a strange book, written all around the subject, though not wanting in force and spirit" — could equally be applied to it. Moreover, Coleridge's themes were in no way unique to him. They could be found in German writings of the times, and echoes of similar themes appeared in works by a variety of writers. Indeed, Coleridge's power may have been that he put into words an intuition that was swelling up among many who were stifling under the heavy weight of mechanistic categories. Coleridge confirmed for his readers what they had already intuited, that there was a greater spiritual reality in the world than surface appearances might imply. Although there are key parallels between the thought of Coleridge and Bushnell, therefore, it seems likely that they were more like two travelers on the same journey than like a teacher and his disciple.

In the summer of 1832 Bushnell became licensed to preach by the New Haven West Clerical Association, and he intended to leave the city immediately in search of a pulpit. But events again intervened. In the beginning of the summer he had agreed to lead a Bible class for the ladies of the Third Congregational Church. There he met an attractive young woman, Mary M. Apthorp, and fell in love. For this reason he wanted to stay near New Haven until he had assurance of a permanent call. Then he would be able to marry.

So he busied himself in writing and in preaching an occasional visiting sermon. His first sermon was to his home church in New Preston, and he took as his text "Why will ye die?" (Jer. 27:13) He also preached in Watertown, Connecticut. Finally in February of 1832 he was invited to preach at North Church in Hartford, whose pulpit had become vacant. If he were successful a permanent call might result.

So for the second time in five years Bushnell left New Haven. He left the city a very different person than he had been in 1823. There he had received an education and found a calling. And he had begun a relationship with Yale that would continue to his death. He also had begun the process of negotiating between a world of homespun and a far more complicated world.

3 Explaining the Faith; Defending the Faith

HARTFORD was the oldest town in Connecticut, and there were still in the 1830s marks that reminded one of its two hundred years of history. The curfew bell was still rung at nine o'clock each evening, as it had been for years. (One visitor earlier in the century had commented that when the bell rang "all good citizens drank their cider, raked up their fires, and returned to their beds." Many still did so, though as a result of the temperance campaign their drink would not have been anything as strong as hard cider.) The Connecticut River still dominated the city, and commerce on the river was still important. But not everything was as it had been in the past. Changes in fashion and public propriety no longer made the town smell of "molasses and old Jamaica [rum]," as it had earlier in the century. And like other towns across the country, Hartford was changing in more important ways, growing in size and complexity. In 1812 it had been a small commercial town of four thousand hugging the banks of the river, but by 1830 it had almost doubled in size. Manufacturing was edging out shipping as the economic center of the city. The first woolen mill in the country was built on the Little (or Mill) River, and residents of Hartford spoke proudly of the fact that George Washington had delivered his first inaugural address wearing a suit made of its cloth. Britannia ware, bells, watches, books, and friction matches were all now manufactured there. Improved roads and a new canal allowed visitors to reach the city more easily, and foreigners were regularly impressed by two institutions that represented the new spirit of humanitarianism and the old emphasis on Puritan order: Hartford's Asylum for the Deaf, founded by Thomas Gallaudet, the first free school for the deaf in America, and, in nearby Weathersfield, the state prison.

If Hartford combined both old and new elements in matters of commerce and industry, it did so as well in things religious. Even though the standing order had ended a decade and a half earlier, the Congregational Church still held sway. The First Church of Christ was as old as the colony itself, and in 1807 it had moved into an impressive new building in the style of Wren baroque. Moving away from the plain style used in earlier buildings, the new meetinghouse sported a central steeple, Ionic columns, and a pulpit on the narrow end of the rectangular building rather than on the wide side that had been favored by earlier generations. All bespoke the prominence and prosperity of the former established church. The spirit of the standing order could also be found in the laws of the state, and strict order was still maintained. No ropedancers, tumblers, or mountebanks were allowed to perform, the theater was illegal, and it was only in 1833 that some of the restrictions on Sunday labor and recreation were lifted.

But all was not what it seemed. Throughout the previous decade Hartford had been a crucial battleground between the orthodox and the Unitarians. As Lyman Beecher, who visited the city to fight against the Unitarian forces, recalled, the Unitarian onslaught had been "systematic, keen, and persevering," and the outcome had not been certain. Another of the orthodox champions in the battle for Hartford had been the Reverend Joel Hawes, minister of First Church. Hawes brought a new and more emotional style of preaching to the church and used it to stem the Unitarian surge. By the end of the decade Unitarianism had been checked, but almost immediately the orthodox began to fight among themselves over the theology of Nathaniel William Taylor, and former allies became antagonists. By the early 1830s Hartford Congregationalists were divided between followers of Taylor and followers of Bennet Tyler, whose seminary in East Windsor had become a bastion of conservative Congregationalism.

In addition, Episcopalians were making their presence known.

Christ Episcopal Church was as least as noble a structure as First Church. Its old building (in use until 1829) had been considered by many the handsomest in town. Not affected by the Puritan proclivity toward plainness, it sported a magnificent steeple adorned with four urns. In 1829 the old structure was replaced by an even more impressive building in the new gothic style. Episcopalians could boast of as much dignity and solemnity as the Congregationalists and did not seem to be so constantly divided. Furthermore, they were attracting a number of the leading families of the town. Lydia Sigourney, the celebrated poet and literary figure, was one such figure, and she espoused with enthusiasm her newly acquired Episcopal theology. In contrast to the emotional preaching of persons like Joel Hawes, the moderation, decorum, and beauty of Episcopal worship had their attractions.

If the presence of a thriving Christ Church reminded all that the age-old opponents of the Puritans were alive and well, there were hints of an even greater challenge. The homogeneity of the Puritan commonwealth was being challenged. Almost since the first settlers arrived, Connecticut had been a bastion of Yankeedom. As late as 1821 only thirty-one foreigners were recorded as entering the state from any of the local seaports, but during the 1830s this had begun to change. Attracted by the building projects of the era, an influx of Irish laborers began to make their appearance. By 1840 Hartford possessed not only two Episcopal congregations but one Roman Catholic one as well.

Hartford, in all of this, was not unique. It mirrored changes happening all over New England as cities grew, manufacturing increased, and the religious and cultural unity that had been a prized part of the Land of Steady Habits gave way to a far more complex society. In this process, many wondered how one could hold on to the traditional values in such an altered landscape.

ESTABLISHING A MINISTRY

North Church, to which Bushnell and his new wife would soon make their way, reflected this mixture of old and new. The congregation was organized in 1824 from members of Joel Hawes's First Church. Although the official chroniclers insisted that it was organized "not because of ill will but lack of space," others have not been so sure. Whatever the reasons, on September 23, 1824, ninety-seven persons left First Church and came together as the new congregation, to be joined by five others. (All told, there were thirty-nine males and sixty-three females.) A meetinghouse was dedicated December 1, 1824, and was designed in the style of First Church. A Wren baroque steeple graced the liturgical west end, and the new church had the added luxury of rounded windows. That building no longer stands, but engravings from the 1840s and 1850s do reveal one distinctive peculiarity of the meetinghouse: on top of its steeple there seems to have been a cross instead of the typical weather vane. The building was far larger than was needed for 102 worshippers, and nearly half of the floor seatings were unoccupied. But it was hoped that a dynamic minister would fill the church.

Who such a minister should be became the question. In October of 1824 the church issued a call to the Reverend Carlos Wilcox, a graduate of Middlebury and Andover. He was a sensitive, poetic, sickly man whose sermons were described as "a beauty of thought and expression." In the pulpit he strove for "tasteful decoration." Sickness (probably tuberculosis) forced him to resign in the Spring of 1826, and he died the next year. He was succeeded by a very different type of minister. Samuel Spring had the vitality and gusto lacking in Wilcox. He had been a sea captain and had even been captured by the British as a blockade-runner during the War of 1812. He was a blunt New England cleric, far more at home railing against drink than writing poetry. He also may have been a devotee of Nathaniel William Taylor's activist theology. Yet by 1832 he too had left.

For a congregation that had first called a poet and then a pilot, the choice of Bushnell — who combined character traits of both men — must have seemed ideal. And indeed Bushnell's later ministry would take up some of the themes of both of his predecessors. First, however, he had to run the gantlet of theology. As he later recalled, the congregation's doyens were almost equally divided between Taylorites and Tylerites. On the occasion of the twentieth anniversary of his call, Bushnell recalled traveling from Litchfield through drifts of snow and arriving at the house of the chair of the calling committee; before he was able to settle in he was immediately whisked off to the house of another committee member. He was only later to learn that the chair had been a Taylorite, and he feared that it would be unseemly for a recent graduate of Yale, such as Bushnell, to be too closely associated with him. "The committee had made up their mind, very prudently, that it would not do for me to stay even one hour with the New-school brother of the committee."

But for Bushnell the division between Taylorites and Tylerites was no more an insurmountable problem than had been his father's carding machine. One simply had to start from a "very small mustard seed of Christian experience" rather than from the received doctrines. The result was one of his earliest sermons, "Duty Not Measured by Our Ability." In their catch phrase "power to the contrary," Taylorites had trumpeted the role of the human will. Seeing in these words Arminianism, Tylerites had rallied to the banner of divine sovereignty. But, as Bushnell explained, this was a false dichotomy. God could empower individuals to acts far beyond anyone's conceptions. He offered as examples to his flock figures dear to the New England pantheon: David, Luther, Cromwell, and George Washington. "How childish," he reminded them, "is it in religion, to imagine that we are called to do nothing, save what we have ability to do beforehand; ability in ourselves to do." In the religious life, God has arranged for supplying "spiritual" or "supernatural" help to meet the challenge. Bushnell's compromise, which combined elements of both human will and divine grace, was apparently acceptable to all concerned. An older Bushnell, looking back at this incident, saw it as reflective of much of his later ministry. "My ruling endeavor has been in all my investigations of truth, to find a form of doctrine broad enough to include, as far as possible, the opposing truths or half-truths which Christian believers are contending."

We should pause and note, however, that Bushnell was revealing something else about himself and his later career in the incident. His solution hung precariously upon the interpretation of his terms "spiritual" and "supernatural." These words bear the load that more technical and traditional categories had for Tyler and Taylor. Bushnell's language was emotive and personal, and would always run the risk of being misunderstood — or at times of being understood better than Bushnell himself had intended — by those of a technical or traditional bent. Bushnell would always be the Yankee tinkerer. Not everyone would be enamored of his handiwork.

THE PROBLEMS OF RELIGION

Bushnell was very much the pastor, and one of the responsibilities he took most seriously was preaching. His sermons (at least in their printed form) are carefully crafted works with a high literary flair, and his contemporaries often commented on his pulpit style. There was a fiery, urgent quality to his preaching, and although he was never the sort of preacher who attracted great crowds, some found his style quite arresting. One contemporary noted that he spoke to his congregation as equals and took them into his confidence in a way that gave life to old ideals. His disdain for the logician can be seen in the way he crafted his sermons. Rejected was any attempt to approach the great truths of Scripture through any biblical or theological system. Instead he offered to his congregation the power of a direct look.

But what is perhaps most striking to the modern reader is Bushnell's preoccupation with the problems of religion. How can one find God? How can one believe? How can one be sure? All of these were recurring questions for him. The central issue of his sermons was not right doctrine but belief itself, and the task of the preacher was not philosophical analysis but shepherding his flock through the threshold of belief. "To mill out a scheme of free will and responsibility," he told his congregation, "to settle metaphysically questions of ability and inability, to show the scheme of regeneration as related to a theory of sin and not to conscious fact may all be very ingenious and we may call it gospel, but it is scarcely more than a form of rationalism." Such questions pleased the head but they did not feed the heart; only true religious belief could do that.

How that religious belief could be appropriated was the theme of many of his sermons. Whether he was speaking autobiographically (as many great preachers have) or with an ear to the doubts and struggles of his flock, a Bushnell sermon often began with a recognition of doubt, of the scandal of belief, or of the problem of faith. He responded in two ways. At times he cajoled his congregation. Religious faith was a practical skill. By doing we become. He likened the soul to a garden that responds to labor. "Religion is cultivation itself," he explained. "No one becomes a Christian who cannot by the cultivation of thought . . . make himself a gift of four fold, and perhaps even an hundred fold value to the church." In another sermon, "The Capacity of Religion Ex-

tirpated by Disuse," he argued that people lose their childhood faith
not because their intellectual world becomes too complicated but because their spiritual lives become flabby from lack of use. If a concern
for things religious is lost, the religious sense is affected; "eyes disused
gradually lose the power to see." He often sounded this theme of discipline. By striving, determination, and dedication one could make faith
grow. One should not sit passively hoping that the Holy Spirit would
miraculously open minds that had been consciously closed to its
power. "It requires a talent . . . for the Holy Spirit to entertain or receive
[an individual]." One must first prepare a place, and that was the
Christian's responsibility.

At other times, however, Bushnell seemed to acknowledge that
the fault did not lie with his congregation's lack of concern; rather,
something was broken. There existed a disconnectedness between the
great truth of religion and the lives of modern men and women. It was
as if a veil stood between his congregation and the power of faith, and
all that existed on this side of the veil were disconnected facts, lacking
power. "The Christian facts," he observed, "are stored in history, and
are scarcely more significant to us, than if they were stored in the
moon." The task of the preacher was to make these real. He was to
evoke this power in his hearers, not to defend it through logic. As he
explained in still another sermon, "a life separated from God is a life of
bitter hunger or even of spiritual starvation. My object will be not so
much to prove this truth as to make it apparent and visible . . . by
means of appropriate illustrations." Throughout the early years of his
ministry Bushnell put his mind to work on the question of how one
could make religion real.

From early on he was sure of what paths not to take. He rejected
the path of moral culture favored by the Unitarians. "Christianity," he
explained, "is not any doctrine of development or self-culture, nor
scheme of ethical practice, or social re-organization." The right school-
ing or the right books could not make one a Christian. If this were possible surely some enterprising Yankee would have mastered the technique. Likewise, the sacramental model of his Episcopal neighbors,
who saw regeneration as being effected by the waters of baptism, was
sacerdotal silliness to Bushnell. "To admit that such a change could be
manipulated, or officially passed, by a priest in the rite of baptism, is
no better than a solemn trifling with the subject." But if Bushnell could

easily dismiss the schemas of those critics of the Puritan way, he was nonetheless uneasy about the paths urged by his evangelical contemporaries. Regeneration could not be effected by "waiting for some new creating act of God, to be literally passed on the soul." The revival method was also flawed. His 1838 essay "Spiritual Economies of Revivals of Religion" was his first public discussion of the issue. Although in the piece he took care to praise much of the good that resulted from revivals, he argued that as a "system" revivalism had two related flaws. What bothered Bushnell first was how temporary the accomplishments were. Almost always after the season of excitement, deterioration and disillusion began to take root. It seemed to him such an inefficient system, with so much loss. But on a deeper level revivalism was but the tip of a greater issue, that of conversion. Revivalism emerged as a means of bringing about the conversion experience that many New Englanders saw as necessary for full church membership. It was part of the genius of the activist spirit of New England Calvinism. But what if all of this were based on a false premise? In this essay all of Bushnell's problems with the concept of conversion began to well up. He explained that the popular saying that the great goal of the gospel and the church was to convert humankind had "as much error as truth in it." "The great business of the gospel is to form men to God," he asserted. Conversion might begin that process, but what mattered was fruition. Like the sower of grain in the Bible story, sowing was not an end in itself, but the beginning of a process that ended in harvest. What men and women truly needed was to learn how to grow. Regeneration was an act of the Spirit, but it was a human action as well. Bushnell wrestled with both how this was to be accomplished and how it was to be explained from within the context of the world of New England theology. The first issue he addressed immediately; the second he would return to.

An early sermon, "Every Man's Life a Plan of God," shows the direction of Bushnell's thought. The essence of the human predicament was choice. God has a destiny for each person — "God has a definite life-plan for every human person," he told his flock — and we have the freedom to accept this plan or not. But if such a plan existed, he continued, why was it so hard to perceive, and why did so many struggle to apprehend God's will? Why was it that God seemed so distant and his plans so opaque? The answer lay in the nature of the human predicament. Men and women must follow God with only imperfect and limited knowledge. God will guide us, "but he will not comfort your distrust, or half trust of him, by showing you the chart of all his purposes concerning you." Belief and doubt were not antitheses, but part of the same process.

If the power of the human will was important, so was the use of language. From the very beginning of *Sermons for the New Life* (a volume of early sermons) one enters a rhetorical world far different from the standard New England preaching of the day. Bushnell's longstanding impatience with logic is present, as is his interest in using rhetoric to move or touch his listeners. But more than this, Bushnell's preaching displays his fundamentally paradoxical view of language. Language is part of both the problem and the solution of the Christian life. It is problematic because it makes up much of the veil that blocks us from true religious knowledge. But when it is properly used language can in turn be a powerful tool for piercing that veil.

PIERCING THE VEIL OF LANGUAGE

He had the opportunity to explore this paradox when the Love of Inquiry Society at Andover Seminary asked him in 1839 to deliver an address. He chose as his topic "Revelation." The preparation for the address was stressful. The Society had moved up the date of the talk, but Bushnell had neglected to record the new date in his almanac. When he discovered his error he had only a day to finish his address, of which he had written only "one or two pages." But clearly this was a topic to which he had given much thought, and the address remains one of his earliest developed statements on religious language.

Revelation was for Bushnell the conduit between abstract truth and humanity. Indeed, the highest aspect of God was neither his knowledge nor his power but his "publicity," his ability to communicate truth to the world. Revelation brought truth into outward exhibition. To accomplish this feat two things were necessary. There needed to be a form to convey the truth — revelation could not be conveyed from mind to mind directly, only through forms such as metaphors and types. And one needed an intelligent mind to perceive the meaning of the forms. Without such perception revelation was impossible.

"An ox grazing on the burning bush," he noted, "would have seen all that Moses saw . . . but it would have been a fire in his eye . . . not the type of an invisible God."

From revelation he turned to language. Language, he explained, had two "stories," a literal meaning directed to physical fact and a metaphorical level used to address issues of thought and truth. To describe moral or intellectual concepts physical images were employed as metaphors. This metaphorical usage grew as civilization grew, and the progress of the human race could be seen as a movement from the physical to the moral. But while moral language transcended the physical it never fully escaped from it. In the language of truth and value the original physical metaphors could still be felt. In the words "right" or "duty" the original image of a straight line still existed, just as in the word "humility" one still heard echoes of the physical image of "humus" or ground.

The ultimate power of language to communicate, he continued, came from God. Earlier, natural theologians had suggested that the order of nature communicated to rational individuals the orderly nature of God. The *Bridgewater Treatises,* for example, were a series of apologetics using the order of nature to prove the existence of God. For Bushnell, language now possessed this power. God had invested the power of communication into the metaphors of language, and humans understood the web of words because they possessed this power of language as a gift from God. "Here then in language we have a revelation of God which shows, as in a mirror, one vast and varied image of his intelligence. Language in fact is the grand Bridgewater treatise of the universe."

Bushnell then turned to the images found in Scripture and argued that a parallel to the two levels of language occurred there. The Old Testament was filled with all sorts of graphic and earthy imagery. Floods, brazen serpents, sacrificing priests, and blood-drenched altars were just a few of the myriad images found in its pages. But in the New Testament all these figures and events became understood to be not finally physical, but signs pointing to the spiritual power of Christ. They provided a vocabulary to help the New Testament writers explain the meaning of Jesus. But just as nature continued to leave its lingering influence on language, so too did the directness of the Old Testament linger in the spiritual message of the New.

One senses that Bushnell's intended audience for this address was not merely the students at Andover but the Unitarian congregations of eastern Massachusetts as well. At the time of the address the controversy over Transcendentalism had been raging for over a year, and only two months earlier Ralph Waldo Emerson had issued his famous (or infamous) Harvard Divinity School Address. In it, Emerson had declared his independence from a religion of Scripture and his loyalty to a religion of nature. Nature, he explained, was real — and through it the reality of the One could be experienced. A religion based on the Scriptures, in contrast, was stale and secondhand. Thus he urged his readers to take up the true religion of Jesus and all other great religious geniuses, which approached the divine directly through nature and not indirectly through religious texts.

Bushnell's insistence on the importance of the biblical imagery was thus in contrast to the Transcendentalist appeal directly to nature. The Bible, he assured his listeners, would stand forever. "It will be the school book . . . of philosophy to the end of time." Indeed, humankind's advances would only serve to make the Bible a richer book. Students would be able to derive from its images and figures more and more meaning. One of the few viewpoints he graced with the term "heretical" was any rejection of the forms of truth that God had provided in the Bible, or "annihilating all the extra natural types and words in which God has come nigh to us."

Yet he did not hold back his criticism of what he saw as the failures of the orthodox in New England. Scripture for them was not a vital series of images and metaphors but a mass of dead facts. In their passion for logical system building they mined the Scriptures, digging for doctrinal nuggets. They then in turn strove to refine the scriptural images into neat ingots of doctrine to be carefully stacked in some convenient theological depository. To do so, Bushnell claimed, robbed Scripture of its power as much as did ignoring it.

Bushnell concluded his address with a reflection on how his view of language affected the role of the preacher. The true preacher, he observed, was neither a dogmatist nor a logician. "Logic is the weakest and most unfructifying of all arts." The preacher must not shy away from the power of the scriptural images, but must use the spiritual power embedded in the language as a tool for conveying the truth. As in poetry, the choice of the right word was everything. When thoughts and words existed in harmony language had the ability to soar. Furthermore, the true preacher must always see the images of Scripture as not simply rhetorical exercises but as the lexicon of divine truth. When armed with a care for language and a love of truth the preacher could become a modern prophet. "His being, in fact, mind and body, look, tone and action become one animate harmonious organ of power." When form and truth came together in preaching, true religion could triumph.

The Connecticut tinkerer in a mere thirty pages had modestly plumbed the nature of language and the meaning of Scripture and had set forth a plan for the triumph of the gospel. In this early endeavor one sees characteristics that would often reappear in Bushnell's later writings: bold originality, impatience with traditional categories, and a willingness to redesign things from scratch. But one sees at the same time his reverence for the Scriptures and his respect for scriptural vocabulary. Tinkering was for the purpose of preserving.

SEEKING A MORAL ORDER

As a minister in the capital city of Connecticut, where the swirl of politics never ceased, Bushnell could not avoid the larger issues of his day. For anyone born in the ordered certainty of the old standing order, the political and social changes of the 1830s must have been mind-boggling, if not disturbing. If proper New Englanders had earlier raised their voices against the radical principles of Thomas Jefferson, their children were even less pleased with one of his successors, Andrew Jackson. Jackson had revolutionized American politics by introducing a new spirit of partisanship and overthrowing marks of the traditional order. The era of the "common man" seemed to threaten the ordered sensibilities of the land of steady habits. These were sentiments shared by Bushnell. As a young graduate of Yale College he had questioned the moral nature of a democracy. "Real merit," he lamented, "has very little to do with political elevation." An insatiable desire for political advantage had polluted public discourse; the only question one heard was who should govern, never what were to be the basic principles of right order.

The tumultuous nature of Jacksonian America made Bushnell's

distaste for partisan politics even stronger. The election of 1840 — with its corruption, huge rallies, and use of campaign techniques like the distribution of hard cider — was embarrassing even by American standards. In these trends, the good Puritan minister saw the shadows of Pilate and the mob. Some said that democracy was sacred — that the voice of the people echoed God's will. But such an attitude, Bushnell warned, led to "Gospel Jacobinism," or a "fanatical storm in which all the elements of religion and politics shall be blended, and their distinction lost." The signs of sickness were there for all to see: the spoils system in which government service was seen as a reward for political loyalty rather than as a public trust, and the rejection of higher virtues in favor of political coalitions.

In addition, the glue that held together the society was being eaten away. Earlier in the century Protestant churches had been united in their emphasis on reforming the moral life of the republic, but that unity was fast disappearing and society was being pulled apart. The 1830s witnessed an intensification of reform movements. What one writer christened "freedom's ferment" poured forth in all manner of panaceas. Conservatives bristled when reforms, such as that of temperance, seemed to surpass the guidelines found in Scripture. The question of slavery was particularly divisive. In Hartford it provoked great agitation, and Bushnell's own church — which contained its share of transplanted Southerners — was not immune to the controversy. Here too there was no clear guide in Scripture. Was there a solution?

It was during this time of questioning that Bushnell was invited to address the alumni of Yale College. In his address, published under the title "A Discourse on the Moral Tendencies and Results of Human History," he applied some of his insights concerning language and learning to the question of the social fabric. He began with his familiar theme that in the development of humanity the physical preceded the moral, sharing with his audience examples he had already used at Andover such as the origin of language and the development of religion. He then noted that the same trend was also true in the case of governance. It too moved from a physical stage, in which the strongest ruled, to an elevation of morality. In this upward movement, he told his listeners, Yale College played a role. "This venerable institution exists for a moral purpose. Letters are here subordinate to virtue."

But how, he asked, did one apprehend virtue? One recalls that in his earlier discourse on revelation he had suggested a relationship between truth and language in which the latter communicates but in a proximate way the former. He suggested that a similar system was at work in the transmission of virtue. On the one hand virtue is an absolute or ideal rightness. But it also exists in the forms of the outward conduct of life. These rules of conduct are what communicate virtue to humanity, but like language they are proximate. "The substance of virtue is not here," he explained, "but only her forms of action." Furthermore, moral sentiment, like language, is also open to the law of development. Just as in our spiritual nature advances give us a deeper insight into revelation, so too do advances in moral sentiment allow humanity to bring our moral laws closer to true virtue. This helps explain the moral advances in the Bible — from the ambivalent morality of the patriarch where birthrights and blessings are happily stolen to the higher morality of the prophets.

He went on to note that such moral progress continues at present, and he offered three examples: attitudes toward wine, slavery, and war. Each had found a place in the scriptural record, and each had generally been tolerated by the Christian church. But increasingly all three were under scrutiny by virtuous individuals. Modern Christians were raising scruples that were not found in scriptural writers. It was not that modern Christians were morally superior to the writers of Scripture, but that they benefited from this moral development. The scriptural record, he noted, contained both positive moral or religious commands and accounts of primitive practices that were (at least temporarily) tolerated. Thus he concluded,

> The real question on these subjects [i.e., wine, slavery, and war] . . . is not on one side whether we can torture the Scriptures so as we can make it condemn all that we desire to exclude, nor on the other whether we are bound, for all time, and eternity to boot, to justify what the Scripture suffers . . . but the question philosophically stated, is whether new cognate inventions and uses, do not make old practices more destructive, old vias more incurable — whether a new age of the world and a capacity of better things, have not so changed the relations of the practice in issue, that they are no longer the same, and no longer to be justified.

In order to solve the problems besetting society, therefore, citizens must desire virtue as much as Christians loved the language of the Bible. If they did so the Scriptures would be not a roadblock to moral advance, but rather its true avenue. The law of growth would provide a way out.

Bushnell must have felt pride in his address before his old college. He had outlined a course of progress in which Yale men and sons of Connecticut were playing an important role: Lyman Beecher had stirred society's conscience about wine, and Connecticut-born David Low Dodge was a leader in the peace crusade. Perhaps most famous was Bushnell's old teacher Josiah Willard Gibbs. In 1839 the *Amistad*, a Spanish vessel manned by Africans, was apprehended in the Long Island Sound. The Spanish claimed that the Africans had mutinied and demanded both them and the ship back. Since the Africans spoke no English their side of the story could not be heard. It was Gibbs's linguistic skills that came to the rescue. He was able to master their native language enough to find an interpreter. The Africans eventually proved that they were unlawfully enslaved, and they were accordingly found innocent in a celebrated legal case. The children of Connecticut could take pride in their role in the great story of moral advance.

Bushnell's contentment, however, was short-lived, as he quickly found himself under attack. An anonymous pamphlet appeared entitled *A Letter to Dr. Bushnell of Hartford on the Rationalistic, Socinian, and Infidel Tendency of Certain Passages in His Address Before the Alumni of Yale College*. The writer's chosen *nom de plume*, "Catholicus," suggested that he was an Episcopalian.

Catholicus began by noting the parallels between Bushnell's schema of development and those of such notorious critics of Christianity as David Hume, Charles Blount, and Joseph Priestley. All three were infamous to pious American Christians, and all three had taught that progress moved from the physical to the moral. Catholicus took particular delight in linking Bushnell's notion that government began in rule by the strong with a similar idea in Hume, and in contrasting both with the judicious (and Anglican) Richard Hooker's idea of an original social contract. Catholicus also faulted Bushnell for failing to take seriously the biblical history of the early chapters of the book of Genesis when formulating both his theory of language and his notion of the development of religion. If Eve had communicated to Adam in the Garden of Eden about knowing good and evil, then conceptual language could not have appeared only late in human development. Catholicus carefully corrected Bushnell's bold assertions by appealing to sober British biblical experts such as Richard Graves and Samuel Horsley. The subtext was clear for all to see — Bushnell was a provincial and unsophisticated thinker and needed to be instructed by British divines.

A third problem, according to Catholicus, was Bushnell's "theory madness" and his attempt to force all evidence into his categories. This led him to a less than reverential approach to the Scriptures. To claim, as Bushnell did, that Noah was a chronic drunkard might delight modern-day proponents of temperance, but it showed little respect for either the facts or the spirit of the Scriptures. Furthermore, if his theory of moral advance were true, then the Pharisees who rejected Jesus were on a higher moral plane than the patriarchs.

Finally, Catholicus suggested that in Bushnell's language about Jesus one could catch the scent of Socinianism. He noted that he had read some portions of the address to a "friend accustomed to Socinian ways of talking" and asked him who might be the author. His friend responded that it sounded like the Unitarian, William Ellery Channing, or more probably a transcendentalist like Emerson or Parker. He was far from challenging Bushnell's sincerity as a Christian, but concluded that Bushnell did not or could not understand the true nature of orthodox Christianity. "Are you one thing Dr. Bushnell preaching in Hartford," Catholicus asked, "and another thing as Dr. Bushnell addressing the alumni of Yale College?" If so it testified to the sad state of affairs within Connecticut Congregationalism. If the orthodox Yale applauded such performances from one of its sons, then its orthodoxy had become questionable at best. "It will soon go . . . to slumber by the side of its sister Harvard."

Catholicus baited both Bushnell and Connecticut Congregationalism in general. His underlying theme was to contrast the mature, conservative, sophisticated biblical faith of the Anglican heritage with the adolescent and erratic beliefs of the Congregationalists, who always tottered on the brink of heresy and disaster. As if such a provocation was not enough, the back cover of the pamphlet advertised it as but one of a series of tracts on "Romanism and Dissent." Not only were the proud heirs of the standing order dismissed as "dissenters" in their own state, but they were put on the same level as Roman Catholics! Something had to be done.

DEFENDING THE RELIGION OF THE PURITANS

Thus for the next three years Bushnell became deeply involved in the battle over episcopacy, which involved both practical and theoretical concerns. In some ways the battles of the 1840s were but another phase in the controversy, begun in the library at Yale College in 1722, that had pitted a Congregational appeal to the language of the New Testament on the equality of ministry against an Anglican appeal to the presence of bishops in the life of the early church. But by the 1840s the issues had broadened. One factor was undoubtedly the Episcopal Church's successful growth in Connecticut. Each decade beginning in the 1820s witnessed a doubling of the size of the Episcopal communion, largely through converts from the old standing order. For Bushnell, the growth of nearby Christ Church, Hartford, was particularly foreboding. Christ Church grew at a faster rate than North Church and was attracting some of the most prestigious citizens of the city. Part of the appeal was the refinement of the worship. The building was a handsome gothic structure and the Prayer Book liturgy combined dignity of spirit and chasteness of expression. The sacramental focus also appealed to many, since the Episcopal emphasis upon entrance into the church through the waters of baptism seemed to sidestep all the thorny theological issues that wrenched Congregationalism. Finally, there were cultural factors. As the anglophobia of the Revolutionary generation began slowly to give way, many were attracted to the Episcopal self-identification with a more refined English culture.

Bushnell was well aware of these appealing factors. As we will see, his writings on the subject of Christian nurture were composed with one eye on the upstart Episcopalians. And he did not simply reject the attractions of refinement; he could see their effects on his own congregants. Earlier in 1843 he had composed an essay that suggested a place for a spirit of refinement in a Puritan culture. "Taste and Fashion" followed the same general theme of both "Revelation" and "A Discourse on the Moral Tendencies" and highlighted the idea of spiritual advance. In the story of the advancement of human society, he explained, there had been two great victories — the freeing of the ideas of truth and reason from mere force and the liberating of taste and beauty from the dictates of fashion. Beauty, like truth, was part of the divine order of the world. "Beauty descends from heaven to be the clothing of spiritual intelligence and the grace of Christian piety." It was natural and wholesome. Fashion, in contrast, was rooted in caste. It was always tied to the court or to the aristocracy. It was both artificial and hierarchical. Furthermore, it was imitative. "The term *fashion* carries a sense of imitation with it, on this side of the Atlantic, which is far less prominent on the other." In his defense of taste and beauty and rejection of fashion, Bushnell went on to add that taste was a republican virtue while fashion was unrepublican. In the case of religion, a refinement of taste could only help. One should never fear such refinements. "If a tasteful religion is dangerous," he observed, "what will you say of an untasteful? — what of a religion that glories in the absence of all order and dignity?"

The underlying thrust of the essay was that good Christian citizens were right to strive for taste and beauty since to do so indicated a high degree of intellectual culture. As the intellectual and moral level of a community advanced so too did its appreciation for beauty. But one must always be wary of fashion. For Bushnell, Connecticut Episcopalians were fashionable in all the odious senses of that term. Their worship was imitative, it stemmed not from a spirit of truth, and it all too often had a snobbery appeal. It was also artificial; it did not emerge out of the culture of New England but was a foreign imposition. "Taste and Fashion" can be read as an indirect rebuke upon his Episcopal neighbors.

But by the end of 1843 Bushnell was no longer satisfied with indirect rebukes. The aggression of writers like Catholicus had added a social and theological element to the controversy. Catholicus' theme that Congregationalism was abandoning the true faith and teetering on the brink of collapse began to be echoed by other voices. The great Catholic revival coming out of Oxford that swept through nineteenth-century Anglicanism emboldened Episcopal apologists. They gleefully pointed to the divisions and disarray of American Protestantism and argued that the multiplicity of sectarian communities confused

69

the populace and allowed many to avoid the religious question. Some suggested that the social and political divisions facing Americans in the 1840s were exacerbated by the fanatical spirit engendered by popular Protestantism. The Episcopal Church, in contrast, was a rock of safety.

It was irritating enough for anonymous pamphleteers to make such charges, but in June of 1843 they were also voiced by Thomas Church Brownell, Episcopal bishop of Connecticut, in his annual charge to the clergy. He entitled his address "Errors of the Times" but it could perhaps more accurately have been entitled "Congregational Errors of the Times." Brownell focused on three issues. First, lacking the Book of Common Prayer as a standard of faith and worship, popular Protestantism interpreted the Scriptures with reckless abandon. The principle of private judgment allowed any person's opinion to have equal authority with any other person's. The seeds of this error lay in the seventeenth-century Puritan migration itself, for in their rejection of the Church of England and its Prayer Book liturgy the Puritans had unleashed this spirit of division. Puritanism, he explained, had bred the "schisms, the heresies, the infidelity, the fanaticism which have everywhere sprung up." Both learned theologians and ignorant mechanics had broken the unity of the church into a myriad of sects in their support for some new doctrine, and "No metaphysical quibble appears too slight to obtain partizans." A second error was the loss of any emphasis on the church as a visible institution. The children of the Puritans, Brownell explained, elected their clergy, which made them subservient to the popular will. Other American religious communities went further and rejected the very idea of an ordained clergy. In contrast, Episcopalians could emphasize their historic ministry. Finally, he noted how the sacramental life of American Protestantism had declined, particularly with regard to baptism, which had lost any real power among the people. He quoted Timothy Dwight, who had lamented, "There is but too much reason to believe that [people who have been baptized] are . . . lamentably ignorant of the nature of this institution, the truths which it declares, the duties which it involves, and the privileges which it confers." The reason for this decline, Brownell went on to explain, had to do with the new view of religion that had taken root a century earlier: according to the "New-Light Theology" introduced by John Wesley, George Whitefield, and Jonathan

Edwards, true Christianity "necessitated a sudden change of heart wrought by the Holy Spirit." Since change was seen as a direct experience of the Holy Spirit rather than something brought about through the ordinary means of the church, was it any wonder that the promises of baptism had been lost?

Bushnell's ire was fueled not only by the nature of such an attack but also by its accuracy. He had expressed reservations similar to the first and third of Brownell's points, and in years to come would address them again. Yet these criticisms were now being leveled by persons who were fundamentally at odds with the Puritan tradition. Indeed, these were persons who desired to root out his cherished tradition and replace it with an exotic foreign import. Brownell himself had earlier been active in the campaign to legalize the theater in Hartford, against the wishes of the clergy of the old standing order. Furthermore, ecclesiology was not the only thing at stake. In their glorification of the faith and language of the ancient Catholic church, the Episcopalians were emphasizing not the principle of growth and development, so cherished by Bushnell, but the normative importance of the past. It was ultimately a reactionary movement, at odds with the true course of history.

Bushnell counterattacked in an anonymous article, "Review of the Errors of the Times." In it he attempted to pull away the mask of moderation and reason from his Episcopal opponents and reveal them for what they were. If one wanted to search for fanatics, one might start with the fanatics in Oxford, he argued. "Laud is alive again at Oxford, and the dead body of high church formalism is seething once more in the blaze of rubrics." The fires of fanaticism were burning in England and "our Anglican clergy on this side of the water . . . kindle up their little tapers to emulate the great fire that is burning in England." But while the English developments were worrisome, those in Connecticut were laughable. "While Oxford roars, Connecticut squeaks . . . in a soft mouse like tenor."

Much of Bushnell's essay lashed out at the pretensions of his Episcopal opponents. To use the term "dissenter" to describe the hereditary church of his home state was a "gratuitous insult" and hid the true nature of the case. The Episcopalians were the true dissenters; they stood opposed to the tradition of the land. He reminded his readers that at the birth of the nation Episcopalians were a "tory clan" while the Congregational Church "was bearing the nation on its shoulders and giving it an existence and a name." To abandon Congregationalism and enter the Episcopal Church (as Brownell had done) was to besmirch one's ancestors; and to attack private judgment "in the state of Connecticut, where every mental habit and every social institution is the distillation of Puritanism," was an outrage. Nor did Bushnell have much sympathy for Episcopal worship. It was fashion at its worst, attracting only those who "love its imposing formalities, and praise it as a tasteful religion; for the dress which the wearer is ever admiring must needs be tasteful."

Brownell was wrong not only in attacking private judgment, Bushnell argued, but in his other charges as well. It was not American Protestantism that was sectarian but the Episcopal Church; the Episcopalians were the ones who would not exchange ministers with others. Despite their separate bodies there was a "real and substantial agreement of opinion" among Congregationalists, Presbyterians, Dutch Reformed, Baptists, and Methodists. In their unity in the faith they stood as an answer to Episcopal pretensions. Yet this "substantial agreement" seems to disappear when Bushnell turned to answering Brownell's third criticism, or his critique of New Light theology. Here Bushnell artfully attempted to distance the religion of the Puritans from the excesses of the Great Awakening. He began by asserting that the New Light theology described by Brownell was the product of the Anglican clerics Whitefield and Wesley and could not be laid at the doorstep of Congregationalists. The great Jonathan Edwards had opposed it, he insisted, and had crafted an alternative that was properly rooted in the theological tradition of the Reformation. Bushnell also attempted to distinguish between Congregationalist teachings and those of Methodists. It was the latter who disparaged the ordinary means of church life and practice, and claimed that the work of the Holy Spirit could be perceptible to the mind. The Congregationalist tradition was more nuanced in its beliefs.

READYING TO MEET A WIDER WORLD

The Episcopal controversy showed Bushnell at his most Puritan. Whenever the ancient religion was challenged, particularly when it was challenged by outsiders, it had to be defended. In the controversy Bushnell put to good use his training in journalism. He was harsh, direct, cutting, and skillful in disputation. But he was also conscious of which of his opponents' blows had drawn blood. Clearly the fractious nature of American Protestantism was a problem. So was the exaggerated New Light view of conversion. And he could not help but recognize that his attempt to separate Edwards from the message of the Great Awakening was far from persuasive. He silently noticed these things that needed to be fixed.

Throughout the middle years of the decade the Episcopal controversy raged. Almost every issue of the *New Englander,* the journal published by Yale, contained at least one anonymous anti-Episcopal article. Some may have been by Bushnell; others were by friends and collaborators such as Leonard Bacon. But during all this time Bushnell found his health deteriorating. Throat problems, an all-too-common malady among clergy, began plaguing him in the mid 1830s. In the winter of 1844-45 he fell seriously ill, and in the spring of 1845 he journeyed to North Carolina in hopes that the milder climate there might be beneficial. Yet the illness continued.

Finally, at the behest of his church, Bushnell decided to try a European trip as a means of cure, hoping that the ocean voyage and the combination of physical activity and a respite from oratory might help contain his sickness. North Church graciously granted him a year's sabbatical with pay and funds to cover all his expenses, and so on July 1, 1845, the now middle-aged minister departed for England. It was twenty-two years earlier that he had discovered New Haven. Now he was to discover an even bigger world.

4 The Puritan-Yankee Abroad

T HE PERIOD of 1845-46 was pivotal to Bushnell's intellectual development; having been granted the opportunity to go on a European tour, he made the most of it. He achieved his first brush with
fame (or notoriety) with his published *Letter to His Holiness, Pope Gregory XVI*. He made contact with the Scottish philosopher John Morell
and through him encountered the new theological trends associated
with Friedrich Schleiermacher. And during the course of the year
many of the themes that would reoccur throughout his later life began
to be heard. A passion for Christian unity, a growing impatience with
stifling orthodoxy, and an awareness of the distinctiveness of American culture all find a place in the diary he kept during his travels.
Through his ruminations we can glimpse a picture of a young pastor
coming into contact with an ever-enlarging world.

Bushnell made this trip alone. By 1845 his family had increased
to five in number. Francis Louise had been born in 1834, Mary in 1837,
and Dotha in 1843, and the three girls took up all of his wife Mary's ef-
forts and prevented her from accompanying him, even if the family
could have afforded to pay for her travel expenses. Clergy traveling
for long periods, and thus being separated from their families, was far
from uncommon during the nineteenth century, but it did not make it

any easier for Bushnell. The separation from wife and daughters was painful, and he wrote back regularly. Similarly painful was the memory of two of his children who had died prematurely. A daughter, Lilly, had died soon after birth in 1837, and the couple's only son, named Horace, had died of "brain disease" in 1842, shortly before his second birthday. That memory in particular was still dear to him.

ENTERING INTO A WIDER WORLD

An ocean journey, however, has a way of putting things in perspective. The vastness of the sea cannot help but dwarf the worries and concerns of human beings. And it was such a journey that Bushnell began on July 1, 1845, aboard the British ship *Victoria*. The trip would take twenty days.

Travel inspired Bushnell, and his notebooks overflow with detailed observations. He meticulously recorded weather conditions on the journey and his mechanical mind led him to describe every structure and contraption he came across. But what interested him most at first was the ocean itself. The vastness of the Atlantic fascinated him, and he pondered its significance. Like Jonathan Edwards a century earlier he sensed that there was something providential in the great ocean that separated the Old World from the New. Had the territory of America been linked to either Europe or Asia, the land would have been merely an extension of the Old World. But providence decreed otherwise, and "when at length, the new world was discovered, then were the race called out, to begin again." Now the same ocean that had once divided became a highway for communication; the oceanic cocoon of protection and separation had become a web of connectedness. Here too, Bushnell believed, one could see the hand of providence; the Old World was now finally prepared to be instructed by the New. Had such instruction come earlier, "Europe was not ready for it." Now the old Puritan emphasis on the well-being and character of the individual rather than on the dignity of inherited institutions, which had become a national trait in America, was being revealed to the larger world. The importance of individual character was a mark of the age, and here the American experience showed the way forward.

As the *Victoria* continued its journey, Bushnell reflected further.

The spirit of progress advanced over the ocean through the extension of both commerce and Christianity. Commerce planted the rule of law in nations, weeding out piracy in favor of honest trade. Through it "one conscious brotherhood" was being formed. Over the same ocean came Christianity, with its elevating and blessing of humanity "in everything that constitutes their moral life." But, as Bushnell noted, in this effort the church itself was changing in a way foretold in the American experience. Lacking an established church, American Christians were tolerant and open to each other, eager to find common ground. This, he explained, was the wave of the future, but it was not yet the case in the Old World. Perhaps remembering his encounters with Catholicus and the Episcopalians of Connecticut, he went on. "The church can never attain to its proper power and beauty till it has become thoroughly catholic in its spirit, a result which is to be continually favored and assisted by the influence of a catholic commerce." Brotherhood and recognition were true catholicism.

His reflections on things English were mixed. While approaching England the *Victoria* was met by a war fleet of ten vessels from the British navy, including a steam frigate. The maneuver, with the ships "rising up like mountains of canvas," impressed the young cleric. It was, he confessed, "a most grand and imposing show." England truly did rule the sea, and she did so according to the rule of law. Off Lizard Point, at the far southwest corner of the island, he and other passengers boarded a pilot boat for Falmouth, as the *Victoria* made its way to its final destination, Liverpool. Surveying the countryside he was impressed at the frugal way in which the land was being used. Every last inch of available ground was cultivated. Likewise, he found the physical setting impressive. The harsh rocky shore made the isle seem like a "fortification or military post in the sea." But as interesting as the landscape might be, there was something strangely missing. He could not refrain from noting in his diary that unlike America, England was "an old country."

If his impressions of the English countryside were mixed, his view of the religious life of the realm was not. Here were the very artificiality, insincerity, and fashion that he had decried in Hartford. He could hardly contain his disgust after witnessing a worship service at Exeter Cathedral. Although he admitted the quality of the organ, the music he dismissed as "Puseyite or Romanist." It possessed emotional power but lacked any moral power. He felt moved but remarked, "I do not conclude that I am any better for it." The music, he added, milked the feeling but did not uplift the soul. At the cathedral in Bristol he experienced even greater dismay as he observed young choristers joking among themselves during the singing of the Lord's Prayer. Nor was St. Paul's Cathedral in London any more edifying. It was "grand" but "cold"; a "beauty that wants a soul." The peers of the realm who dutifully attended the service struck him as hopelessly listless, but well they should be (he added) since nothing intelligent was to be heard in the service. "All this array of music, pomp, priesthood and architecture for what? I could not but ask what Jesus Christ would say to this."

Perhaps as a tonic for this fashionable faith, Bushnell in early August headed for Scotland. Scotland was much more reminiscent of village New England, and Bushnell described in a letter to his wife the keeping of the Lord's Day in the rural countryside. With no church nearby he had originally intended simply to offer some private devotions, but he fell upon three country folk headed for the Free Church at Tarbet. They offered to take Bushnell there, but he was hesitant, and offered a series of excuses including the threat of inclement weather. All his doubts vanished when to this worry an old woman said, "Yes sir, but ye main trust Providence for that." Bushnell accompanied the others to the church and later gave a lyrical description of the worship there.

> The whole scene was so primitive and picturesque, and withal so beautifully Christian, that my heart overflowed with delight. . . . Nothing could exceed the reverent manner of the worshippers. They sang from their old version of the Psalms . . . a plain homespun fellow, sitting in a little desk under the pulpit led the singing. . . . Then followed a prayer, very laborious and fervent, three quarters of an hour long. . . . Then came the sermon, about an hour and a half long . . . rank limited atonement, Scotch orthodox, and yet all divine love to a guilty world. . . . I was carried straight back to the time of the Covenanters, and saw, as I never expected to see, that Sir Walter [Scott's] pictures are no caricature. . . . It was a good day, the best and sweetest I have spent since leaving home.

The allusion to Sir Walter Scott reminds us that we should take such a narrative with a grain of suspicion — a suspicion that might also serve as an antidote to an overdose of romanticism. But standing as it does in juxtaposition to his jaundiced view of English cathedral worship, the description serves as a rebuke to the fashionable religion of Exeter and London. Authentic singing, true preaching, and heartfelt piety put Anglican pretentiousness to shame. The description also foreshadows Bushnell's more famous description of village piety in "The Age of Homespun"; in the singing clerk in particular one sees his elevation of the simple. Indeed, in all his writings, whenever homespun is mentioned one invariably finds an oasis of true religion. The nostalgic yearning for a lost past that would be a regular part of Bushnell's message to his flock was already present in his description of this Scottish church.

But bucolic faith was not all he found in his journey to Scotland. When he first arrived in the city of Glasgow he was amazed at the grandeur of the old medieval cathedral — the "Presbyterian Cathedral," as he called it — which was every bit as exalted as any in England. Nor were the urban clergy in Scotland any friendlier to a visiting American than those in England had been. He had brought with him seven letters of reference to introduce himself to various dignitaries, yet none deigned to meet him. Indeed, the only persons who showed any spark of Christian hospitality were some of the "unorthodox" (to use his phrase) that he met. To the Scottish dignitaries (representatives of a church as well established north of the Tweed River as Anglicanism was in the south), Bushnell felt himself destined to be "forever a stranger." But with the few individuals he did get to know, there was a sense — despite their lack of "proper" doctrine — of spiritual fellowship.

THE PROBLEM WITH ENGLAND

Bushnell's sense of isolation was only greater when he returned to England. As an educated New England minister he had access to social circles many of his countrymen would not have had, but the hierarchical, stratified nature of the society, descending from the lofty monarch down to the lowest knave, rankled his Puritan soul. The social order seemed to have little if any place for an American such as he, and throughout his sojourn he felt all the many snubs and condescensions he received from the English. When he first arrived he attended a meeting of the "Evangelical Society" only to find (much to his surprise) snobbery even there in an alleged community of faith. The persons he met there knew precious little about the religious situation in America but that did not stop them from belittling their American cousins. Such events would multiply. Toward the end of his stay he learned of a "Dr. [John] Campbell" who had decided to preach on the deplorable state of religion in the United States, and whose sermon was later printed in the English *Congregational Magazine*. When the American theologian Albert Barnes (along with the noted cleric Ezra Stiles Ely) tried to challenge the accuracy of some of his claims, Campbell haughtily refused even to look at their objections. "What an ass," Bushnell wrote.

One day Bushnell strolled to St. James' Park to see the queen and royal family. He stood surveying the scene with a tourist's amusement until startled by a policeman's cry of "off with your hats!" It had only been a little more than a decade earlier that the American artist and inventor Samuel F. B. Morse had found himself in a similar situation. While visiting Rome he made the mistake of remaining hatted as Pope Gregory passed. A stern papal soldier then proceeded to knock Morse's hat off with a rifle and bayonet. Earlier the young Morse had decided not to attend any worship services but merely to observe events from the street. He reasoned, "If I go into a church, then I feel bound to remove my hat as a mark of civility, and if I stay they may rightfully, if they choose, force me to kneel . . . but in the streets I have my rights as a foreigner; no man has a right to interfere with my rights of conscience." The soldier's bayonet instructed him (he later confessed) what absolutism thought of rights of conscience, and he became after that a leading anti-Catholic advocate. Bushnell's clash was not as violent, but for him, too, it was something of an epiphany. "Confound these English. They are willing to have a testimony of respect or courtesy by force," he wrote. He concluded his journal by noting that he had been "of a good mind to stand erect with my hat on." The connection between a religion buttressed by the power of the state and a loss of republican virtue was present for all who had eyes to see.

Still other things bothered him about the English. Unlike Americans, they seemed oblivious to the advantages of the cold-water pledge. He felt awkward when he was expected to drink to a person's health at formal dinners, and the culture of the grog house bothered him. It led to a decay in demeanor; "the shops and people are dirty beyond recognition." In New England the use of alcohol was increasingly seen as a major point of division between evangelical Christians and others, but in England tippling affected even the church. "Two or three barrels of beer or wine are part of the [Sunday School festivities] . . . and this for the children." Even the tract societies provided drink for children and workmen.

These clashes of culture perhaps provide the background for Bushnell's response to one of the great issues of the day, the union of evangelical Christendom. By the late 1830s voices in favor of a pan-evangelical union began to be heard on both sides of the Atlantic. In America, evangelicals from the various denominations increasingly saw themselves in a common position against non-evangelical forces in the society, and in the early 1840s a number of American Protestants, including Bushnell's friend Leonard Bacon of Center Church in New Haven, began calling for an international gathering of representatives of evangelical bodies. Bushnell's run-ins with the Connecticut proponents of the Oxford Movement had made him an early convert to the cause. He served on the board of governors of the "Christian Alliance," an American Protestant ecumenical organization dedicated to extending evangelical Christianity into papal lands. The hope of furthering the connectedness between evangelical Protestants had been one of the purposes of his European trip, and he had urged his friend Leonard Bacon to accompany him to prepare for the scheduled meeting of a proposed "Evangelical Alliance" in late 1846. But throughout his time in England he began to have second thoughts about any such international alliance. The stumbling blocks concerned politics, ecclesiology, and theology.

The legal establishment of the Church of England troubled Bushnell. The state of evangelicalism in England in the 1840s resembled George Orwell's famous description in *Animal Farm*: all were equal, but some were more equal than others. Clergy of the established church looked down on all other ministers and behaved as if the defense of the legal establishment were their central concern. Any plan of union that even suggested an equality among ministers of the gospel would be vigorously opposed by Anglicans; in private, many clergy told Bushnell that "churchmen" would unite en masse against any evangelical union if the issue became linked with disestablishment. Although Bushnell did often attend Anglican worship, its exclusivity bothered him, and he privately chafed at worshiping among a group "which unchurched me and denies my office." As if this were not bad enough, other English Christians, rather than rejecting these pretensions like good Puritans, meekly submitted. The weight of the establishment crushed their spirit of independence. Far worse, they all too often aped the fashionable worship of the established church. Bushnell was disgusted with a Methodist church he attended while on the continent. Rather than offering truly spiritual worship, the congregants read a set service of prayer — "with all the bows" — in the hope of appealing to traveling Anglicans. "They lick the feet of them that say they are naught and secretly uphold the hierarchy who declare they are pests and schismatics." As he had noted in an address he gave to his fellow passengers on the *Victoria,* a religious establishment all too often produced a spirit of bigotry and illiberality. England bore such fruit.

A second issue centered on ecclesiology. In England the native Nutmegger saw the ominous signs of the Oxford Movement's Catholic revival wherever he turned. As appalled as he was, however, he was more appalled by the lack of any concerted action against it. Among the Anglicans he met who professed an allegiance to evangelical principles, there seemed to be little if any movement either to purge these abuses or to separate themselves from those who indulged in them. Some established clergy privately admitted to him that the High Church Catholic revival was destroying fellowship between "churchmen and dissenters" but no one was taking action against it. What was one to make of those who spoke of union but practiced disunion and exclusion?

Finally, there was the issue of theology. The perennial question for evangelicals was that of definition — what constituted an evangelical? On one level the answer was easy. Evangelicals stood over against corrupt Catholicism, and Romanists and Puseyites were clearly outside the pale. They refused fellowship with Protestant Christians so any future alliance should avoid them. But what of boundaries on the other side? Should persons and churches be excluded from the fellowship because of differences in doctrine? The heirs of the Puritans in

America had divided on a series of doctrinal questions, with the orthodox and the Unitarians distinctly separate. Should this division exclude the Unitarians from an international evangelical alliance? Here Bushnell's impatience with theological finery began to show itself. Throughout his journey he was impressed with his contact with Unitarians, who on the whole were far friendlier to him than those with a higher pedigree of theology. At meetings of the proposed Evangelical Alliance he bristled at the theological minutiae of some of the conversations. A Dr. Curry, for example, stopped a procedure to ask whether language concerning God's manifestation of himself to the world in Christ "was not too much like Sabellianism." In his diary Bushnell confessed, "The more I see of the Evangelical Alliance, the weaker and shallower does it seem." He much preferred attending groups like the "Italian Asylum," which focused on the practical goal of establishing schools for poor Italian children. Such tangible acts of charity seemed to him more appropriate and worthier of Christian endeavor than the flights of theological fancy so many indulged in.

It must be emphasized that Bushnell's reaction to England and its culture was not uniformly negative. He admired many aspects of its tradition in art and music as well as its material progress, noting in particular the fineness of the macadam roads. He also acknowledged that as a New England Puritan he had a filial connection with Old England. He wrote home, for example, to share the delight he experienced in Coventry when he came upon a portrait of the patriarch of the Davenport family, pictured "between Queen Elizabeth on one side and James I on the other." Davenport was an ancestor of his wife. He was also an ancestor of one of the founders of the New Haven colony. The bonds between the two Saxon lands lay deep. But still, England convinced Bushnell that he was an American.

EXPERIENCING THE WORLD OF CATHOLICISM

After almost a month in Britain, Bushnell journeyed to the continent. His aim was to reach the fresh mountainous air of Switzerland before the Autumn chill set in. His first stop was Belgium, a land more different from his New England home than even Old England had been. While traveling he met a fellow American, a Mr. Haddens, who invited him to attend a Sunday afternoon concert. Having already been overwhelmed by the artistic riches of the city (he marveled at the works of Reubens and Van Eyck), he readily agreed to sample its musical offerings. Since it was a Sunday afternoon event he assumed the concert would be of sacred music, as would definitely have been the case in Hartford, but much to his shock he learned that secular music was going to be performed. The dilemma was perplexing, particularly since, as Bushnell (always the Yankee) noted, "the tickets cost five franks." The lover of culture now stood at cross-purposes with the pious Sabbath observer, and both claims were judged by the frugal Yankee. Finally he reached a decision. Since he had already attended worship that day he concluded "that my sabbath was over [and] I should see all the fashions of Antwerp." But still his conscience would not let him rest, and he confessed in his journal that the last five pieces of music "were lost upon me."

In the cities on the continent he saw other things that caused him to reflect on the differences between the Old World and the New. He found little charm in the medieval cities he encountered, for, while the new parts of these cities were "spacious, beautiful, and comfortable," the older parts struck him as "dingy, cramped, and miserable." Furthermore, the walls surrounding some of the old cities led him to reflect on the triumph of the spirit of law. At one time, such walls provided the only method of protection in a violent world, but now "the pacific reign of law has become a better wall."

If Sabbath customs and urban architecture seemed foreign to the provincial parson, the practices associated with Roman Catholic worship were even more so. As always, he was fascinated by architecture, but he found perplexing the dichotomy between the noble architectural setting of the worship and the message of the worship itself. "The two most striking objects in Belgium . . . are the magnificent churches or cathedrals and the profligate looking priests." Like many nineteenth-century figures he truly believed that one could judge a book by its cover, or at least judge a person by his or her countenance. The priests he observed revealed a "certain sensual air" and a "greasy look [of] the loss of that virtue which it is their office to maintain." As was the case for so many other Protestant writers of the time, the practice of the confessional inflamed all of Bushnell's prurient speculations. He described the practice in a letter that was later published back in Hartford: "On one side an ingenuous looking boy, or simple conscientious-looking woman; on the other a red-faced, sensual son of Eli, in his dirty habiliments, receiving the whisper of a simple story, perhaps of its struggle with evil, — those struggles which to the mind of God are the purest incense that ever rises from the world of mortals."

But he was forced to admit that the service of worship did evoke strong and true emotions despite the decrepitude of the clergy, and so his experience of continental Catholicism disturbed him. On the one hand it was clearly false. After visiting one of his first services he wrote, "I was never so impressed that Romanism is idolatry." Yet on the other hand he could not help but acknowledge its power. After a few weeks he confessed, "I began to be so much a Catholic myself that I am [compelled] to prefer the Romish to the English Church." Anglicanism had tried to rectify the erroneous doctrines and false superstitions of Rome by the use of reason in its theology, and to correct the errors of Roman worship by a "moderate" use of ritual. "But men are not stirred by their reason," he wrote, "or by the halfwayedness of the English Church." The power of Roman Catholic worship was real, and Bushnell could sense its attraction.

A NEW REFORMATION?

While on the continent Bushnell began to hear of a movement that would stir his excitement — a new Reformation. Although today Johann Ronge and Johann Czerski may not be household names, for Bushnell and other mid-century New Englanders they were heralds for the coming of a new age. The details of their lives and of their movements are, from the perspective of the twenty-first-century historian, vague and not always consistent, so perhaps it is best to recount the story as Bushnell himself would have heard it from contemporary Protestant sources. What such a storyline may lack in historical objectivity it gains in imaginative power.

Both Ronge and Czerski had been Roman Catholic priests in central Europe, but each had broken with Rome over abuses in practice and discipline. Ronge served in Trier (or Treves), a Roman Catholic city then under the jurisdiction of Protestant Prussia. The city was perhaps best known for its prized relic — the holy coat that was alleged to be the seamless cloak worn by Jesus at the time of the crucifixion. The coat purportedly had miraculous powers and was publicly exhibited at times for veneration. The year 1844 was such a time, but the young Ronge denounced the event as a "heathen festival." The denunciation ignited popular approval, just as Martin Luther's denunciation of indulgences had three centuries earlier, but the political authorities (despite their Protestant affiliation) preferred civil quietude to theological reform and acquiesced to the Roman Catholic demand to silence the young priest. Czerski had launched a similar protest in western Prussia that, like Ronge's, stirred public excitement while garnering official reproach.

While Bushnell toured the continent the movements of these two men began to coalesce into a "German Catholic Church." Although doctrinal agreement was only eventually worked out, it ultimately involved the rejection of not only the authority of the pope but such doctrines and practices as auricular confession, priestly absolution, clerical celibacy, the use of images, the Latin mass, the idea of priesthood, and prohibitions against mixed marriages between Catholics and Protestants. The movement spread throughout Germany, with one printed account claiming that within a year of its founding the new church possessed 321 congregations and over 40,000 followers in Silesia (a German-speaking area now part of Poland) alone. Bushnell heard that by August of 1845, 130,000 persons had been attracted to the movement. Noting its exploding popularity, he wrote that he had hoped to visit the "new Catholic Church" (which was then meeting in a Protestant church after the scheduled Sunday services), but was told that seats were impossible to attain. "I must have gone as early as 8 o'clock to get a seat, such is the crowd." People reported that 130 individual congregations had already joined the movement.

The German Catholic movement excited a man like Bushnell because it kindled the fire of reformation in the very heart of Catholic Europe. But he (like others) admitted that the movement was of questionable orthodoxy. Ronge, for example, had voiced his protest in the name not of the gospel but of human freedom and dignity. Such "human freedom," however, led him (it was alleged) to call into question not only Catholic "superstitions" like the holy coat but gospel stories as well. Like other "rationalist" critics of the time he often questioned "the miracles and doctrines of Christianity itself" in denouncing the

85

errors of Rome. Czerski, it was claimed, was more orthodox, but even he had his difficulties. In a letter to the faithful back in Connecticut, Bushnell admitted that the movement had its problems: "Ronge, it is said, is a rationalist; whether justly, or because of the strong antagonistic expressions he would naturally use in his conflict with the mystical and ghostly doctrines of church authority and the church legends of Romanism, I cannot say." Yet whatever the failings of these two men as leaders, the movement served a purpose and merited encouragement. The new reformation was real, but "the common remark is that a Luther is wanting."

MORE TRAVELS, MORE THOUGHTS

Bushnell's ambivalent response to the Old World continued as he made his way across the continent. As usual the natural vistas and the architectural wonders overwhelmed him. The valley of the Meuse he described "as the most beautiful country I ever surveyed" (though Bushnell in fact spelled the last word as "cerveied"!). The great unfinished cathedral at Cologne so inspired him that he went to great pains to describe almost every aspect of it. Also in Cologne he experienced for the first time the Byzantine style of architecture and observed that it might be more adaptable to the needs of Protestant worship than would the Gothic. He occasionally spoke warmly of the religious spirit he found — such as when he witnessed a rural church crowded with "men and women all in their Sunday dresses of homespun" — and he was moved by some monuments he found that testified to the historic faith. In Lausanne he visited the tomb of Andrew Broughton, clerk of the Puritan court who sentenced Charles I to his death in 1649. At the time of the restoration of royal authority, Broughton fled to the Swiss city, and the town leaders steadfastly refused to surrender to the authorities of the English crown one whom they considered a Protestant patriot. But more often he found only the husk of true faith remaining. His travels in Switzerland, which had once been the great mother of the Reformed faith, were particularly disturbing. Now the home of Calvin, Zwingli, Bullinger, and Beza presented but a shadow of its former religious glory. He recorded with shock how the allegedly Protestant authorities in one Swiss canton had banished a person for the crime of holding a prayer meeting. "These [authorities]," he wrote, "are nominally Protestant but really Socialists and infidels." In Switzerland he found not so much errors in belief as a loss of spirit. After explaining the agenda of the Christian Alliance to one cleric of the city, the latter scoffed and proclaimed that any opposition to Rome was doomed to failure: "'Mont Blanc will stand' i.e. Rome 'after all the speeches and resolutions.'" Rather than being moved by the crusade against Roman Catholicism, this successor of Calvin pooh-poohed any possibility of progress in Christianity and warned American Protestants of their "worldly" orientation. A few days later Bushnell did meet a band of Swiss peasants whose faith was robust and true, but they were headed to America.

Nor did his travels solve for him the paradoxical ambiguity of Catholicism. He could easily dismiss the relics collected by Charlemagne, such as a piece of Christ's cross and a part of the girdle of the Blessed Virgin Mary, and see them as a confirmation of the idolatrous spirit of Rome. Yet while in Switzerland he witnessed a Catholic pilgrimage to the "black virgin" of Einsiedeln that seemed to combine both heartfelt piety and doctrinal error. He was similarly ambivalent in his observations of a Catholic funeral. The death of his only son a few years earlier had impressed upon Bushnell the grief of separation and the pain of the grave. After watching the funeral procession of torches and tapers and the sprinkling of the grave with holy water by all present — "including the children" — Bushnell was of two minds. The priest's work was of course "mummery"; but the profound devotion of the laity impressed him, as did the bridge the ritual offered between the living and the dead. "Can it be less than a merit of the Catholic religion," he asked, "with all its attending superstitions, that it keeps up so close and intimate a relation between the living and the dead?"

From Switzerland he entered Italy. Here again the physical beauty of Lake Como, with its kaleidoscope of colors, the stateliness of the great cathedral of Milan, and the treasury of artistic abundance he found in Florence all merited his comments. So too did the clutter and filthiness of Naples, which disturbed him so greatly that he returned to his hotel and "sick of heart and stomach together went to bed." His Puritan sensitivities recoiled at the great public religious festivals, known as "festas," that were so popular in Italy. "What a burden are these festas on the industry and well being of a people — not to say on their character also — for what breeds illness and spendthrift is next door to vice itself."

ON TO ROME

Then on to Rome. Perhaps no city on the continent better epitomized and stirred the ambivalence Bushnell was experiencing than Rome. The city in some ways summed up that sense of development he had tried to convey in his Yale College lecture on the moral tendencies of human history. It was the city of "Old Rome and New, Pagan and Christian . . . here sat the mistress of the world amidst her temples, conscious of her power. . . . Here, too, come the first emissaries of the cross. Paul trod these streets, and, by virtue of a message not his own, gave law at length to the ministers of the world herself." There was so much to admire in Rome. The organ music he heard was like no music he had ever experienced, and the chanting of the services enthralled him. The priest would lead the chant and the people would respond with a fervor that thrilled him. "Would to God that I could have a liturgy and responses in my church if they could be used in this way." He contrasted it with the English service he attended, which was mumbled in a dull, unfeeling manner. "When I go for prelacy I shall join the church of Rome," he wrote.

The physical arts also impressed him, and the artistic collections of the Vatican were awe-inspiring; "there could hardly be a greater show of magnificence than such a vast collection of art." He wrote that he found Michelangelo strangely unreligious — more interested in muscular mass than in the mysteries of holiness — but on the whole he was overwhelmed by the display. As always, however, something was wrong. Why did Rome stand athwart the law of progress? In his reflections he increasingly focused on the papacy. His description of the worship he experienced in the Vatican contained no acknowledgement of any latent inner power. He catalogued the service, from its architectural setting, its array of tapers and incense, right down to the cardinals reverencing the pope. "It was on the whole," he concluded, "one of the most painful of sights I ever witnessed — so absurd, so pompous, so far from all consideration of truth such as ought to actuate an intelligent being and more than all so wholly wide of the humble life giving gospel of Christ." When he later visited the special dining room of the pope, where the pontiff always dined alone, "being in fact above all kings and there being none of a rank to be his guest," he contrasted the pretentiousness of the setting with the humility of Jesus. For Bushnell the fundamental problem of the Roman system seemed to be not false doctrine per se but a profound misunderstanding of the true religious spirit of Christianity.

Paris, in contrast, was a pleasant surprise. A loyal alumnus of Yale College, whose President Dwight had systematically condemned French political errors and gross irreligion, Bushnell found himself pleased. The people had an intelligent look about them, a sober and serious appearance "as in the United States." There was also a surprising lack of beggars. "You meet more beggars, more bloated faces, more rags and dirt in London in one day than here in ten." The changes of the revolution had in fact led to a real change for the better. Property was better distributed than in any other country in Europe, the class distinctions that had been so painfully present in England were eliminated, and a republican spirit was emerging. True progress had taken place. But now France needed a religion that could move that progress along. The old religion could not do this, but no new religion had yet appeared to take its place.

Bushnell's continental travels planted in him a number of perceptions. The first was that Roman Catholicism possessed a mixture of strength and corruption. If its views of priesthood, sacraments, and relics were all idolatrous, there was still a power in its religious life that moved him. If that power could be purified and linked with a true spirit of the gospel, who knew what might be the result. The second was that Anglicanism in general and Puseyism in particular misunderstood the nature of this power. They mistakenly believed that it was somehow connected with the external forms and that by reduplicating the forms they could recapture the power. The coldness Bushnell perceived in the continental Anglican congregations he visited testified to the failure of this notion. Finally, Bushnell became increasingly convinced that the old Protestant churches on the continent were of little use in bringing about the needed transformation. They were either spiritually moribund or hopelessly tied to the idea of political establishment, as were, for example, the Protestants of Prussia who would

not back the German Catholic movement for fear of political consequences. In the new movement of Ronge and Czerski, however, despite all their problems, one did sense the spirit of transformation.
They did engender an enthusiasm that the older Protestant churches
did not. The multitude sought out the new movement, "for the state of
the Lutheran church offers no attraction." In these revolts lay a power
that might transform even Rome.

By early February Bushnell was back in England. The nation
seemed aroused by the controversy over Oregon; both Britain and the
United States had laid claim to the territory north of the Columbia
River, and war hawks on both sides of the Atlantic predicted conflict.
Bushnell, in an open letter published in the *London Universe*, explained
the American point of view. He went to great pains to distinguish the
responsible citizens of New England, who paid their debts, from the ir-
responsible citizens of other sections of the country who happily de-
faulted on payments to English creditors. He also continued to involve
himself in the discussions concerning the upcoming meeting of the
Evangelical Alliance, though his continental visit had made him no
more sanguine about the possibilities of success. In addition to the
questions concerning establishment, there now arose the complication
of slavery. English evangelicals were protesting any participation by
American slaveholders in any public meeting. Bushnell, now thoroughly disgusted with the English, chalked it up more to self-
righteousness than to any great moral stand. He had recently been
present when the great Irish patriot Daniel O'Connell addressed parliament and had been shocked to learn how the British had so misgov-
erned that island nation. The English had an "incapacity [to empathize
with] anything different from themselves." As distasteful as he found
slavery, he found English hypocrisy more so, and far more present. In
the face of their many failures, the moral posturing of the English left
Bushnell cold. "Let them go for religious liberty like men and then we
shall all be against slavery."

THE PROBLEM OF THE PAPACY

During the spring of 1846 Bushnell also published *A Letter to His Holiness, Pope Gregory XVI* — a work that was eventually both translated

into Italian and formally condemned by the Vatican. The mid 1840s were a time of inflamed anti-Catholicism among American Protestants, and scores of American clergy were penning pieces on the threat of Rome. Bushnell's contribution, however, was somewhat different from the others. His letter was deferential in tone but took as its focus the question of religious freedom. He began his open letter by explaining that he was a member of the board of America's Christian Alliance. The Alliance, which dedicated itself to translating and distributing in Italy Protestant pieces such as Merle D'Aubigne's *History of the Reformation*, had been condemned in a papal bull issued in the spring of 1844. Any cooperation with the Alliance by Italian subjects was forbidden; the faithful were called to destroy all of the Alliance's translations they might happen upon, and those "who govern churches situated in Italy" were called to be vigilant in preventing the organization from taking root. "Such endeavors on your and our part," the pope explained, "we doubt not will be aided by the help of the civil powers, and especially by that of the most potent princes of Italy." The papal course of action stemmed from a profound misunderstanding of the aims of the Christian Alliance, Bushnell explained. The Alliance was not trying to foster any secret plots but only to disseminate ideas. Rome should desist in the use of force and participate in the discussion. "We believe that the time for using church penalties in place of Christian arguments, dungeons instead of doctrine, has gone by." The world now demanded the freedom of open discussion.

In the course of his letter many of the issues raised privately in his journal were made public. He highlighted the political failings of Rome: The papal governance of central Italy was the worst government in Christendom. The number of clergy and officeholders overwhelmed the populace and corruption reigned. "Every center of power is the seal of some cabal; and creatures, male and female, glide about the precincts, who are able, by the base and criminal secrets in their keeping . . . to open or shut at will the gates of favor." The result was a land destitute in fortune and spirit. "Nothing wears a look of thrift and happiness: no sign of improvement meets the eye, which is not refuted by signs of decay and deterioration." Those who brought such malediction to the land had further left their mark on the populace. The high rate of taxation, the awarding of monopolies in trade, and the mandatory saints' day observances, which robbed one day in three from useful production, all served to destroy any spirit of ambition. Recounting a conversation he had with "a brilliant accomplished youth," he quoted the lad as saying, "Sir, there is no hope for us here; the priests have taken everything away from us." Furthermore, if the regiment of clergy had destroyed the political and economic fabric of the land, the confessional had poisoned the family. The priest was set between husband and wife, parent and child. As if this were not bad enough, all this had been done in the name of Christ — or so claimed the great pontiff who in turn also declared himself to be Christ's own vicar here on earth. "If Christ is indeed represented in you, then is Christ one of the most malignant obstacles to the advancement and happiness of mankind." The Christian world could not long tolerate such a stain on its reputation, and Bushnell solemnly pronounced, "in the name of the Christian world, I protest against the delinquencies by which you furnish so baleful an argument." The course of human progress could go forward only when Christianity was freed from such a linking of the powers of religion with those of the state.

In the second half of his letter Bushnell focused on the religious abuses of the papacy. One finds the standard charges here: relics, idolatry, the substitution of pomp and ceremony for the simplicity of the gospel. But two charges do merit mention since they touch on two of the aspects of Roman Catholicism that Bushnell himself was most attracted to: art and music. He had spent hours appreciating both, and his journal bulges with accounts of his great enjoyment. But here, both are described as ultimately still further signs of papal corruption. The store of fine art found in the Vatican was indeed impressive, but what did it signify? The very immensity of its presence suggested a passion for accumulation rather than an innocent interest in beauty. The viewer of such a collection "will fancy the priest engaged to rival the prince and not displeased with his victory." And what connection was there between "the apostle of the fine arts and the apostle Peter"? Likewise, concerning the music, of which he had also spoken movingly in private, it too was a source of corruption. The music of the Sistine Chapel, he wrote, had left him cold. It was marred by pomp; it was also marked by exclusivity. Women were banned from passing beyond the choir screen, and laity could not enter save properly dressed. But the worst corruption became apparent only at the time of the choral anthem. "When the anthem rose . . . my ear was caught by notes of a strange quality, — not the voice of a woman, not of man." Well into the nineteenth century, Italian choirs made use of castrati, choristers gelded as young boys to preserve a soprano voice. Bushnell looked upon them and lamented. They were "the poor beings whom you have damned to a fall even out of nature, to serve the luxury of your worship." Even the beauty of music was corrupted through the influence of Rome.

In all these ways, Bushnell argued, the forces of history were moving against the papacy. It strove to keep people in ignorance — hence its fear of the Christian Alliance — but ignorance was impossible at the present. The same ocean that carried Bushnell to England also brought persons and ideas to Catholic Europe. Every traveling visitor from England or America brought witness to a new and more progressive world. The march of progress and liberty was the true message of the age. Rome was mistaken if it believed that the Catholic revival in the Church of England was bringing the English-speaking world closer to Rome. "The very signs by which you are cheered . . . foretoken rather an attitude of firmness and more compact resistance; nay it is well for you if they do not rouse a continual movement sufficiently vigorous to overwhelm you."

A VISION OF TRUE UNITY

In his conclusion Bushnell stated that he was arguing in favor not of "Protestantism" but of religious liberty. Liberty, for him, was what the spirit of the age called for, and, as we will see, it was a message he would direct not merely at Rome. In his last weeks in England he composed an essay on the proposed Evangelical Alliance, from which he read excerpts to at least one gathering while he looked for a publisher. This essay in all likelihood served as the basis for his essay "The Evangelical Alliance," published a few months after his return to America. In it, he evaluated the organizational meeting of the Evangelical Alliance, which had gathered in London in August of 1846.

He applauded the Alliance as a visible symbol of evangelical unity and as a "visible confutation of the outcry of schism, perpetually echoed by the Romish and Anglican priesthood and all the adherents of church authority." He also praised the meeting for avoiding ecclesiastical pretensions; it saw itself simply as a Christian assembly of individuals rather than as a "council of the church." Nevertheless, the Alliance manifested not only some of the strengths he had predicted but many of the weaknesses as well, and the essay is permeated with his distaste for both religious formalism and the political establishment of religion, a distaste that had become a passion for Bushnell during his European travels. The issue of church and state had not disappeared, Bushnell wrote, as established churches vehemently protected their privileged positions (as he had feared they would). Furthermore, divisions over doctrine and slavery had arisen. Ronge was denied a seat because of questions regarding his orthodoxy, and Czerski was not invited out of consideration for the established Protestant churches of Germany, who feared that a recognition of the German Catholic movement would provoke the wrath of Roman Catholics. Quakers and Unitarians were also excluded on doctrinal grounds. The committee professed to practice the unity of the spirit in the bond of love, "and yet they dared to love only by their creeds and catechisms." As he had predicted, orthodoxy rather than spiritual life had become the governing rule for the Alliance. "They have done what they could to tighten the bigotry of Protestantism and modernize its title to odium." Bushnell willingly acknowledged the doctrinal errors of these communities, but it was clear that in the great struggle between priestcraft and republican religion Ronge, Czerski, and the others were clearly on the side of progress.

He similarly condemned the exclusion of slaveholders as still another example of English moral posturing. He did not sympathize with slavery, and he took pains to criticize its corrosive effects on the Sabbath and the sanctity of marriage, but to deny that a slaveholder could be an evangelical Christian (as the English seemed to claim) was to deny an obvious fact. Those who knew no slaveholders could judge in abstract, just as those who had never witnessed the ministries of Ronge and Czerski could judge on pure doctrine alone, but Bushnell chose instead to judge on life. To separate based on abstractions was not only facile but prevented any chance for continued growth and change. Persons and groups who communicated with one another affected and influenced each other in a way that divided communities weren't able to. He prayed that the day would come when slaveholders would see the error of their position, but until that time came inclusion was a wiser policy than exclusion. The English, in contrast, seemed to want to take a symbolic action rather than to try to influence Southern slaveholders. The reason the Evangelical Alliance went down the road it did, Bushnell concluded, was that it was not ultimately concerned with *doing* anything. Like so many of the clergy he met in England during his visit it was more interested in making distinctions and in defining itself precisely according to some abstract measure than it was in practical action. And here, he noted, is where the superiority of the American Christian Alliance lay. It led to *action* and not simply discussion. It saw itself as involved in a struggle against popery and Anglicanism at home and against popery in Italy. In such a struggle disagreement on specific questions was not as important as unity on the fundamental issue, or the struggle for religious liberty.

Others agreed with Bushnell in his criticism of the narrowness of the Evangelical Alliance, particularly regarding its exclusion of Ronge and Czerski. Many American evangelicals saw the German movement as the great hope for the future. It was a movement based on congregationalism and on the autonomy of the people over the claims of prelacy. "The people have here exercised their right," noted one writer in the *New Englander*; "the people have given their judgement against Rome." But the German Christian movement excited the heirs of the Puritans for one additional reason. For centuries the Christian world had been deadlocked between Catholicism and Protestantism. There had been movements and developments within Protestantism but the division between Protestants and Catholics had remained constant. If there was not an iron curtain separating the worlds of Protestants and Catholics, there was, one could say, a curtain of Belgian lace, the material commonly used for Roman Catholic eucharistic vestments. But in Germany the "lace curtain" seemed to be collapsing. In the reforms of Ronge and Czerski there emerged "a sort of universal church, assimilating Protestants and papists to each other, and uniting all sects, churches and doctrines in a sort of 'Christian Freemasonry.'" Possibilities were opening up that had been closed for centuries. Bushnell sensed this, and would make his contribution to this new unity.

To understand better Bushnell's concerns, we might do well to look at a sermon he gave near the close of his visit. If his letter to Pope Gregory and his essay on the Evangelical Alliance shed light on his public mind, his sermon "Unconscious Influences" reveals his more private thoughts.

The topic of the sermon was one dear to him: how human beings communicate. He began by observing that communication comes through two different means, rationality and intuition. The former is willful and works primarily through words, but intuition flows not from what one says but from who one is. It is therefore pre-rational, involving "that which flows out from us unawares to ourselves." It comes to us not through the ear but through the understanding and is revealed by "looks, tones, manners, and general conduct." Such unconscious influences, he continued, are social in nature. Communities are held together through their power. In social organizations "all adhere together, as parts of a larger nature, in which there is a common circulation of want, impulse and law." Communities cohere because they share certain presuppositions and attitudes, which they intuitively recognize in each other. It is not so much rational agreement as this mutual recognition that serves as a basis of fellowship. Such intuitions are the reason we feel comfortable in some families and communities. A visitor to France could feel "the spirit of infidelity." And "What is the family spirit in many a house," Bushnell asked, "but the spirit of gain, or pleasure, or appetite?" The particular power of unconscious influences in family culture, he believed, lies in the fact that they provide the earliest form of education for children. "We begin our mortal experience, not with acts grounded in judgement or reason, or with ideas received through language, but by simple imitation, and under the guidance of this we lay our foundation." As we will see, this interest in unconscious influence became the basis of Bushnell's interest in Christian nurture.

The essay went on to suggest that part of the failure in effectively communicating the gospel lay in conflicts between our words and our unconscious influences. The contrast between word and intuition may help us understand why Bushnell reacted as he did to the religious scene he found in his travels. The superiority of unconscious influence over the world of words defined precisely his reactions. The words of Ronge and Czerski were admittedly flawed, but Bushnell nonetheless believed he saw in the movement they led the face of true Christianity. Indeed, he even saw such a face at times in the Catholic worship he experienced on the continent. In contrast, when he came into contact with representatives of the established Protestant churches, despite the agreeable words, he found no Christ-like spirit reflected in their unconscious influences. Furthermore, the intuitive recognition of a spiritual connection made him recognize the limitations of verbal divisions. The fellowship experienced when one could sense "that the Lord is in this place" emboldened one to assault the walls created by language. Without such a recognition, however, formal doctrinal agreement meant little.

A LEARNED FELLOW

In April, about a month before he was to return to the United States, Bushnell met a young philosopher, "a truly learned and accomplished fellow," John Daniel Morell. Morell was a young minister who, after graduating from Glasgow in 1840, studied German philosophy at Bonn under the tutelage of the younger Fichte. He later returned to Britain to begin a career as a philosopher. When Bushnell met him he was in the process of preparing for publication a *Historical and Critical View of the Speculative Philosophy of Europe in the Nineteenth Century*. Bushnell was drawn to the young philosopher for a number of reasons. For one thing, Morell too had doubts about the Evangelical Alliance's attempt to unite on the basis of creedal conformity — "Unions of creeds," he wrote, "being so less broad and deep than unions of hearts." He was also a young minister who like Bushnell had known the force of doubt, and he had a strikingly original theological mind. (For example, Morell believed, as some had in the early church, that evil souls were annihilated upon death rather than suffering eternal punishment.) But it seems to have been philosophy that was the two men's true point of interest. They spoke together of language theory and Bushnell was intrigued by Morell's suggestion that notional (or abstract) words, and not those of mere relation, had a physical base. Bushnell eagerly read the preface to Morell's manuscript and made suggestions for an American publisher.

The significance of Bushnell's encounter with Morell is that the latter was one of the early and vigorous proponents of the religious philosophy of Friedrich Schleiermacher in Britain. He enthusiastically accepted Schleiermacher's starting point that religion was fundamentally a feeling outside the region of intellectual activity. As one American reviewer of the young philosopher's writings noted, "Schleiermacher is the oracle of Morell." Furthermore, both in his discussion of revelation and in his understanding of the relation between theology and religion Morell offered far more nuanced analyses than Bushnell had earlier set forth in "Revelation," the address he gave before the Love of Inquiry Society at Andover. Religion, Morell explained, presents itself immediately to the intuition, "while the propositions of theology are the best representations we can make of that truth, in definite and abstract terms, to the understanding."

Bushnell's encounter with Morell is the first documented encounter between him and an individual intimately connected with the thought of Schleiermacher in particular and of German Romanticism in general. As a person who read no German Bushnell would have been limited to the small handful of Schleiermacher's works that had been translated into English, but through Morell, his "learned and accomplished" companion, he now had greater access. Furthermore, Morell shared with Bushnell a distaste for the scientific or Baconian approach to theology and an interest in the possibility of Christian union based on a renewed Christian life. Baconian scientific methodology stood between the individual and the real truths of Scripture, both believed. "The form, the phraseology, the whole scientific tone comes from the *schools!*" argued Morell. "The plain, pure, primitive, spiritual fact, comes directly from the Bible, in which we have presented, not the formal doctrines, indeed, but simply *information* respecting the merciful dealings of God in the recovery of man." It would be through the recovery of this reality that questions of religious life could be authenticated and the unity of the church achieved. On each of these points Bushnell would have given a heartfelt "Amen."

By the end of April Bushnell was ready to return to America. His health was only marginally better, so in that sense the trip had not fulfilled its purpose. But through his European sojourn Bushnell gained a sense both of what was happening in the larger Christian world and of what further steps needed to be taken. Even more, he gained insight into how the American Christian community, and in particular the children of the Puritans, could contribute to the change, and how he, the provincial pastor, might set the direction.

5 Rescuing the Children and Reuniting the Puritans

THE Horace Bushnell who returned to his family, church, and community in the summer of 1846 was a changed man, and he came back to a changed society. When he had left, his country had still been at peace. It was now involved in a war with its southern neighbor, Mexico — a war that evoked little approval among the proper citizens of New England. He also returned to find the flood of poor Roman Catholics entering his land even greater than when he had left. The great Potato Famine had struck Ireland (and to a lesser degree Germany) with horrendous effect, producing widespread starvation and prompting mass migration to the New World. The religious world of New England had certainly not settled down since his departure for England, and it was to this world that he returned with all the insights and understandings he had gained during his time abroad. The stage was set for the most explosive period of his ministry.

THE VISION OF UNITY

The impact of his trip could be seen in the spurt of publications that flowed from his pen in the months after his return, including a revised version of his lecture on the Evangelical Alliance, which he had re-thought in light of the group's first meeting. It is in his Thanksgiving sermon for the year, however, that one finds his most explicit reflection on his travels. "The Day of Roads" was in some ways a literary travel-ogue of his trip, and it offered a sweeping view of the progress of civi-lization and his opinions of the various states of Europe that he had visited, all through the prism of the road. "The Road is that physical sign or symbol by which you will best understand any age or people," he explained. Here in this address the traveler who had praised the English for their macadamized roads now lauded the ancient Romans for constructing "roads themselves . . . hardened to a floor macadam-ized before the time of McAdam by sand, gravel, and cement." Roads were the vehicles of commerce and communication; they epitomized progress and freedom. He described how medieval rulers would have viewed the roads and the new commerce that sprang up during those years as a threat to their power. "How many of the fine conservatives of that age," he asked, "were lamenting over a degenerate mercenary age of merchandise and money, raising up a class of upstarts to rival the fine old nobility and destroy ancient precedence?"

He noted that travel and motion were signs of life and vitality and went on to describe what life he had found on his journey. In En-gland he discovered a "land of roads, new roads, and that everybody there as here is in motion." It was not the old things that struck the vis-itor to England, but the new. Roads were part of the struggle between the old order and the new order. The more communication and move-ment flourished, the more possibility there existed for improvement. "If it [is] to be a question as some will say between Roads and Cathe-drals, which in one sense it certainly is, what chance have the dead against the living?"

After discussing England, Bushnell took his listeners to the conti-nent and led them along a journey such as he had experienced: from Belgium, through the Rhineland and Cologne, to Switzerland, and fi-nally to Rome. In Belgium as in England roads were challenging the power of the cathedrals. The Belgian people might be "degenerate," but "the roads are coming, and without doubt are bringing something of consequence with them." Mobility would usher in progress. In con-trast, a lack of mobility led to moral stagnation, even where true reli-gion was formally present. Concerning Switzerland he observed that "all the world are traveling in Switzerland except the Swiss." The lack of movement took its toll. The Swiss, he observed, were a "fine people," only they did not understand the meaning of liberty. "They think it is liberty in the canton Vaud to compel Christian ministers to read their state proclamations against themselves, and do the bidding of the state in all respects." But even there in that "little nation of republicans . . . locked within their mountain fastnesses" things were changing, religion was reviving, and true liberty was taking root.

In Italy the clamor for roads bespoke a clamor for freedom. The people demanded of the papal government roads, "but roads were not all they wanted, it was only safer to speak of roads; they had some want of law, personal safety, freer marts of trade, tribunals clear of bribery." The current pope tried to offer roads while clinging on to his powers, but it would be in vain. Bushnell prophesied the day when locomotives would finally enter the Eternal City, "and rolling their smoke over St. Peter's will come as new ideas and types of modern power."

But Bushnell did not stop at simply discussing the social and political implications of roads, proceeding to sketch out how the new communication was changing the face of a future Christianity. In doing so he returned to a theme he had already touched on in both his letter to Pope Gregory and his address on the Evangelical Alliance — his vision of a reunited Christianity that would transcend the old divisions. All the older churches would contribute their special gifts: England, its sense of liturgical order; Germany, its "Scripture learning and all possible views on Christian doctrine"; Rome, its solemn conviction of the need of Catholic unity; and France, "if she returns to religion," a sense of social grace and Christian refinement. The American church would offer "the element of spiritual simplicity and practical activity." In mentioning Germany he noted that many feared the strange teachings emanating from that land, but he assured his listeners that despite the occasional eccentricity, there was in German thought a movement toward truth that would ultimately be of greater value than the stone cathedrals of old, since "truth is more divine than stone and her temple more magnificent than anything made by hands."

"The Day of Roads" focused more on social progress than on the church of the future, but within a few months Bushnell returned to the theme of Christian unity in a more systematic way in an article entitled "Christian Comprehensiveness." In the essay he employed the "eclectic" method of the French philosopher Victor Cousin, who had helped bring the ideas of the German Romantic tradition into the New World. Cousin's eclecticism attempted to find an alternative to the idealist/empiricist impasse in philosophy. Idealists began with the abstract or ideal while empiricists started with the specificity of the conditional. The eclectic attempted to live within this tension. Bushnell showed scant interest in the technical aspects of Cousin's writings but latched on to one key principle: for Cousin, every form of belief that existed contained within itself some truth. How to approach that truth and connect it with other truths was the task, and Bushnell saw this as particularly relevant when it came to Christianity; how could Christians who disagreed nonetheless theologically unite? One approach would be to forge agreement on the lowest common denominator. Bushnell referred to this as "neutering" and dismissed it because it gave up the power of the original claims. Another approach, which he called "liberalism," he dismissed because it tried to solve the problem by expanding the boundaries of the truth. The need, he continued, was not to *mediate* extremes by finding some middle position, but to "comprehend" the extremes. To comprehend extremes "offers no disrespect, but the highest respect rather, to the great and earnest spirits that have stood for the truth and fought her battles." The individual truth claims of the various communities were real and vital. They were like "the right and left wings of the field which it now remains to include in one and the same way." The task of comprehension was to take and preserve whatever good and whatever truth there might be in a given position.

To describe how this could be accomplished, Bushnell returned to a favorite theme: the relation between image, word, and symbol. Many of the most violent divisions within Christianity stemmed from a concern to defend truths that were ultimately only partial. Christians latched on to one of the various images in Scripture to help them define a theological issue such as spiritual regeneration or the doctrine of the Trinity. From the image they shaped words, these words became hardened into dogmas, and the dogmas divided. One needed now to reverse this process. "If our schools of theology could, by three years of exercise, get into the minds of their pupils a right understanding of this one simple matter, — the relation of a thought to a word, — they would do more to quicken their intelligence and prepare them to a skillful resolution of the great questions pertaining to religion, than is often done in their own course of discipline." To understand the limitations of language allowed one to identify the truth expressed only semi-adequately in the words. And to do this would allow for the possibility of a "new church . . . that shall comprehend the uses of all." Nowhere were the chances better for such a church to emerge, Bushnell believed, than in America, where already the different communions lived together in peace.

Bushnell then proceeded to distill the essence of the different religious bodies around him, suggesting what each might contribute to a comprehensive Christianity. Baptists, for example, could bring the virtue of Christian individualism in its highest and most perfect degree. It was true that at present the spirit of individualism lapsed occasionally into an exclusive and anti-social spirit, but in the future that would pass away. Congregationalists could offer the vision of the church as a brotherhood, equal to the work of self-government. Congregationalism was firmly republican and "denies all priestly dignities, and suffers no lords over the heritage of God." Presbyterians displayed this same republican spirit, as did Methodists.

Roman Catholicism, too, could contribute something to the new comprehensive church, and it is striking to see the remarkably charitable view of the Catholic church found in Bushnell's vision. In an age when anti-Catholic riots were not an unusual event, Bushnell strove to be evenhanded. Echoing his earlier observations concerning the city of Rome, he described the Church of Rome as a "monumental Christianity." Its rites, prayers, and devotions were a monument to the long Christian past, in both its good and bad. Rome did not so much reflect the content of the gospel of Christ as it did "the history of the Gospel." If American Protestants (and particularly Bushnell's own Congregationalists) emphasized the future of Christianity, Rome offered a link with the past, and a true church needed both. "As Protestants, we seem to imagine a new beginning of Christianity. We assert a future seemingly disrupted from the past, and Romanism confronts us with a past disrupted from the future. And this is a condition of death for both; for every social body, whether civil or Christian, is *of* the past and *for* the future, and cannot properly live save as it connects with both."

If the modern reader is struck by the charity displayed toward Rome, she is also struck by the harshness of Bushnell's critique of Anglicanism. Of all the religious groups only Anglicanism was bucking the flow of history and moving in an opposite direction. The catholic revival in the Church of England, occurring as it did in one of the most advanced nations of the time, troubled Bushnell. It was understandable for benighted European peasants to cling to a hierarchical church; they lacked the benefits of roads and learning. But for cultured English men and women voluntarily to embrace such ideas was scandalous, and for their American cousins to do so — and, even worse, to lure good Protestants into these erroneous beliefs — was ominous. "The phantom of a priestly succession . . . a superstition cherished with so great industry in England, as the last hope of a priestly fabric outlawed by time, can never get possession of this nation," he claimed. "Not one in fifty of the Episcopal sects of this country," he assured his readers, believed in such retrogressive ideas. But still they must be abandoned. If a comprehensive church were to be realized it would necessarily reflect the political genius of the land — and here that would be the embracing of the principles of republicanism and equality. The American experience had created Christian churches far closer to the apostolic model than were the state churches of Europe. The Puritans had labored to achieve this, and "since Puritanism has been a root in our history, let some honor be ascribed to Puritanism." American Episcopalians needed to accept this heritage. They had to give up the superstitions of priestly succession and apostolic bishops and eschew their exclusiveness. They had to "cease to Anglicize and consent to be Americans!" If Bushnell returned from Europe with a vision of a greater Christianity and the role of America in bringing it about, he also returned with a heightened suspicion of Anglicanism as a counterrevolutionary force.

One finds these ideas surfacing yet again in "Barbarism the First Danger," an address Bushnell delivered before a number of Home Missionary Society Meetings. Fifteen years earlier, Lyman Beecher had published "A Plea for the West"; it urged those living in eastern America to support western missions to secure the great American heartland for Protestantism and to prevent it from falling into the hands of Rome. In "Barbarism" Bushnell argued that the great threat was not Rome but the loss of civilization through "ignorance, wildness, and social confusion." Immigration always wreaked havoc with communities, and extraordinary care through education and religion was necessary to preserve culture. He offered as historical examples both the Israelites of Scripture and the Puritan fathers of New England. Many of his contemporary examples were taken from life in the American Southwest, where the great moral traits that had governed American character seemed to be giving way and a social order of rashness and violence emerging. He christened it "the bowie knife style of civilization" in which "the code of honor" was all that remained of virtue. Echoing the comments he made in England on the Oregon question, he noted that the inhabitants of the Southwest were "prompt to resent an injury, slow to discharge a debt." The unfortunate war with Mexico was in large part a result of this type of citizen.

But toward the end of his address he offered hope. Just as religion had saved the Puritan forebears, so too would religion be the salvation of the great American West. But religion must reflect the age. The old Puritans relished in the hard Calvinism of their catechism, which contained "doctrines that were incorporated in their souls as the spinal column in their bodies." He admitted that this heritage was a key part of the foundation of a true religious character, but claimed that now it had to be updated. "God means to finish out this character by uniting it in the softer standards of feeling and the broader compass of a more Catholic and genial spirit. . . . We cannot, therefore, spend our strength now upon exclusive and destructive dogmas, but we must proceed in a Catholic and comprehensive spirit." As earlier, he warned that this catholic comprehensiveness could not be a "vapid liberalism" based on indifference; rather, Catholics must with forbearance and charity join with other Christians "when we clearly find the spirit of Jesus in their life." That "spirit of Jesus" must take precedence over doctrinal differences. Only then could a united church take on the task of reforming society.

QUESTIONING THE ANXIOUS BENCH

Although the idea of a united Christian body possessed Bushnell at this time, he had not forgotten the question of revivalism. Shortly before he left for England he had published an essay in the *New Eng-*

lander, "The Kingdom of Heaven as a Grain of Mustard Seed," that pushed further his criticism of the revival system, and in the months after his return he took up the question again. He was not alone. The issues of revivalism, spiritual regeneration (or conversion), and the proper relation between children and regeneration were increasingly becoming sore points, and were being examined by forces both within and outside of the world of orthodox New England.

The necessity of a supernatural transformation as a mark of re-generation had been a crucial part of the Puritan experience that the orthodox party proudly honored. It linked the orthodox to the first generation and distinguished them from their black sheep Unitarian cousins. Furthermore, ministers like Lyman Beecher saw the revival system as one of the distinctive characteristics of American Christian-ity and as one of the strongest tools for bringing persons to a recogni-tion that they needed to be converted. While English Calvinists waited their American cousins pushed. A contemporary of Beecher's summed up nicely this view of the revival system as the great genius of Ameri-can Christianity:

> If I were asked why revivals are so frequent in America and so rare in Europe, my first answer would be, that Christians on one side of the Atlantic expect them, and on the other side they do not expect them. These seasons of "refreshing from on high" are part of the blessing that rested on our fathers; and the events of the last forty years, especially, have taught us, that if we seek their continuance in the spirit of those with whom they commenced, we shall never seek in vain.

But there were always lurking difficulties in yoking Calvinist theology with revivalism. If human will was marred by sin (as Calvinists taught), and if regeneration was a supernatural act, how could any hu-man activity affect the divine plan? New England theologians like Nathaniel William Taylor had tried to allow for enough freedom of the will to anchor human responsibility and a theology of revivalism. Like a fine sculptor, Taylor carefully tapped away at the Calvinist tradition with his scholarly chisel to open a place for his purposes. Charles Grandison Finney, on the other hand, used a sledgehammer. Finney was the greatest revivalist of the second quarter of the nineteenth century. Although an ordained Presbyterian minister, he had little patience for the niceties of Calvinist theology. For him, the freedom of the will to choose was paramount, and it lay at the foundation of his theology of revivalism. As he explained, "the sinner should consider that the change of heart is a voluntary thing. You must do it for yourself or it is never done." Coupled with his belief in human freedom was his confidence that the use of new tools and techniques could make the work of the revivalist far more effective. By the 1820s he began to employ a number of novel procedures. Trained as a lawyer, he made use of his legal skills in his preaching style, which was direct and colloquial. He also sharpened his appeal by praying for sinners by name. He set up enquiry meetings for sinners under conviction, and an "anxious bench" where persons "anxious to be saved" might be prayed for in the course of the service. Together these were known as the "New Measures."

They made revivalism both more effective and more controversial. The success of Finney's labors in Rochester, Philadelphia, and New York testified to the former. The opposition he invoked spoke to the latter. Lyman Beecher threatened (perhaps only figuratively) to "call out all the artillery-men" of Connecticut and fight Finney "every inch of the way to Boston." Others were more pointed in their criticisms. To strict Calvinists, Finney's theology seemed like a rank abandonment of any notion of supernatural regeneration, resting as it did entirely on human freedom and the revivalist's technique. To others, the New Measures seemed not only a break with the past but a coarsening of the revivalist tradition. One of the aspects of revivalism in nineteenth-century New England had been a balancing of heartfelt piety and social propriety, but Finney spurned talk of propriety, and none of the New Measures were as distasteful to his critics as his encouragement of women to actively participate in mixed assemblies. As one writer noted, "there can be no surer sign of grossness and coarseness in religion than a disposition of this monstrous perversion under any form." Modern readers may find such sentiments odd and offputting, but they touched on a crucial issue: to what degree should religion strive to undergird a culture that saw itself as modeled on Christian values, or to what degree should it challenge those values? The debate over the New Measures would serve as a foretaste of greater controversies over the social implications of Finney's notion of the new birth. For Finney, conversion could and ought to inspire the human will to a new thirst for holiness. It would lead the newly converted boldly to attack evils over which other Christians compromised. In particular it would link revivalism with the crusade to abolish slavery, the most explosive issue in American social and political life.

Revivalism also raised the question of children's proper relationship to the church, a difficult issue for the heirs of the Puritans since the seventeenth century. New England Congregationalists doggedly held two positions that to outsiders seemed contradictory: they practiced infant baptism while at the same time insisting upon a distinct experience of saving grace for church membership. They maintained this teaching in the face of opposition from both the right and the left. Episcopalians insisted that baptism itself offered regeneration and generally insisted upon no evidence of later conversion for church membership. Baptists, in contrast, restricted baptism to professing believers. The nature of the tension had been apparent since the time of Henry Dunster, the first President of Harvard College, who resigned that office in the 1650s to become a Baptist. The growth of both Baptists and Episcopalians in New England during the middle decades of the century indicated that the tension had not gone away.

The question of the place of children, however, was not merely a theological problem but a practical one as well. Foreign visitors at the time regularly commented on the place of children in American culture, since children were given far more freedom in the United States than they were in Europe. This fact appealed to some observers; Harriet Martineau believed that the "independence and fearlessness of children were a perpetual charm." Frances Trollope, in contrast, was less amused, and wrote of the "total want of discipline and subjection which I observed among children of all ages." If American society in general seemed obsessed by children, middle-class America was even more so. The changing social world of antebellum America questioned traditional patterns of child rearing. No longer could parents dutifully pass on to their children a particular set of practical skills that would equip them for the public world. The new, increasingly urban society demanded not particular skills as much as general social skills and a developed character, and the home was to provide this need.

The shift in child-rearing methods one sees developing in the

1830s was partly the result of the new understanding of regeneration offered by Finney. The older view called for the parent to break the sinful will of the child in order to re-form it, much as regeneration was seen as a supernatural work of God. But just as Finney elevated the power of the individual to choose, and suggested that with the proper techniques that choice could be helped along, it was now suggested that the child's will could be shaped for the right development of character. The mother of the Christian home was seen to have a particular role in the shaping of her children, and a flurry of magazines — with names like *Mother's Monthly Journal* and *Mother's Magazine* — began to advise middle-class women on the art of child rearing. All of this change co-existed precariously with the old theology of conversion; for followers of the new models of child rearing, particularly those outside the theological world of Calvinist evangelicalism, the traditional theological views of children seemed scandalous. The idea of the damnation of infants seemed particularly odious, and Lyman Beecher, for one, had to go to great lengths to absolve the orthodox from this charge. In many quarters outside of the world of theology children were viewed as innocent rather than depraved.

Revivalism and revival-oriented piety found itself under attack on a number of fronts. John Henry Hopkins, the Episcopal bishop of Vermont, criticized revivalism as an innovation and offered in its place the regular worship of the Book of Common Prayer. Unitarians dismissed revivalism and its "inflammatory, or we should say, ferocious style of preaching" and argued instead for the rational incorporation of children into Christian culture. But perhaps the most celebrated attack on revivalism was John W. Nevin's *The Anxious Bench*, published in 1843. Nevin, though reared and educated a Presbyterian, was at the time professor of theology at the German Reformed Seminary at Mercersburg, Pennsylvania. He had been attracted to a number of aspects of the German tradition: the sense of history in the community, its close roots to the theology of the sixteenth century, and its emphasis on the unity of the Christian community. His vantage point made him a strong critic of contemporary developments and he viewed the revivalism of Finney as a serious perversion of Protestant Christianity. *The Anxious Bench* was both an attack upon the New Measures and a plea for an alternative model for understanding the Christian life.

The true spirit of the anxious bench, he argued, was not that of

the "Reformation" but that of "Methodism," and he traced its anteced-
ents back not to the great Reformers such as Martin Luther and John
Calvin but to the Radical Reformers who strove to stir up the people
rather than instruct them. In its current form, the movement taught
that people's feelings could be manipulated through certain techniques so as to bring about a desired result. Its goal was "mechanical
conversions" accomplished by "justification by feelings rather than
faith." The heightened emotionalism of the anxious bench served little
if any good for true Christianity, Nevin argued, for a false method
could only produce a false view of religion. He rejected any empirical
claim of the method's effectiveness; a decision brought about by a rush
of emotion could not sustain true Christianity, and he noted how many
"converted" souls eventually fell away. But the anxious bench erred
not only in its practice but in its principle as well. It rested upon a radical individualism. In its concern for converting souls it lost sight of the
corporate nature of the Christian message. True religion is ultimately
connective, not individual. "The true theory of religion carries us continually beyond the individual to the view of a deeper and far more
general form of existence in which the particular life is represented to
stand."

In contrast to the anxious bench Nevin proposed the system of
"catechism." One must start, he explained, with a right understanding
of the church. "The church is truly the mother of all her children." Infants born in the church and incorporated in baptism were to be
treated as "members from the beginning." The individual, growing up
in the church "under the faithful application of the means of grace,
should be quickened into spiritual life in a comparatively private
way." He cautioned that baptism was not an end in itself and if left un-
attended could be a "barren sign," but it was a true beginning. Patient
teaching through catechesis, the labor of parents in instilling religious
faith, and the means of grace provided for by regular worship would
bring about true religion.

Nevin's critique of the anxious bench would have been on the
whole pleasing to Bushnell. His interest in development in religion
and his movement away from an insistence on a dramatic conversion
meshed nicely (we shall see) with many of Bushnell's own thoughts.
There were two sticking points, however. The first was that Nevin's
emphasis on church and sacraments would have sounded a bit too

much like that of his Episcopal adversaries. More important, Nevin and others who criticized revivalism rested their arguments upon a historical claim. If true Christianity (and in Nevin's case true Protestantism) had taught the catechetical method, and viewed with disfavor the principles of the anxious bench, seeing them as a perversion, then this perversion must have been brought about by some other party. And revivalism's critics were clear who the guilty party was. The Puritans were to blame. And they carried the blame not only for the religious problems facing America, but for many of the social problems as well.

THE PROBLEM OF PURITANISM

The question of the Puritan heritage became an increasingly debated topic during these decades. As the Presbyterian Charles Hodge observed, "the name Puritan . . . is rapidly becoming a term of reproach." To understand why, we must briefly note some religious and social factors, each of which made its mark.

As scholars have come to recognize, nineteenth-century Americans' understanding of their own religious past was a continually evolving phenomenon. The idea of an eighteenth-century "Great Awakening" only gradually developed, and became crystallized only in Joseph Tracy's 1842 publication *The Great Awakening: A History of the Revival of Religion in the Time of Edwards and Whitefield*. But a historiographical issue constantly lay underneath this growing idea of a "Great Awakening": was this Awakening a restoration of an earlier religious vitality, or was it, rather, a fundamental revolution in American Christianity? In other words, was the religious story of America one of continuity or discontinuity? The general tendency of New Light evangelical authors was to stress the idea of continuity. For Benjamin Trumbull, author of a *History of Connecticut*, for example, an "experimental" or conversion-oriented piety connected the first generation with the supporters of the Awakening. By the time Robert Baird wrote his *Religion in America*, the importance of revivalism and conversion had become one of the defining elements of American evangelical Protestantism, which was seen as having its origins in New England Puritanism. This insistence upon a continuity between the faith of the

Puritans and evangelicalism was particularly important for the orthodox party in New England in their debates with Unitarians. The inaugural issue of the *Spirit of the Pilgrims* proudly announced, "the orthodox feel themselves to be the proper and legitimate representatives of
the pilgrim fathers." By arguing for a fundamental continuity between
the Puritans and nineteenth-century evangelicalism, the orthodox
could simultaneously claim both the mantle of the Puritans and a preeminent place in the great Protestant evangelical enterprise.

One sees this agenda at work in Lyman Beecher's 1827 Plymouth
Sermon, "The Memory of Our Fathers." He begins by emphasizing
how important the Puritans' doctrine, polity, and piety were to them,
saying that "Their peculiar doctrines and views of experimental religion and church order were dearer to them than life." He then connects them with revivalism, moral societies, and other fruits of the Second Great Awakening. The pan-evangelical nature of this filial
observation is seen in his call for all Christian denominations "to cooperate for the preservation of religion." To be true to the memory of
the Puritans a religious principle "must be applied throughout the nation and no one denomination can do it." But the Unitarians were not
being true to that Puritan memory. He warned that "the attempt is
now openly made to destroy the religious and moral energy of the
churches which our Fathers planted, by perverting their doctrines,
[and] changing the qualifications for membership." For Beecher, doctrine, church order, and social reform connected the world of the Puritans to that of their nineteenth-century descendents, while at the same
time creating a wall of separation between them and the "apostate"
Unitarians.

By the 1840s, however, many had a far more ambivalent memory
of the Puritans. Most were not as pointed in their language as the
young George Templeton Strong, who spoke "of those great humbugs,
the Pilgrim Fathers . . . a more detestable set of men never existed" —
but criticism was increasingly heard. The critique of the Puritans came
from a variety of sources and involved not only religious but political,
social, and cultural factors. Quakers forgot neither the persecutions
they had received from the early Puritans nor the hostility they still felt
from the Puritans' descendents. One Quaker compared a contemporary Calvinist who had attacked the legitimacy of his faith to "his
brother Calvinists, who came to America in the settlement of New En-

gland, who 'whipped the Quakers, men and women, cut off their ears, and . . . hanged four of their preachers . . . in the last century.'" Others saw the Puritan heritage as warping the American character, giving to the culture a cunning utilitarianism with no appreciation for beauty. For novelists like the New Yorker James Fenimore Cooper, Puritans and their Yankee offspring seemed vulgar, self-righteous, and parsimonious. One later commentator on Cooper felt that by becoming a deacon in a Congregational Church, one of Cooper's characters had found "a fitting sequel to a life passed largely in committing acts of doubtful morality." Southern writers often saw a similar connection between Yankee character and Puritan roots. The image of the Connecticut Yankee peddling wooden nutmegs in the rural South was often recalled with disfavor. Writing a few years later, the southern writer George Fitzhugh caustically commented, "The Puritan fathers had lived in Holland and probably imported Norway rats and Dutch morality in the Mayflower."

In the religious context there emerged what we might call an "ecclesiastical" critique of Puritanism. The Puritans were criticized for the severity of their piety; far from having been friends of liberty, they were considered extremists. "Fanaticism is the more appropriate term," wrote one critic, "which compelled the Puritans to seek a home in the wilderness of the New World." They were also attacked as being the source of the problems of the day. If the revival system was a heritage of the Puritan experience, then its failures belonged to them. During the 1840s there were two fronts of this type of criticism: one from High Church Episcopalians (with whom Bushnell had already crossed swords) and another from Nevin's own Mercersburg Seminary. For both groups Puritanism was a perversion of true Christianity and the heritage of the Reformation. In his *The Principle of Protestantism*, Philip Schaff, a professor at Mercersburg Seminary, used the term *Puritanism* to characterize the sectarian nature of American Protestantism, one in which "any one who has . . . some inward experience and a ready tongue may be persuaded that he is called to be a reformer, and so proceed at once, in his spiritual vanity and pride, to a revolutionary rupture with the historic life of the Church." But, Schaff continued, Puritanism resulted not merely in sectarianism, but in rampant individualism as well. "The principle of Congregationalism . . . leads legitimately to full Atomism." As such, Puritanism was at war against the organic principle of the Bible.

Although High Church Episcopalians had been attacking the divisiveness and individualism of modern Puritanism and its emphasis upon a radical conversion experience for decades, by the 1840s Episcopal writers began also concentrating on the connection between Puritanism and the social ills facing America at the time. The children of the Puritans were quickly falling into competing movements divided by theological bickering, and dubious moral reform movements such as temperance, all because of the Puritan belief in the sanctity of private judgment. "I consider," wrote one author, "this a faithful representation of the progress and issue of that society, which looks up to [Puritan minister John] Robinson with as sincere filial veneration, as Methodism to Wesley." But this divisive fanaticism was not merely a religious problem. In an America fearing civil war, the same author dryly noted, "South Carolina has had her nullification, and New England her Hartford Convention; but having lived in a southern state as well as a northern one, I am free to say, that if rebellion must come . . . let it not begin among the posterity of the Puritans. The little finger of rebellion there would be thicker than the loins of nullification elsewhere." Thus Puritanism was seen as the source of both the religious and social crises facing America. That centrifugal quality of American life, which so many critics had commented upon, was the fault of the Puritan spirit.

If the reputation of the orthodox heirs of the Puritans was under assault, the situation among their liberal descendents, the Unitarians, was even worse. Throughout the early decades of the century Unitarians had striven to maintain a distinctively liberal but nonetheless recognizably Christian faith. They upheld the importance of Jesus and the Holy Spirit while rejecting the formal doctrine of the Trinity; they continued to honor the cross while rejecting certain views of the atonement that cast dishonor on God; and they respected the authority of Scripture (including the miracles it describes) while rejecting certain Calvinistic interpretations of it. Furthermore, with Boston as their center, they were leading promoters of a genteel American Christian culture. But the comfortable world of New England Unitarianism was torn asunder in the 1830s by the revolt of the Transcendentalists. Ralph Waldo Emerson, Theodore Parker, Bronson Alcott, George Ripley, and others challenged the Unitarian marriage of Protestantism and Enlightenment reason, dismissing it as a "thin porridge" of "pale negations." Inspired by the spirit of Romanticism, they rejected much of the spirit and many of the doctrines of the past. Emerson urged people to stop following a religion centered on Jesus and to instead seek to recapture the faith that inspired prophets like Jesus. That, he believed, would be an authentic religion. Parker separated the permanent aspects of Christianity from the transient, and included in the latter the idea of the miraculous and most of the traditional doctrines. The Transcendentalists began a discussion that would, by century's end, largely transform Unitarianism. Their call was to reject a historic, particularistic Christianity in favor of a more universal religion.

If in the long run Transcendentalism would refashion Unitarianism, in the short run it shocked it. Parker in particular was violently denounced and systematically shunned. He was excluded from the Boston clerical association and ostracized by his fellow clerics. The rancor against him is perhaps best epitomized by the decision of the alumni of Harvard Divinity School not to convey a message of sympathy to the dying Parker in 1857. In reaction to the transcendentalist critique of historic Christianity there was a revival of Christian self-consciousness within the Unitarian community.

In all of his discussions of Christian comprehensiveness, Bushnell had largely ignored the Unitarians, but he was certainly mindful that they as well as he were inheritors of the Puritan tradition. Their division weakened the witness of the Puritan vision at a time when he felt it needed to be vigorously trumpeted. Thus in the year 1847 the Yankee tinkerer saw a number of issues that needed to be attended to: the problem of revivals, a better place for children in the church, how to defend the reputation of the Puritans, and the reuniting of their children. To fix all these problems would be a tall order.

GROWTH, NOT CONQUEST

During the summer of 1846, as Bushnell began to reacquaint himself with his congregation and with the rhythms of life in Hartford, he began to hear reactions to his 1844 essay "The Kingdom of Heaven as a Mustard Seed." The essay, a follow-up to his earlier work on revivals, linked together religious and social issues and discussed two different ways of enlarging the church. The first, which he called increase through "conquest," involved the rapid accumulation of members through conflict. The second and, he believed, better method he described as organic growth. True Christian growth, he argued, came from the organic spirit within; it grew as the mustard seed grew and did not make use of external forces. In organic growth the family played a fundamental role.

In the course of his essay Bushnell made three important points. The first was to be expected: he went to great lengths to distance this organic growth from the High Church belief in baptismal regeneration. True growth occurred in the organic life of a community and had nothing to do with the mechanical workings of a priestly sacrament. Bushnell's other two points were new connections. In the essay he argued that models of piety had social implications; a piety based on conquest whetted the soul for the hope of conquest in other arenas as well. The revivalists' emphasis on speed and force bled into other areas, and Bushnell suggested that a connection existed between revival piety and the cries of the war hawks calling for the annexation of Texas.

> Our only idea of increase is of that which accrues by means of certain abrupt technical experience. Led away from all thought of internal growth . . . efforts to secure conversions take an external character. . . . Accretion displaces growth. . . . Immediate repentance proclaimed, insisted on and realized in an abrupt change, proper only to those who are indeed aliens and enemies, is the only hope or inlet of the church. We can not understand how the spiritual nation should grow and populate and become powerful within itself; — nothing will serve but the immediate annexation of Texas!

Near the end of the essay Bushnell made his final point. The great failure of revivalist piety was that it concentrated exclusively on the feelings of the heart to the neglect of character or "those duties of society, of good neighborhood, and good citizenship, in which human life is spent, — the kind of graceful feelings, honesty, mercy, generosity, — every thing that is necessary to outward dignity and beauty." He then went on to add that the concern for character was a hallmark of Unitarianism, though Unitarians in turn undervalued the role of warm, inward piety. He concluded by observing, "we have sometimes thought, that if a practical Unitarian and an orthodox disciple could be melted into one, they would make a Christian." Each of the heirs of the Puritans had something to offer the other.

CHRISTIAN NURTURE

Bushnell's essay stirred discussion among the clergy in the Hartford Central Association. In response he penned two discourses on Christian nurture, which he first preached to his own congregation and then proceeded to deliver to his brother clergy in August of 1846. The audiences apparently found little if anything objectionable in them and requested that they be published. But rather than publishing them in Connecticut Bushnell accepted the offer of some members of the Committee of Publication of the Massachusetts Sabbath-School Society to publish them in Massachusetts. In April of 1847, *Discourses on Christian Nurture* appeared.

Bushnell's *Discourses* are paradoxical — bold yet traditional, simple yet highly complex. His thesis is simply stated. The true idea of Christian education is "That the child is to grow up a Christian." (In later editions he would add "and never know himself as being otherwise," but in 1847 the first clause stood alone.) In contrast to the revival system, which assumed that the child would grow up in sin before undergoing the "technical experience" of a conversion, Bushnell believed children could love the good from their earliest years. This did not mean that the process of becoming a Christian was automatic: "I do not affirm that every child may, in fact and without exception, be so trained that he certainly will grow up a Christian. The qualifications it may be necessary to add will be given in another place."

The idea of Christian nurture, Bushnell assured his readers, was not a novel teaching. It had deep roots in Christian history and was the dominant model in much of the Christian world at present. It was, for example, the reason deep religious piety continued to flourish in Germany despite the eccentricities of that church's theology. Christian nurture assumed that the seed of right principle would be planted by the family and church, and when rightfully cultivated would bring forth a true faith. Christianization involved not so much a dramatic decision as a process of formation. The Christian, he explained, was simply a person who had "begun" to love the good for its own sake. The process of growth lasted a lifetime, but it was possible and appropriate for a child to begin it. But again, he cautioned that it was not automatic. "The growth of Christian virtue is no vegetable process, no mere onward development." If parents or pastors failed in their duties, growth would not occur. If the child was not willing to struggle with evil, growth was not possible. "The soul becomes established in holy virtue, as a free exercise, only as it is passed round the corner of the fall and redemption, ascending thus unto God through a double experience, in which it learns the bitterness of evil and the worth of good."

Perhaps the most subtle aspect of the *Discourses* was Bushnell's discussion of the "law of organic connection" as it related to parents' influence on the character development of their children. As we have seen, the role of the family in shaping character was a popular topic. Bushnell yoked it to the task of theology. The relationship between parent and child was not simply didactic and rational, he believed; it was a true example of the work of unconscious influences. Indeed, he went so far as to suggest "that the character of one is actually included in that of the other, as a seed is formed in the capsule." Long before a child could intellectually acquire formal learning, the character of the parents was shaping the offspring. For Bushnell, the home more than either the church or the school was the true locus of character formation. In that sense Christian character was a divine gift passed down by God through the institution of the family. The individual did not earn it, but received it through nurture. In his earlier essay Bushnell had invoked Hebrew imagery, seeing the family as a covenanted community and the children as "included in the faith of their parents." The failure of the revival system was that it ignored this organic connection and emphasized a radical individualism, according to which only rational individual souls could be brought to the decision of conversion. Bushnell dismissingly referred to this as the "Baptist" view of human development in which a person "becomes, at some certain moment, a complete moral agent, which a moment before he was not." The working out of character, he argued, was actually a long process, and was communal rather than individual. "The Christian life and spirit of the parents shall flow into the mind of the child, to blend with his incipient and half formed exercises," and the result would be a distinctive

Christian character. In his advice to parents Bushnell echoed themes he had earlier made in his sermon "Unconscious Influences." Parents must convey Christ-like love and the importance of religion to their children. "And it must be first not in words and talk, but visibly first in your love — that which fixes your aims, feeds your enjoyments . . . beautifies and blesses your character."

At the conclusion of his *Discourses* Bushnell suggested that Christian nurture was not only a viable message for families but offered a fresh start for the American Christian world. The emphasis on the mechanical workings of revivalism had come to a dead end. "We have worked a vein until it has run out." The fever of activity had exhausted the churches. "No nation can long thrive by a spirit of conquest; no more can a church." "We preach too much," he observed, "and live Christ too little." To return to the method of Christian nurture would revivify the church. It would bring forth a generation "ardent without fanaticism, powerful without machinery."

Christian Nurture bears the unmistakable traits of the tinkerer's handiwork. It was intuitively bold, particularly when discussing the dynamics of the family relationship. Decades later scholars would acknowledge that Bushnell had touched on many facts developmental psychologists later discovered about how children learn. The work was sharp and journalistic, particularly in his willingness to caricature alternative views. (To describe traditional piety as having children "piously brought up in sin" — though admittedly clever — was hardly fair.) But *Christian Nurture* also simply sidestepped the classic theological questions. Issues such as human depravity and freedom of the will that had long been points of debate among learned theologians were treated in a most cavalier way. There was no attempt to place the thesis of *Christian Nurture* within the wider context of the New England theological tradition. It stood alone, and beckoned others to follow. Finally, the work was frustratingly opaque at crucial points. Bushnell's discussion of the "organic connection" and his image of character being passed on "as a seed is formed in the capsule" are intriguing and evocative, but they are so incomplete that they raise more questions than they answer. As before, Bushnell was better at offering an intuitive solution to a problem than in rationally explaining his method to his learned peers.

His critics pounced on these problems. The strict orthodox journal, *The Christian Observatory*, chided him for his inventiveness. "Dr. Bushnell is by nature an original genius," it wrote. "But like a conscious beauty, who makes too lavish a display of her charms, he offends against truth and propriety by straining and exaggerating his turn for originality, until it becomes an affectation and a vice." At best, the work was but a fancified version of a truism everyone recognized, that family life shaped children. "Stripped of its strange costume, the naked principle is triteness itself, and hackneyed to the very bones. This is what ten thousand tongues are talking every day. The 'Mothers' Magazines' and 'Assistants' are filled with nothing else." When the work was read as theology, the *Observatory* claimed, it was hopelessly confusing. Although Bushnell paid lip service to the doctrines of depravity and regeneration, his answers always fell short.

The theological weaknesses of the work were also taken up by Bennett Tyler, who was in many ways the antithesis of Bushnell. A plodding, if unimaginative, traditionalist, Tyler was more concerned with logical consistency than was Bushnell. Despite all of Bushnell's rhetorical flurry, Tyler argued, his case ran aground on the question of regeneration, or how and when a person became a Christian. Evangelicals were clear on this point: regeneration occurred at the point of conversion. Anglicans were also (if wrong) at least clear: it occurred at baptism. But Bushnell was vague. If a child was to "grow up a Christian" she must necessarily already be a Christian. But to assume that a child was a regenerated person without any signs or evidence was a dangerous presupposition. It would "lead persons to flatter themselves that they are Christians, while they are strangers to genuine piety."

RESCUING THE PURITANS

Such criticisms caused the publication of the work to be suspended and the book to be withdrawn from circulation by the Massachusetts Sabbath-School Society. In response to these criticisms Bushnell penned his *An Argument for "Discourses on Christian Nurture,"* in which he added a historical dimension to his proposal, jettisoning the cherished New England orthodox claim of continuity between the Puritan Fathers and the Great Revival of the 1740s. He claimed that both John

Calvin and Richard Baxter were in fact proponents of his vision, and that the practice of seventeenth-century Puritanism was far closer to his idea of family nurture than his critics assumed. The present mode of religious piety emerged not in the seventeenth century but in the eighteenth, Bushnell argued; it was not until the 1740s that "Jonathan Edwards, followed by Whitefield, the Tennants, Davenport and other inferior teachers [came forward], *introducing a new religious era,* the same which was continued to the present day — the era of extreme individualism, of adult conversion, revivals, angular experiences, hard and violent demonstrations, painful exhaustions, and now at least a growing disrespect to spiritual piety itself." The individualism and emotionalism which had been seen as fruits of Puritanism by his critics were in fact a product of a religious revolution scarcely a hundred years old.

The idea that Christian initiation was tied to a dramatic conversion experience was not, he argued, a Puritan belief but a product of the eighteenth-century Awakening. Only with Edwards was the idea popularized that conversion could be brought about only by the agency of the Holy Spirit and apart from individual initiation and choice. "Hanging everything thus on miracle, on a pure *ictus dei* [i.e., a divine action or blow], separate from all instrumental connexions of truth, feeling, dependence, motive and choice, there was manifestly nothing less than to wait for the concussion." So great was the authority of Edwards, however, that he introduced a new era in New England religion, "and what is not a little remarkable, we have theological professors, and other distinguished teachers, sworn to the maintenance of orthodoxy, who are actually defending, as synonymous with all antiquity, notions and practices, which are scarcely more than a century old!" Even worse, by rejecting traditional Puritanism in favor of a radical, conversion-oriented piety, New Light advocates opened the way for even stronger proponents of revivalism like the Methodists and the Baptists. Commenting on Nevin's jab, Bushnell admitted the weight of Nevin's criticism but argued that Nevin misidentified the culprit. "The development of this precise style of religion [i.e., the 'ictic' theory of grace] he considers with me to be the great misfortune of Puritanism as seen in the history of New England. In a word it has made us all Baptist in theory, which is the same as to say we ought to be in fact." The direction of evangelicalism since the 1740s had been away from the genius of the Puritans and toward the individualism and emotionalism represented by the Baptists.

In the course of his *An Argument for "Discourses on Christian Nurture"* Bushnell thus took arguments that had earlier been made by Schaff, Nevin, and his Episcopal critics *against* the New England Puritan tradition and transformed them into criticisms of the *abandonment* of the Puritan tradition. While three years earlier he had maintained the continuity of Jonathan Edwards's teachings with the Puritan tradition, and attacked Bishop Brownell's criticism of Edwards as a New Light Theologian, Bushnell now adopted Brownell's position, distancing Puritanism from the entire Great Awakening movement. The present-day failures in church and state were thus a result not of Puritanism but of the Awakening's rejection of the vision of the Puritans. But this raises the inevitable question, what precisely was the essence of Puritanism for Bushnell? To answer this we must turn to an oration Bushnell delivered two years later and published in 1851 under the title "The Fathers of New England."

In that address, Bushnell tried to recast the image of the Puritan, arguing that the Puritans were a people shaped by a distinct character. They did possess a strong theology, but unlike the followers of Luther and Calvin on the continent, they were not characterized by their theological beliefs. Rather, their faith reflected the parting words of Pastor John Robinson that "God hath more truth yet to break forth out of his holy word." It was the character and culture of Puritanism that set it apart, not individual theological doctrines.

Furthermore, the institution in which people and culture met was the family. Bushnell contrasted the advice given by seventeenth-century philosopher Francis Bacon, who in his "Of Plantations" urged that only single men be sent to start new colonies, with the homely wisdom of the Puritans, who emphasized the importance of domestic establishment. "Bacon is there — Robinson is here. There was the deep sagacity of human statesmanship — here is the divine oracle of duty and religion." The existence of families allowed the Puritan colony to grow in a natural or organic way.

But much of Bushnell's oration concerned how the Puritans were to be understood as the foundation of American order. Their key contribution was their respect for law. They always recognized that law was not a human creation but was of divine origin. They understood that "law is law, binding upon souls not as a human will or the will of just one more than half the full-grown men over a certain age, but a power of God entering into souls and reigning in them as a divine instinct of civil order. . . . This it is that makes all government sacred and powerful, that it somehow stands in the will of God."

We will see how Bushnell would elaborate upon this theme in the decade that followed, particularly to explain the causes of the American Civil War, but what is striking is that for Bushnell these cultural attributes marked the true genius of Puritanism, and absent from the discourse is any real emphasis upon the church as it had been traditionally understood. Indeed he ends his oration with a striking image:

> And so the "Church of the Future," as it has been called, gravitates inwardly towards those terms of brotherhood in which it may coalesce and rest. I say not that Christendom will be Puritanized . . . but what is better . . . it will be Christianized. It will settle thus in a unit, probably not of form, but of practical assent and love — a commonwealth of the Spirit, as much stronger in its unity than the old satrapy of priestly despotism as our republic is stronger than any other government in the world.

The true end or *telos* of Puritanism was a transcendence of the inherited idea of the church and the emergence of the church as a true spiritual commonwealth. Puritanism was not a system of fanaticism and harsh doctrine but a forerunner of the comprehensive Christianity of the future. Church identification becomes, in Bushnell, no longer tied to the distinct "qualifications" of a Lyman Beecher or the sacramentalism of the ecclesiastical critics but to a cultural vision. The future church was to be transformed from an ecclesiastical satrapy to a "commonwealth of the spirit." For Bushnell, peoplehood took the place of ecclesia, just as families took priority over sacraments and policy. Traditional concepts of the church, which so moved Beecher, Chapin, and Nevin, he completely rejected. The Puritans were most essentially a people. Moreover, according to Bushnell this merging of church and peoplehood was not unique to Puritanism but was the ultimate vision of true Christianity. In one passage at the end of his "The Kingdom of Heaven as a Mustard Seed," for example, Bushnell likened the church to a great heavenly colony:

> Imagine the church of God to be to be a spiritual nation, founded
> or begun by a colony descended from the skies. It alights upon our
> globe as its chartered territory. Can this Spiritual Colony spread it-
> self over the whole territory of the planet, and absorb all the hu-
> man races in its dominion?

The experience of the church universal was the experience of Puritan
Connecticut writ large, and the church would expand organically by
growth, through the institution of the family, just as the children of the
first Puritan generation had expanded through the continent.

Bushnell in *Christian Nurture* offered an understanding of the Puritans far different from either the panegyrics of Lyman Beecher or the
criticisms of the ecclesiastical critics. Puritans were the foundation of
American order not through their doctrines or their ecclesiastical institutions, but in their contribution to character. The church as a people
or colony was for Bushnell an alternative to both the fractiousness of
revivalism and the formalism of ecclesiasticism.

REUNITING THE PURITANS

Contemporaries were aware of the radical nature of Bushnell's
agenda, both its ecclesiology and its historical claims. But why did
Bushnell propose such a reconceptualization, and how does one explain such an agenda in the middle of a work on Christian nurture?
One reason was of course Bushnell's fear of the growth of Catholicism,
a growth witnessed to by both increased immigration and the growing
interest in Puseyism. We have already noted that his European travels
had left him profoundly suspicious of the pretensions of the Church of
England and the corruptions of the Church of Rome. But perhaps there
is something more going on here. Indeed, there seem to be two hidden
agendas in Bushnell's reinterpretation of the Puritans.

First, by seeing the principle of organic growth as the true Puritan principle, Bushnell recast the figure of the Puritan from a dangerous fanatic to a sober conservative. Both church and nation advance by
growth, not conquest. Indeed, when he included his earlier essay on
growth like the mustard seed in *An Argument for "Discourses on Christian Nurture,"* he sharpened its title by renaming it "Growth Not Con-

quest the True Method of Christian Progress." Puritan New England became a mighty province not through "forces and instruments that were really external to the church" — that is, not by external forms — but by the internal development of the spirit, in which the family played a key role. This, too, was the genius behind the growth of the nation. A true religious spirit led to "simplicity in manners" and "mental vigor," and, as a result, "population multiplied, wealth increased, the forest fell away at the sound of their axes, the natives retired before the potent and prolific energy of the Saxon life, as before the Great Spirit himself." A true religious spirit (such as Puritanism) allowed for proper natural growth in both church and state. But just as there was a connection between a true religious spirit and proper national growth, so too were their opposites linked. The fractiousness of American political life was an outgrowth of the New Light piety. Christians impatient with the slow growth of the religious spirit were also citizens upset with the slow organic growth of the nation across the continent. They were the proponents of "bowie knife civilization" and were the advocates of the annexation of Texas. Bushnell's recasting of the Puritans made them an anchor of sober solidity in a society running amuck.

Bushnell's second agenda is a more hidden one, and here we must speculate, but Bushnell does provide one intriguing clue. Toward the end of *An Argument*, Bushnell heaped criticism upon the decision of the Massachusetts Sabbath-School Society to withdraw its support, claiming that their decision had prevented the possibility of healing the breach between the orthodox and the Unitarians. The great debate over Transcendentalism had shaken New England Unitarianism, which was, Bushnell noted, "not content with itself." This presented an opportunity for the Congregationalists, but they were not taking advantage of it. He warned darkly, "But what do we see, if any among the Unitarians become dissatisfied and desire to find some form of religion more adequate to their spiritual wants? Seldom do they stop with you, but they pass directly on to the hands of the bishop. They prefer to take a type of religion foreign to New England, and one that has no sympathy with our institutions, rather than to stop with you who are bound up with them in the ties of a common history." Note the language. Episcopacy is a religion "foreign to New England," while Unitarianism and orthodoxy have the "ties of a common history." The Congregationalists and the Unitarians were really one community of the children of the Puritans, who had tragically divided over theological questions earlier in the century. But the threat of ecclesiasticism and atomism reminded them that they still bore familial marks, and that reunion was still possible. Unfortunately, Congregationalist intransigence was providing an opening for the growth of a religious tradition at odds with the genius of New England. Is it not possible to see Bushnell's recasting of the Puritans as a means by which to elevate this common history of New England? Bushnell's vision of the Puritans is one that would have been acceptable and attractive to both orthodox and Unitarian. Furthermore, such a recasting would derail the "ecclesiastical" assault on the Puritans. He noted that an Episcopal writer had recently published a volume on "the radical defects of our religion, as illustrated in our history." In it, the writer pointed to many of the same defects that Bushnell had noted. "The impression left by the tract is that Episcopacy is the proper remedy. I have endeavored to suggest a remedy consistent with our history, and the ecclesiastical frame of our churches." In this way Bushnell uses the Puritans in the opposite way from Lyman Beecher. Whereas for Beecher the memory of the Puritans supported pan-evangelical unity in the face of Unitarianism and unbelief, for Bushnell it was a symbol of pan–New England unity in the face of both revivalism and episcopacy.

Christian Nurture should be seen not only as the beginning of the Christian education movement in the United States, but also as a work Bushnell used to further his notion of a comprehensive Christianity. Reuniting the children of the Puritans, and bringing together the orthodox emphasis on piety and the Unitarian concern with character, was one of his goals. It was the goal that he would continue to pursue in the next year when he was invited to give theological lectures at the three great theological centers of New England: Harvard, Yale and Andover. There, the tinkerer would try his hand at theology.

6 Reimagining Theology
   in the Name of Religion

N EW ENGLANDERS were proud of their religion. It seemed admirably to reflect the flinty character of the people. Noah Porter Jr. of Yale College, in a jaundiced review of Coleridge and his American disciples, aptly described the regional tenor: "Ours is a Puritan theology. . . . Ours is severe in its simplicity, plain in its nomenclature and sternly logical in its arrangements. . . . The New England theology is stern in its love of truth, and rigid in its scrutiny of evidence. . . . Above all the eloquence of the New England theology is found[ed] on convictions, and warmly and frequently addresses the conscience, which it carries with its solemn appeal and its awful earnestness." The ancestral faith, loyally kept by the orthodox, was tough, rigorous, and sober. It was the mettle in the soul of all true New Englanders.

Or so it was praised as being. But for people like Bushnell, that character of toughness seemed more like cloddishness, and its logic and rigor more like marks of intellectual rigor mortis. Furthermore, the people who sang the praises of New England religion were tragically divided on issues of religion, and the divisions robbed the people of much of the power of their witness. While there appeared to be a fresh spirit in the air, a sense of new possibility that the divisions might yet be overcome, all too many still preferred the old paths of separation to the new idea of unity.

Thus for Bushnell it might have seemed providential that in March of 1848 he received an invitation to address the Divinity School at Harvard that summer, and that this offer was quickly followed by invitations to deliver the *Concio ad Clerum* at Yale College's annual commencement and to speak before the Porter Rhetorical Society at Andover Seminary. Not only were these three distinguished invitations, they came from the three great centers of New England theology. Cambridge was the hub of Unitarianism, Andover still the home of the heirs of the New Divinity men, and New Haven the stronghold of Nathaniel William Taylor and the Taylorites. If any three institutions reflected the divided state of New England religion it would be these. They witnessed to the brokenness of New England culture, with their constant feudings and in-fightings. But they also provided a challenging arena for a tinkerer to try his hand at repairing the brokenness.

EXPERIENCING THE GOSPEL

Immediately before receiving Harvard's invitation Bushnell experienced a great spiritual epiphany. He had taken to reading the writings of Madame Guyon, who, along with François Fénelon, Archbishop of Cambrai, had struck a new spiritual course in late-seventeenth-century France. Guyon and Fénelon offered the vision of a mystical union between the soul and God through a pure love in which the soul lost any ability to distinguish between itself and God. Condemned by Rome, their writings found favor in the Protestant world throughout the eighteenth century. Guyon was published in America as early as 1809, primarily by Quakers who saw parallels between her way and their emphasis on the inner light, and by the 1830s interest in Guyon had spread beyond the Society of Friends. Thomas Upham, a Congregationalist minister and professor of philosophy at Bowdoin College in Maine, took up her cause and published in 1846 a life of Madame Guyon and an account of the history and religious opinions of Fénelon. Through this volume Bushnell encountered a glimpse of the pureness of the mystical vision and a sense of the certainty of the divine presence that he had striven all his life to achieve. At one point

Upham quoted Guyon as proclaiming, "I had a deep peace, a peace that seemed to pervade the whole soul. A peace which resulted from the fact that all my desires were fulfilled in God." In another place she described true prayer as "that state of the heart in which it is united to God in faith and love. The heart that has faith and love is the true praying heart." This sense of abandonment to God's being must have sounded strange to the self-reliant Yankee, but the power of such words thrilled him, and the effect was profound. As his first biographer (and daughter) described it, "On an early morning in February, his wife awoke to hear that the light they had waited for, more than they watch for the morning, had risen indeed. She asked 'what have you seen?' He replied, 'The Gospel.' It had come to him at last after all of his thought and study, not as something reasoned out, but as an inspiration, a revelation from the mind of God himself."

In a sermon preached soon after the event, he attempted to describe the experience. His language was intensely personal and differed in tone from both the activist advice of his sermons of the 1830s and early 1840s and *Christian Nurture.*

> Some persons imagine that nothing is wanting in us, save to do what we may in and upon ourselves in self-reformation, self culture, a life of duty and good works, and a faithful endeavor to polish and beautify ourselves. . . . What a joy and relief it should be to the soul to find the incarnate Word descending to its aid, to go out of herself and rest herself in a love not her own, and thus to form herself unto a new and noble life by adherence to another.

This was Bushnell's third "conversion." The first, in Bantam, led him to membership in the community of the church. The second, at Yale, opened to him the ministry of the church. This third appears to have been an experience of divine reality, and it offered him a depth of assurance he had always longed for. As we shall see, that event of February of 1848 would shape many aspects of his later career — particularly his opinions on the supernatural. But it would also serve to brace him for his immediate task. The story of Madame Guyon reminded him that truth bearers could be both prophetic and unpopular at the same time. Fénelon and Madame Guyon scandalized the worldly church of Louis XIV, and they felt its wrath and suffered its scorn. But

129

their vision prevailed. Furthermore, Madam Guyon's writings, coupled with the experience Bushnell had undergone, convinced him of a truth he had long suspected — that lying beneath theology and logic was a deeper reality. Beneath all lay the experience of the divine.

EXPLAINING THE CROSS

His three addresses went to the very core of Christian theology. For his address to the Divinity School at Cambridge he chose the doctrine of the saving work of Christ, or soteriology. Perhaps no subject has deeper roots in the Christian experience than the atonement, or Christ's death on the cross, through which sinners are reconciled to Christ. Early in the Christian era the apostle Paul offered as a summary of the Christian faith, "God was in Christ reconciling the world to himself," while in the Fourth Gospel, upon seeing Jesus, John the Baptist proclaimed, "Behold the Lamb of God, which taketh away the sins of the world." No belief set Christians more apart from others than this belief that Jesus had performed an act of reconciliation between God and humanity, a reconciliation which sinful human beings could not bring about themselves. Such was the mystery of the cross — a mystery that puzzled philosophers, perplexed followers of other religions, and confounded many over the centuries. To describe the mystery the Scriptures employed numerous images. Jesus was the lamb who was slain, the one who set the captives free, the one through whose stripes we were healed. But as theology developed, the question increasingly became not one of "whether" but "how." How did Jesus take away the sins of the world and put humanity in a new relationship with God? For a millennium Christian writers and preachers proposed various explanations, but none seemed to adequately address the mystery.

Soteriology as a systematic discipline of inquiry emerged first in the writings of Anselm (1033-1109), a medieval monk and Archbishop of Canterbury. His treatise *Cur Deus Homo,* or *Why God Became Man* (meaning human), was the first systematic attempt to explain why the coming of Christ was necessary to free humans from the bondage of sin. In the present era, Anselm explained, Christians could not rely upon the images of Scripture alone. Reasons needed to be given why such a death as Jesus suffered was necessary. Of the biblical imagery he noted, "all of these statements must be accepted as beautiful and like so many pretty pictures. But if there is no solid foundation for them, unbelievers do not think them adequate to show why we ought to believe that God was willing to suffer what we described." One needed to go beyond pretty pictures. Thus Anselm explained that in Christ's death upon the cross the debt to God's honor, which had occurred because of human sinfulness, was fully rendered, and because the debt of sin was paid the relationship between God and the human race was altered. *Cur Deus Homo* became foundational for much of the later soteriological writings in the Latin West. Protestants and Catholics in the sixteenth century might differ on many points, but they agreed on this understanding of the work of Christ.

Anselm's theory lay at the core of the New England concept of a governmental theory of the atonement. The governmental theory was recognized as perhaps the most original contribution of the New England theological tradition. The New England theologians, one recalls, shifted the metaphor from the idea of a payment of a debt to the idea of justice in government: God required a sacrifice to maintain the principle of justice; no evil could go unpunished in a just society. In Christ, God himself suffered the penalty and restored the moral order.

The penal or "objective" theory of Christ's saving work was not, however, without its critics. From the very time of Anselm himself, theologians such as Abelard chafed at the implications of this theory for the divine nature. That God would require blood sacrifice to appease his honor seemed cruel and unloving. Such criticisms became louder in the eighteenth century when evolving attitudes concerning sovereignty and justice cast the traditional soteriological theory in a cruel light. The satisfaction view of the atonement offered the picture of a cruel God who would allow his own son to suffer to appease the divine honor. As we already saw, this traditional view of Christ and the cross was one of the most noxious things about the old orthodoxy for liberals in New England, and in its place they championed a subjective view of Christ's work: Christ's death was not directed to God but to humanity, and it demonstrated the depths of divine love.

Two opposing views of Christ's work thus divided the children of the Puritans: an objective view taught by the orthodox that emphasized Christ's death as a sacrifice to restore order, and a subjective view held by the Unitarians that saw the death as an example of divine love directed to humanity. But, asked Bushnell, was such an impasse necessary? Bushnell, the tinkerer, suggested that there was a relationship between the objective and subjective theories. "If the . . . subjective view of Christ, that in which I state the end of Christ's work, is true, that end or aim could not be effectively realized without the second or objective view, in which the whole work is conceived in the altar form, and held forth to the objective embrace and worship and repose of faith."

Before his (mostly) Unitarian audience at the Divinity School, he willingly acknowledged the problems involved in orthodoxy's attempted systematic explanations of the biblical imagery of sacrifice. However the penal view was rendered — either as a substitutionary death or as Christ's suffering and death as an expression of God's abhorrence of sin — it involved great moral problems. It assumed that God punished the innocent to let the guilty go free. Indeed, in their attempts to rationalize this view its advocates made it even more grotesque by quantifying the suffering. "Calvin maintained the truly horrible doctrine that Christ descended into hell, when crucified," he wrote, "and suffered the pains of the damned for three days. A very great number of Christian teachers, even at this day maintained that Christ suffered exactly as much pain as all the redeemed would have suffered under the penalties of eternal justice." But if the orthodox ran the risk of losing God's true nature in their insistence that Christ's death paid some debt, the Unitarians had their own problems. They suggested that Christ came into the world to bring humanity into union with God and reconcile them to God; but if that were God's plan why was the cross necessary? What organic relationship did it have to the divine plan?

Responding to the problems implicit in both of these approaches, Bushnell offered his own view. The work of Christ, he explained, was for humanity. Christ was an example, showing to the human race the sanctity of God's law and character and revealing God's righteousness. But we find the meaning not in the human explanation of the event but in the images themselves. Indeed, Bushnell called for a reversal of the process begun by Anselm. Anselm had claimed that the biblical images were meaningless until they were rationally explained; as "pretty pictures" they possessed no power. Bushnell proclaimed to his listeners that in those pictures lay the true power.

Here . . . the value of Christ's mission is measured by what it expressed. And if so, then it follows of course, that no dogmatic statement can adequately represent his work; for the matter of it does
not lie in formularies of reason and cannot be comprehended by
them. It classes as a work of Art more than a work of Science. It addresses the understanding, in great part through the feeling of sensibility.

In Christ's nature and character perfect life was revealed. In God's entering of the world through the revelation of Christ the way of the
cross was prepared. And here Bushnell returned to themes he had
raised over a decade earlier in his address at Andover. There he had
described how the physical rituals of the Old Testament, particularly
those concerning sacrifice, had served as the foundation of the moral
imagery of the New Testament. In the death of Christ, he explained,
one saw the fulfillment of God's justice through the mode of sacrifice.
Throughout the Old Testament the law of sacrifice taught not a message of punishment but one of reconciliation. "The value of sacrifice
terminated principally in the power it had over the religious character
and the impressions, exercises, aids, and principles, which as a liturgy
it wrought in the souls of the worshippers." Sacrifice impressed upon
the religious conscience the sanctity of the violated law. In the Old Testament the law of sacrifice was manifested through the blood of ani-
mals; in the New Testament it is reflected in the death of Christ. In
Christ's obedience and suffering, and finally in his death, humanity
saw this in its most perfect form. Only such a sacrifice could both
cover the sins of humanity and reveal the full cost of human sinfulness. Without the cross a true and full reconciliation would have been
impossible because humanity would not have had to confront the
depths of its sinfulness. "Were they simply assured, instead, of God's
fatherly benignity and His readiness to forgive sins freely, the assurance would be virtually a declaration of impunity, and a half century
of time would suffice to obliterate even the sense of religion."

In elevating the altar imagery as a focus for the meaning of
Christ's death, he continued, one could still speak of an "objective"
component in the work of reconciliation. The Old Testament elements
of altar and sacrifice, although superseded, nonetheless continued as
images and gave a sense of inward objectivity. These images were

foundational to Christian belief. "Instead of a religion before the eyes, we have now one set up in language before the mind's eye, one that is almost as intense as the other only that it is mentally so, or as adheres to thought." If the orthodox would reject their attempts to translate the pictures into logical theory, and the Unitarians would return to the sharp and powerful images of Scripture, unity might still be possible.

APPROACHING THE MYSTERY OF THE GODHEAD

For his second address, before the Connecticut clergy gathered in New Haven, Bushnell chose as his topic another venerable issue in Christian theology — the divinity of Christ. Here too was a subject ripe with importance and loaded with controversy. If before his Cambridge audience he had addressed the second half of the famous Pauline dictum, "God was in Christ reconciling the world to himself," or the issue of reconciliation, here he returned to the first half. What did it mean to say that God was in Christ?

In posing such a question Bushnell joined a great and famous company of Christian writers. How "God" and "Christ" were related had been a hotly debated topic in the early Christian era. All manner of explanations had been offered, and each was found wanting. Was the human Jesus "adopted" or infused with the divine spirit at the beginning of his ministry? This was rejected as adoptionism. Was Christ's human nature merely an illusion to help cloak his true divine identity? This was rejected as Docetism. Were they really the same being in two different modes or manifestations? This was rejected as Sabellianism or patripassianism. Was Christ a lesser creature, a bridge between God and humanity? This was rejected as Arianism. Christian writers strove to balance a number of concerns that at times seemed irreconcilable: that God was one, that God was truly manifest in the person of Jesus, and that Jesus was fully human. The debate became the source of the fourth-century struggle to clarify the question. As a result of the first four universal or ecumenical councils, beginning with that of Nicaea in 325 and ending with Chalcedon in 451, careful formulae were crafted to explain the mystery. Christ was of the same substance with the Father but was a distinctive person. Together with the Holy Spirit, Father and Son made up the Godhead, one God in three persons. Furthermore, the person of Christ possessed two distinct natures: one human and one divine. These definitions rested upon a number of concepts — such as substance, person, and nature — borrowed from Greek philosophy, and reflected the coming together of philosophy and theology that was the characteristic mark of the age.

Just as with Anselm's theory of soteriology, the Christological definitions of the first four councils became normative and survived the conflicts of the Reformation. By the end of the seventeenth century, however, they began to attract criticism. What did such definitions really mean? Could modern men and women honestly subscribe to professions of faith they could not understand and which could not directly be found in Scripture? Critiques of the traditional formulas increased throughout the eighteenth century in the English-speaking world, and by the nineteenth century the Unitarian rejection of such categories was but another point of division between them and the orthodox. Both the doctrine of the two natures of Christ and the identification of Christ with God were rejected as unscriptural by the Unitarians. For them there was one God — God the Father — and their view of Christ was aptly summarized by their maxim, "one mind, one being, and a being distinct from the one God."

Here, in New Haven, Bushnell attempted to mend this problem as well. Speaking for almost one and three-quarters hours he boldly charged into the thicket of Christology, but his tack must have surprised many of his listeners. Even more so than in Cambridge he took the role of the anti-theologian. "No person," he announced, "would ever doubt for a moment, the superhuman quality of Jesus, if it were not for the speculative difficulties encountered by an acknowledgement of his superhuman quality." Indeed, he claimed, the divinity of Christ was never seriously questioned until the "easy free representations of scripture" gave way to the definitions of the "Nicene theologues." The metaphysical Trinity, worked out so carefully by generations of theologians, far from helping the gospel, hid it. He proclaimed, accordingly, that one should begin not with the Trinity of the metaphysicians, which attempted to solve the paradoxes of Scripture, but with the Trinity of revelation. Here, too, he drew upon ideas from his Andover address. God, in his true nature, was infinite and unknowable, so the only God we could know was the God of revelation. But the revealed God could not be the infinite or absolute God. "It must be to us as if Brama were waking up," he explained, "as if Jehovah . . . were dividing off himself into innumerable activities that shall dramatize His immensity, and bring Him within the molds of language and discursive thought." The revealed God, although real, was ultimately symbolic, since language about him always pointed back to the greater reality beyond human comprehension. Only when God spoke did humans grasp his fatherhood, and only at the time of the incarnation did they glimpse the idea of the Trinity. All these images represented the ultimate being but none encapsulated it. "In these three persons or impersonations I only see a revelation of the Absolute Being, under just such relatives as by their mutual play, in and before our imaginative sense, will produce in us the truest knowledge of God."

Such a revelation of God was neither confusing nor contrary to reason, said Bushnell. The only problems emerged when theologians attempted to conform it to logic. The two great questions addressed by the councils — the relation of Christ's divinity and humanity, and the relationship between the persons of the Godhead — were in fact red herrings and contributed confusion rather than clarity to the scriptural picture. Theologians had painstakingly analyzed what of Jesus' nature was human and what divine, and because of philosophical concerns they strove to make sure no human qualities were posited to the divine nature; but such concerns missed the great message of Scripture. "The reality of Christ is what he expresses to God," Bushnell explained, "not what he is in his physical conditions or under his human limitations. He is here to express the Absolute Being . . . in a word to communicate his own life to the race, and graft himself historically into it." Bushnell did not deny that Christ possessed a human soul but insisted that the picture of Christ in Scripture was one of unity rather than of division. As a unity his human soul could not have a distinct subsistence, such that it might live, think, and suffer by itself. All these activities when experienced by Christ were experienced through a single unified person. For over a thousand years theologians had assiduously held on to the twofold nature of Christ in order to avoid certain metaphysical errors. If Christ were truly God, it was argued, then he could not experience pain or emotion in his divine nature, since philosophers agreed that God was a being without body, parts, or passions. But such metaphysical musings over the relationship of Christ's humanity and divinity were fruitless; "Christ is not here for something accomplished in his metaphysical or psychological interior, but for that which appears and is outwardly signified in his life." Theologians might be interested in such questions, but they missed the true religious power of the gospel.

The same problem surfaced regarding the question of the Trinity. The elaborate language concerning personhood had led to confusion. It had turned one God into three. One of course could use the language of personhood in a limited sense to describe the Godhead; Scripture did employ the personal language of "I," "Thou," "He," and "They" to describe the manifestations of God. But language of personhood could all too easily be pressed by theologians to create a separateness Scripture never intended. "We need to abstain from assigning to these divine persons an interior metaphysical nature, which we are no way able to investigate or which we may positively know to contradict the real unity of God." In place of metaphysical speculation he offered the biblical picture: a real father, a real son, and a real spirit, all manifestations of the ultimate, infinite God.

He went on. To rest solely upon scriptural imagery did not mean the hard questions were avoided; rather, it called believers to consider exactly of what the revelation of Scripture consisted. The Bible presented not an intellectual puzzle to be solved but a gift to be received. To press for logical explanations was to destroy the gift. "It is killing the animal, so we might find where the life is hid in him, and to detect the mode of its union with his body." Thus in place of the metaphysical Trinity of the "Nicene theologues" Bushnell modestly offered up his own solution, an "INSTRUMENTAL TRINITY" which was composed of "INSTRUMENTAL PERSONS." He admitted that his views might be "controversial" and that his rendering of Christ and the Trinity differed "from that which is commonly held," but since his new understanding had helped deliver *him* from confusion and mental darkness concerning God, it might prove of value to others as well.

REVIVING RELIGION

For his Andover address Bushnell took on not another particular doctrine that divided the children of the Puritans but a much larger subject. "Dogma and Spirit or the True Reviving of Religion" offered a grand panoramic narrative of where the Christian church had been and where it could be heading.

With the coming of Christianity the spiritual life of the world was dramatically changed, said Bushnell. Christianity introduced a power, a "Life" and "Spirit" from God. The Jewish community at the time of Christ had missed the power, focusing on the words and syllables rather than on what the words and syllables suggested. In contrast, the immediate experience of God's power vitalized the life of the early Christian church. The church was alive through contact with the Holy Spirit, who continually led it. It lived in a world of "gifts, utterances, and mighty works," and its preaching centered on testimony and prophesying, not on theology. The early Christians had no theology in the modern sense of the term, Bushnell proclaimed; "the[ir] doctrine has no dialectic or scholastic distribution . . . it is free out of the heart, a ministration of the Spirit." They spoke of Father, Son, and Holy Spirit but did not concern themselves with the Trinity, and they rested on such simple statements as the Apostles' Creed.

Things, however, began to change. As the church moved into the world it came into contact with "the Rabbis of Greek philosophy," along with their concerns for logic, precision, and abstraction. In this context theology as we now know it was born, and Spirit began its slow decline into dogma. The simplicity of the Apostles' Creed gave way to the technical language of the Nicene and Athanasian Creeds, "till at last, the truth of Jesus vanishes, his triumphs are over, and his spirit even begins to die in the world." The descent into the darkness of the Middle Ages was swift, with councils being called against heretics and bishops taking up arms. And there was more; in a passage echoing his experiences in Europe Bushnell wrote, "as all bishops have exalted themselves above truth, the bishop of Rome exalts himself above the bishops — the church becomes a vast human fabric of forms, offices, institutions, and honors; a storehouse of subtleties and scholastic opinions, a den of base intrigues and mercenary crimes, as empty of all mercy and humanity as of Christian truth itself." The problems were only partially corrected at the time of the Reformation. The Reformers did succeed in cleansing doctrine, but as great as their accomplishments were in rescuing the imprisoned gospel from Rome, Luther and Calvin failed to address the equally imprisoned Spirit, bound by the tyranny of dogma. Only a few at the time recognized the failure, but among them were the greatest of the Puritans. Bushnell reminded his listeners of the words of John Robinson, pastor to the Pilgrims, who had bewailed the condition of the Reformed churches on the continent: "Luther and Calvin were great and strong lights in their times but they penetrated not into the whole council of God. I beseech you to receive whatever truth should be made known to you from the written word of God."

The present challenge, Bushnell continued, was to reclaim the power of the Spirit, and to do this the church needed a revival far different from that offered by modern revivalists. A true revival could not look to the past. Christians could not reclaim the power of the Spirit by reentering the world of the apostles, but had to act as men and women of the nineteenth century. But part of claiming the power of the Spirit was freeing the church from the shackles of dogma, which, he explained, was only the work of human opinion or, worse, human opinion set up to govern and control other human beings' opinions. The core of Christianity was not dogma but a new life, the life of God manifested in the world, which was kept alive by inward and immediate connection with God. When dogma was elevated over Spirit, the spiritual life was strangled and people were robbed of their access to spiritual truth. Theologians for centuries had believed that they could stack their dogmatic statements like bricks to build a tower to ascend to heaven, but the true science of God, Bushnell argued, rested on an experience of the divine presence and not on rationality or logic. "If there ever is to be anything produced here that can reasonably be called a science, it will more resemble an experience than the dry judgments and barren generalizations hitherto called theology." A rekindling of true Christian experience could be the foundation for a new science of religion. This would have a liberating effect. Accordingly, when the time came that Christian experience provided the entry into Christian knowledge, a humble child might have surer entrance than the most learned of formal theologians.

A second advantage of reclaiming the Spirit involved the revitalization of ministry. Theology could import nothing into the soul, but rather confused it. Theology led the student to weigh and evaluate the opinions of others instead of searching out her own heart, and theologians spent their time "storing the mind with cognitions and judgments" rather than "contesting with the sins that make a Savior neces-

sary, and in those sublime realizations of his power that reveal him as
the inner light and peace of the soul." Dogma cluttered the mind with
useless details that kept it from reflecting on the true nature of Christianity. Bushnell added rhetorically that it would be better to have all
the libraries shut down and "give the weeks to prayer, shave the
crown, [and] put on hair girdles" than to try to build the spiritual on
scientific theology. A true minister must first seek the immediate
knowledge of the Spirit.

Dogma led not only to a loss of life but to division as well. If in
the Spirit there was union, in dogma there was disunity. The divisions
of New England testified to this fact. If the children of the Puritans had
relied upon the simple faith of God as expressed in the Apostles'
Creed no cause of division would ever have been found. Metaphysical
bickering over Trinity and atonement, in contrast, provided the
grounds for disagreement. Individual opinions hardened into dogmas
and the result was a broken body. But the era of disunity was passing.
"No longer is it possible for any man to think it a matter of ambition to
become the founder of a sect." And the possibility of the great work of
reunion was in the air. "If I am right," he proclaimed, "nothing is
wanted now, in order to realize a grand renovation of the religious
spirit throughout Christendom, more glorious, probably, than the Reformation itself, but to recover from this ancient lapse into dogma —
not to uproot opinions, not to stop the intellectual and scientific activity of the church, but simply to invert the relations of dogma and
spirit." To do so he urged his listeners to take up the great spiritual
writers of the past, particularly Fénelon, and to his fellow New England clergy he suggested the study of mysticism.

Although throughout his address he did try to make a place (if
only a modest one) for dogma, he clearly saw the church entering into
a new era. Just as he had in earlier writings, he prophesied an organic
reunion of Christendom in which the churches of New England would
play a great role. They alone among Protestant nations did not have
dogma mired in civil statutes. They could claim the future and could
carry out the work that Luther had left incomplete. Thus he concluded, "If I have suggested the possibility of a reunion of the separated churches of New England, who can estimate the effects that
would follow such an event, the influence it would exert on the religious well being of the nation, and also the world?" The children of the

Puritans could be reunited, but it would be a reunion of Spirit and not of dogma.

Here in "Dogma and Spirit" one finds a strong echo of Bushnell's earlier reading of Coleridge's *Aids to Reflection*. Bushnell's distinction between dogma and Spirit parallels Coleridge's distinction between the understanding and the reason. For Coleridge "understanding" was the lower form of human cognition — empirical, and rational in the narrow sense of being based on calculation and precedent. Reason was that intuitive sense that saw beyond the mundane to the larger reality behind it. For Bushnell, the limitations of dogma were precisely those of the understanding. It was pedestrian, petty, and perfunctory, and lacked depth. Similarly, Spirit and reason shared like strengths. Both permitted a sure connection to ultimate reality, an immediate insight not tied to the mess of ordinary details. Both were the quality of the expansive soul, and were intuitive in nature. But whereas Coleridge, the philosopher, saw reason tied to speculation, the ever-pastoral Bushnell tied Spirit to the experience of the Christian life.

WAITING FOR THEIR PREY

With his September address at Andover Bushnell was finished. Reaction to the talks themselves was muted. One theological student who heard Bushnell's address at New Haven supposedly proclaimed, "I could kiss the soul of Dr. Bushnell," but such a response — if not apocryphal — was rare. The nearly two-hour talk at Andover must have been difficult to follow and the editorial comment of the *New York Evangelist* was probably more typical; apologizing for its reporting of the address it confessed, "We are painfully aware of the obscurity and the inadequacy of the sketch; but the recondite nature of the themes he discussed, as well as the abstruse method and language . . . rendered his discourse intelligible only to a few of his hearers." Even an admirer of Bushnell's admitted that after hearing the New Haven address he left "more mystified than edified." The public would need the written texts in order to render an opinion, and they eagerly waited while Bushnell prepared the addresses for publication.

But as they waited the New England religious community did find things to like and dislike in Bushnell's addresses. His claim in the Andover address that one could not know Christ if one were not in the spirit of Christ must have found favor with New Englanders. It was, after all, a similar claim that had led their forebears out of their parishes in England and into New England, and it had become the cornerstone of evangelical religion. But its context seemed very different here, and, in addition, Bushnell's style seemed quite odd. It had nothing of the logic and simplicity that were seen as the hallmarks of New England religion. The three addresses also demonstrated the boldness of analysis that characterized Bushnell's thinking. His tendency to address issues from his independent point of view, rather from any community of discourse, was obvious, and his willingness to jettison the past as useless was troubling. For those who knew him it was a typical Bushnell agenda — forging quickly ahead on his topics, eagerly cutting new paths, but with little regard for the troublesome details. Then there was that troubling tendency to link the sacred with other things; good New Englanders, unlike their Transcendentalist black sheep cousins, did not yoke Brama and Jehovah as Bushnell had done. Finally, what was one to make of the audacity of his central claim: that New England theology was bankrupt and that its piety was dying? These were bold charges. New Englanders had invested much in their systems, and they were not in a hurry to dismiss them at the urging of a Hartford pastor. Bushnell's claim that dogma strangled the life of the Spirit and that New England clergy preferred stacking doctrines to examining their hearts must have sounded strange to the New England clergy. Did New England pastors deserve such an insult? Had they not striven to hold up both doctrine and true religion of the heart? But here they were challenged for destroying the religion of the heart by a Hartford pastor whose own church had little to commend itself for, if there were any correlation between spiritual life and parish growth. One would have to look at these addresses carefully when they were published. As one editorialist noted during the weeks of waiting, the reviewers throughout New England were "sitting at their desks with their pens fresh cut and nibbed, waiting for their prey."

WORDS AND THINGS

While he prepared his addresses for publication Bushnell added an introduction or a "Preliminary Dissertation on the Nature of Language as Related to Thought and Spirit." The "Preliminary Dissertation" was billed as an introduction but was longer than any of the three addresses. Its twentieth-century reputation has in large part eclipsed the discourses themselves, and many have argued that it is the most important of Bushnell's writings. His daughter wrote in bold letters, *"Here is the key to Horace Bushnell."* But any biographer should pause before granting the piece such weight. It should be noted that it has not always been granted such importance; theologians in the nineteenth century regularly dismissed it as a failure. Furthermore, more than any other of Bushnell's writings, the "Preliminary Dissertation" is a Rorschach test in which people have seen what they have wanted to see. It is perhaps best to view the introduction as Bushnell's contemporaries saw it.

The "Preliminary Dissertation" attempted to do many things. It offered an overarching theory of the origin and development of language; it brought together a number of the themes found within the individual addresses and presented them in a much fuller form; and it attempted to forestall criticism of some of his more controversial claims.

His theory of language elaborated a number of themes, some new and others lifted from his earlier address entitled "Revelation." To explain the workings of grammar he posited a spiritual connection between the human mind and the outer world. "The outer world," he wrote, "is seen to be a vast menstruum of thought or intelligence. There is a logos in the form of things, by which they are prepared to serve as types or images of what is inmost in our souls, and there is a logos also of construction in the relation of space, the position, qualities, connections and predicates of things, by which they are framed into grammar. In one word, the outer world, which envelops our being, is itself language, the power of all language." As earlier, he saw in the mystery of language the handwork of God. He also continued to assert that there were two levels of language: the language of physical things and the language of thought. The latter must be based on analogies from the physical world and consisted of image and figure. As before, he claimed that these original physical forms continued to have an effect on our understanding. Words of thought were conceptions of things signified and not "naked vocal names of those truths." In a word like "prefer" the physical meaning — i.e., to set before — always exercised influence and shifted perception of the word in a way an author might never have intended. Hence there was an inherent imprecision that prevented any common meaning. "We think we have the same ideas [in these words] . . . but we find continually, that when we come to particular uses, we fall into disagreements, often in protracted and serious controversies; and whether it be said that the controversy is about words or things, it is always about the real applicability of words."

Bushnell's theory rested upon a number of questionable assumptions that weaken it as a formal theory of language. That forms never disappear over time and that they exercise an influence on persons who have no knowledge of the original language root is not self-evident. His example, that persons "of only common education" would recognize the discord in a sentence such as "I prefer being behind," since "prefer" meant in its original Latin "to set before," is unconvincing at best. Furthermore, the presupposition that persons could not both use a metaphor and use it with clarity is open to question. A scientist might speak of the "flow" of electricity or a jurist of the "force" of law, and would assume that a common meaning was being communicated. Indeed, all sorts of professions are based upon the assumption of a comparative clarity of language concerning thought. If not, books such as this would not be written. Taken at face value, Bushnell's theory of language is as bold as that of the literary deconstructionists at the end of the twentieth century in its claim that language of thought could convey no common meaning between author and reader.

But this would be a misreading of Bushnell's real intent. His claim at the very beginning of the "Preliminary Dissertation," that many of the theological difficulties could be tied to a misuse of language, suggests that despite the boldness of the title and claims in the first part of the essay, what is really being attempted is not a theory of *language* but a discussion of the function of *religious language*. In religious language, he suggested, symbol and metaphor played a major role. Metaphorical language was always limited, and to counteract this contrasting metaphors needed to be used to reflect adequately the greater truth. Concerning God alone the Bible used a wide variety of images, including Shepherd, King, Lord, and Father. Bushnell, however, through his theory argued that metaphor did not simply play a role in religious language, but that all religious language was metaphorical. This emphasis upon the metaphorical nature of religious language had a number of practical implications. The first was the analogy he made between religion and poetry. "It ought not to be necessary to remind any reader of the bible," he wrote, "that religion has a natural and profound alliance with poetry. Hence a very large share of the bible is composed of poetic contributions." The poetic nature of the biblical record was filled with conflicting and contrasting metaphors, all pointing in different directions. Traditionally exegetes had tried to iron out these contradictions to arrive at a common rational interpretation. But to flatten out the metaphors of Scripture was like translating poetry into prose; the intuitive connection with the great truth was lost. Instead, one should allow oneself to be open to the paradoxes, because in them the truth resided.

Pushing his argument beyond the metaphors of Scripture, Bushnell claimed that multiple (and contrasting) metaphors lay behind doctrinal language as well. Statements of doctrine, despite their apparent rigor and precision, did not set forth a clear elaboration of Christian truth, but were like poetic metaphors, true in their own way yet limited. No single statement was ever adequate. He noted that among the seventeenth-century Puritans no one creed was dictated; they were required to subscribe to either the Westminster Confession of Faith, the Savoy Confession, or to the doctrinal articles of the Church of England. The truth, he continued, could be found in all of these documents even though they were quite different. This idea lay behind the boldest claim found in the "Preliminary Dissertation": "If . . . creeds of theory, or systematic dogma, must be retained," he professed, "the next best arrangement would be to allow assent to a great number of creeds at once, letting them qualify, assist, and mitigate each other."

As we will see, few statements scandalized his readers more than that one. Anyone who could swear allegiance simultaneously to creeds as explicitly different as the Calvinistic Westminster Confession of Faith and the Tridentine creed of Pius IV would appear to have little respect for truth. But the expansiveness of Bushnell's rhetoric must be checked, because it rested upon an unspoken presupposition. Words could hang loosely upon spiritual things because the spiritual reality itself was immediately perceivable. Words about religion might be cloudy but the reality was not. In Europe, one recalls, Bushnell had intuitively sensed fellowship with those such as the followers of Ronge and Czerski, and this convinced him that disagreements over language in theology were not ultimate. The same principle seems to be operating here. Because he had seen in the divided children of the Puritans — Unitarians and orthodox alike — marks of a common family, he could strive to show that it was only words that divided them. Bushnell nowhere attempts to do the same with his Episcopal adversaries, however. With them the division was not just in words but in spirit.

If one focus of Bushnell's "Preliminary Dissertation" was the relation of metaphor to both religious language and doctrine, another was his critique of logic and his appeal to intuition. His lifelong frustration with logic poured forth like a river. To trust in definition as the foundation of truth was to display oneself devoid of truth or genius, and to be "a mere uninspired unfructifying logicker." Proponents of the logical method, he noted — perhaps having in mind the Common Sense philosophy he had been taught at Yale — foolishly believed that if they could classify and define precisely, their endeavors would take on a scientific rigor. On this belief he heaped scorn. "It seems to be supposed, or rather assumed, by the class of investigators commonly called logical, that after the subject matter of truth has been gotten into propositions, and cleared, perhaps by definitions, the faculty of intuition, or insight, may be suspended, and we may go on safely to reason upon the forms of the words themselves." The logician was the enemy of paradox. He attempted to organize, synthesize, and systematize the images that fed the imagination, and to work out the order of salvation in the same way he worked out an experiment in chemistry. The result was that inspiration was sacrificed for consistency, and the life of faith was destroyed. For those alive in God, to speculate whether faith preceded repentance or followed it was as foolish as discussing which bodily organ came first, the heart or the lungs. Both were necessary for life. He noted that both the orthodox and the Unitarians in their own ways had succumbed to the errors of logic. The orthodox seized on some image in the Scriptures, such as Christ's death upon the cross as the slain lamb, and logically worked out a system of soteriology based upon the principle of penal substitution. The Unitarians, in turn, reduced the mystery by domesticating it. They "decoct the whole mass of symbol, and draw off the extract into pitchers of our own; fine, consistent, nicely rounded pitchers, which, so far from setting out any where towards infinity, we carry at pleasure by the handle, and definitely measure by the eye."

Since logic, he believed, had failed, Bushnell proposed a role for intuition. The Scriptures should not be read as a series of propositions but as "inspirations and poetic forms of life." To read the Bible with a sense of intuition was to be always open to its living quality. The difference between the old method and the new, he explained, was the difference between inorganic chemistry and biology. Inorganic chemistry attempted to break things down further and further until one discovered the foundation of reality, but in the process the living creature was destroyed; the biologist, in contrast, was anxious to study the plant or animal as a living being. In abandoning our logical categories we let the Scriptures speak to us in all their vitality and spirit, Bushnell believed. He chided those logicians who attempted to nail down fixed and certain meanings. A great work of writing was always changing in meaning as different persons at different times read it. Indeed, the greater the figure the more open to interpretation would be her words. "What, in fact, do we see in the endless debate kept up for these eighteen hundred years, over the words of Jesus, but an illustration of the truth, that infinitesimals . . . are not the best judges of infinites."

Was it any wonder that those who followed the truth were often not clear and simple in expression? The known was rooted in the unknown; hence clarity and simplicity came about only when partial truths were stripped from their roots in mystery. It was easy to be clear and simple, he explained, "if one is either able to be shallow or willing to be false." We should note here that Bushnell was not only a preacher of but also a practitioner of this gospel of opaqueness. His "Preliminary Dissertation" is at times an overly complicated and indeed an almost orphic work in which bold claims are made from very personal experiences. But Bushnell claimed that his "Dissertation," and indeed all of his addresses, needed to be read in the spirit in which all religious texts should be read — that is, as an organic whole and not in parts. If Jesus could be interpreted in various ways so too could Connecticut preachers. Indeed, Bushnell could almost feel the opposition emerging. "I see the terrible sylogisms [sic]," he wrote, "wheeling out their infantry upon my fallacies and absurdities." He offered what he expected would be one criticism: "Dr. B. says that the trinity is involved in the process of revelation — that the Absolute Being becomes Father, Son, and Holy Ghost, in the way of communicating himself to knowledge. God then is really One, and apparently Three; that is the trinity is a false appearance." With such arguments the logic choppers could attack Bushnell's work. But he urged them to refrain. If one looked at what he had done as being addressed to the feeling and imagination, rather than to logic, one might sense his true meaning. If one looked at the effect of the whole, his purpose could be discerned. Finally, if one honestly compared his solutions to the present problems of both the orthodox and the Unitarians, one could see why he had undertaken his tinkering. He came not to bury the great doctrines of the Trinity and the atonement, both so deeply part of the religious heritage, but to save them. "If we now wish to be clear of scripture, made into logical jargon on one side, and unmade or emptied of divinity or grandeur on the other, I know no better method than to accept these great truths of trinity and atonement as realities or verities addressed to faith; or, what is not far different, to feeling and imaginative reason — not any more as logical and metaphysical entities, for the natural understanding."

DROPPING INTO THE WORLD

In February of 1849 *God in Christ* was published with the three addresses (albeit slightly rearranged, and the Andover address significantly rewritten) along with the "Preliminary Dissertation." The public could now view the many aspects of Bushnell's thought that had previously been seen only in snippets. There was Bushnell the student of language, Bushnell the critic of revivals, Bushnell the ecumenist, and most of all Bushnell the tinkerer. But connecting all of these was Bushnell the student of religion. From his early years he had been fascinated by the mystery of religion, and from the first days of his pastorate he had been grappling with the question of how it was to be communicated. His solution to the problem of communication was slow in coming, but his rejection of the logical methods of men such as his teacher Nathaniel William Taylor had been immediate. What one might say of *God in Christ* is that on one level it was an assault on theology in the name of religion. "Theology" (or that which most people at the time called theology), Bushnell claimed, all too often blocked religion and separated the churches. Worse, it seemed to be seen as an end in itself rather than an imperfect expression of something far more real. Theology was at best like a commentary on a poem, and at worst like a prose translation that took the place of the poem. And here we can see the preacher in Bushnell. A sermon was no more an end in itself than was theology; its purpose was to affect its hearers. The effect was far more important than the individual parts of the sermon. The task of the preacher was like the task of the poet: to translate the absolute into a web of words, using all of the reality of language — with its weaknesses as well as its strengths — to make its mark on the totality of the human. If theology were to serve its true purpose, it, too — along with preaching and poetry — must adopt this method. Thus Bushnell's message to his audience was twofold. First, the old theology had failed and the era of dogma was over. Second, there was a way out, and that was to use the power and limitations of language to enter the power of the Spirit.

But that way out came with a cost. Not only did Bushnell call upon his readers to admit the failure of the old theology, but also to accept a new model for the vocation of the theologian. Theologians had traditionally seen themselves as analogous to practitioners of other learned professions. A rational, professional method shaped the way theology was approached, just as it did the way medicine or law was approached. This was how members of a profession could work in union, recognizing common methods, and how learning could be advanced, as one solution to a problem built upon another. Bushnell, however, proclaimed that a theologian was not like a doctor or lawyer but more like a poet plumbing his soul. Such a claim was not only intellectually shocking but also culturally disturbing. Poets were not the solid, respectable figures that doctors and lawyers were coming to be. What might be the social cost of such a change? Would the cherished identification of the ministry as a learned profession be lost? And what did it mean for the community of theologians? The idea of theological disputation did not begin in New England. For at least a thousand years disputation had been seen as a way in which theological claims could be tested, honed, and proven. Disputation bespoke the communal nature of the theological task, indeed the progressive nature of theology. But if religious truth was like poetic truth, how might one progress from a poem? And what sort of community might theologians now become? These were questions that ran alongside more specific questions concerning the adequacy of Bushnell's particular proposals.

In the concluding paragraph of his "Preliminary Dissertation" Bushnell had written, "I drop [these addresses] into the world, leaving them to care for themselves, and assert their own power. If they create disturbance I hope it may be a salutary disturbance. If they are received and find advocates ready to assert them . . . I shall rejoice. If they are rejected universally, then I leave them to time, as the body of Christ was left, believing that after three days they will rise again." *God in Christ* did not lie quietly in a grave.

7 The Bushnell Controversy

I T DID not take long before all the fresh cut and nibbed pens took
their aim. The controversy over *God in Christ* was one of the great
theological donnybrooks of mid-nineteenth-century America, and the
debate serves as a snapshot of the state of theology in the northern
states, since almost every theological community among the Reformed
churches in America weighed in on the question of Bushnell's orthodoxy. Furthermore, the controversy the book engendered would be the
trial of his life — intellectually, ecclesiastically, and personally.

WHAT DOES DR. BUSHNELL MEAN?

The theological community was quick to respond to Bushnell's bold
claims and on the whole found little to commend in the volume. Some,
such as the Baptist Robert Turnbull, were mild in their rejoinders. He
chided Bushnell on his views of the imperfection of language, remind-
ing him, "when our knowledge is clear and definite, then our words
are clear and definite." He thought Bushnell was a bit confused, and at
points misleading, but that his heart was in the right place.

Most, however, were not so charitable. By rejecting many of the traditional theological categories, it was argued, Bushnell opened himself up to the ancient errors the categories had been set up to prevent. The picture of Christ Bushnell presented in his New Haven address, for example, was fundamentally flawed. His insistence on the unity of Christ's character seemed to lead him into the ancient heresy of patripassianism, the claim that God suffered physically in Christ. Did Bushnell really mean that God grew and developed as the human Jesus grew and developed? Even more problematic was Bushnell's understanding of Christ's humanity, since he was very unclear about whether Christ did or did not possess a full human soul. To some critics his picture of the incarnation merely described God occupying a human body rather than revealing a true uniting of full humanity and divinity. As one writer noted, "[Bushnell] believes that Christ is God in a human body, manifesting himself through it without the instrumentality of a human soul in that body." There was no true incarnation in Bushnell's Christ, only God taking possession of a human the same way an ancient Greek god would take on the form of a bull. Likewise, in his discussion of the Trinity many believed Bushnell revived the ancient heresy of Sabellianism, the teaching that the three persons of the Trinity were only modes or expressions of the oneness of God. Christian orthodoxy maintained that the persons of the Trinity existed in the oneness from the beginning, but Bushnell seemed to imply that the second person of the Trinity emerged only with the incarnation.

Even worse, he had combined an ancient heresy with a modern one. In his address Bushnell had invoked an article by Friedrich Schleiermacher (one of the few works of the German theologian available in English) that had been published over a decade earlier by Moses Stuart, professor of sacred literature at Andover. As a representative of nineteenth-century German theology Schleiermacher was suspect enough, but to boot he was also a defender of pantheism, and Bushnell's critics saw this pantheism lying behind Bushnell's work as well. Bushnell's language for God (that of an Absolute Being) and his depiction of the Trinity as emanations suggested a pantheistic identification of God and all creation. Quoting the passage from the New Haven address in which Bushnell claimed that God will "live Himself into the acquaintance and biographic history of the world," one critic added, "we forgot for a moment that we were not in a German lecture-

room, taking notes to the effect that 'God is the ever streaming immanence of Spirit in matter.'"

The oft-made claim that Bushnell was dabbling with pantheism
merits further reflection. Why did no similar cry go up when Moses
Stuart first published the Schleiermacher essay? Stuart had published
it in the midst of his controversy with the Presbyterians at Princeton
over the relationship of the persons of the Godhead, but he was never
accused of pantheism. Stuart's gravitas helped, as did his care in noting some key places where he differed from the German, but perhaps
the most important factor was timing. Stuart had published before the
full impact of the Transcendentalist revolt was felt. In the 1830s pantheism had been an odd notion propounded by a few metaphysically
possessed Germans; by 1849 it was a doctrine that had torn apart the
proper world of Boston Unitarianism and pitted church against
church. Orthodox divines were vigilant that it would never infect and
wreak havoc in their churches, yet Bushnell seemed to be doing just
that. As another critic noted, "if he does not consider himself a pantheist, has he done anything to prevent his readers from becoming pantheists, by carrying out his statements into their literal import? German pantheism is coming into our country. . . . It is deeply deplorable
that . . . men should find any [such] expressions in the writings of a
Christian divine."

Critics likewise found fault with his discussion of the atonement,
which abandoned the cherished evangelical belief that the cross offered a real propitiation for sin. The sacrificial nature of Christ's death
had been a major point of contention in the debates with the Unitarians, and for Bushnell to speak so critically against the objective view of
the atonement was seen as traitorous, particularly considering that the
speech was given at the very center of Unitarianism. Critics were particularly troubled by Bushnell's willingness to caricature the theological traditions of Calvinism and of the New England theologians in particular. Furthermore, in his rejection of the objective view Bushnell set
up a terrible perversion of the doctrine of justification by faith. In the
address he had claimed, "Justification is that which will give confidence, again, to guilty minds; that which will assure the base and hu-
miliated soul of the world, chase away the demons of wrath and de-
spair it had evoked, and help to return to God in courage whispering
still to itself — soul be of good cheer, thy sins are forgiven thee." What-

ever one might say of such a view of justification, it bore no relation to the evangelical understanding. The great work of Christ had become reduced to something that might bolster the confidence of sinners. "If I can by any means obtain a feeling of confidence that my sins are forgiven me, then I am justified," is how one critic summarized the teaching. "The Universalist who really believes that all will be saved, the idolater who has found release to his fears by self torment, the dying papist consoled by extreme unction, all having obtained confidence are justified." There was no need for true belief, nor was there any need for true repentance. Critics also dismissed as a failure Bushnell's attempt to keep the objective imagery of the cross and sacrifice. "The atonement thus objectively considered becomes little else but a magnificent show," wrote one, and it was foolish to believe that an "imaginary altar" could offer a true remission of sins.

Finally, they found little good to say about his theory of language. The whole "Dissertation" puzzled them. "Why is the preliminary Dissertation here?" asked one irate reviewer. "Is it necessary to enable the reader of the discourses to understand them? Then why was it not at least as necessary for the hearers, for whom those discourses were primarily prepared? How could the orator venture to address those multitudes, until they had been initiated into his peculiar view of language?" Others argued that Bushnell's broad claim that all second department language, or language concerning intellectual categories, was derived from sense language was an empirical claim and could be validated only through a complete survey of the languages of the world. Indeed in some cases the claim seemed certainly false. "The sensation of hunger," wrote one, "is a reality and one with which man, in the early stages of his existence, would be likely to become as soon acquainted as with any external object whatever; and why should he not as early give it a name?" Another offered as a counterexample to the claim that all words of thought were rooted in physical metaphors the term "Bushnellite" meaning one who like Bushnell offered "a peculiar doctrinal or speculative system." Still others challenged his assertion that the symbolic nature of language persisted over time, thus permanently preventing language from being a tool of intellectual precision. They argued instead that the ambiguities slowly faded and that agreed upon conceptual meanings took their place. Some writers attacked Bushnell's idea of a logos connecting the world of things to the world of thought. But the most frequently sounded criticism was that if Bushnell's theory were true, it would strike a deadly blow to all discourse. All admitted that language was imperfect, "but if one-tenth part of what Dr. Bushnell has said about the vagueness of language were true, society would long since have been thrown into inextricable confusion, by the misunderstanding of men as to the use of terms." Another critic added, "we are of the opinion that if a book of the same character with this had been written by a member of the medical or legal profession on subjects connected with his department of science, a question would have arisen at once whether the writer were wholly sane." Bushnell's theory of language destroyed any real ability to communicate on any intellectual issue, and if true would be the end of the learned professions. Without a common, clear, and comparatively precise meaning to conceptual language, not just religion and ethics would suffer, but other concerns as well. "The whole fabric . . . of religion and ethics, of jurisprudence and social life is annihilated at a stroke."

WHAT MANNER OF MAN IS THIS?

But there was a second type of criticism that focused not so much on Bushnell's substance as his style. Here one senses more than a touch of wounded pride in responses to the pastor, for Bushnell's pretensions enraged his critics. Some of his more self-important lines, such as "the true reviving of religion [is a] theme . . . dear above all others . . . not to me only but to the heart of God Himself," received wilting criticism. "He does not stop to join himself with other men," wrote one. "He seems like the highest Alpine summit which receives the earliest rays of sun." His perception of his own loftiness gave him leave to cast away all earlier thought on the topics on which he spoke, and his condescension toward his critics was annoying. In one place he dismissed those who pressed him for logical consistency in his picture of Jesus by comparing his views with the revelation of the angels to Abraham in Genesis 18. To ask for logical explanations "is as if Abraham after he had entertained as a guest the Jehovah angel . . . instead of receiving his message had fallen into inquiry into the digestive process of the angel!" To such rhetoric another critic responded, "When Dr. Bushnell brings with him evidence, like that of the angel Jehovah, that he comes with a message of God, we shall cease our inquiries, and bow humbly beneath his rebuke," but until then he would be treated like any other mortal man.

Another set of criticisms surrounded Bushnell's dismissal of logic and his lack of clarity. One critic noted that he understood why Bushnell was so critical of logic, "for certainly that science, judging from this book, has conferred but few favors upon him." He might dismiss clarity and simplicity but that too had to do with his own limitations. The Transcendentalist turned Roman Catholic Orestes Brownson wrote, "Dr. Bushnell evidently writes in the dark, and strikes hither and thither, he knows not at what."

Finally, critics faulted Bushnell for his lack of reverence in touching holy things. His casual linking of Brama and Jehovah scandalized many, as did his overfamiliarity in speaking for God. Bushnell lacked the gravitas of a real theologian and seemed to say outrageous things for their shock value. Nowhere was this as true as in some of his statements concerning the Bible. Critics cringed at his *bon mot* that no book contained as many inherent contradictions as the Gospel of St. John. Nor were they any happier with his attitude toward inspiration. Indeed, there were passages in which he seemed to lower the inspiration of Scripture below that of other writings. In one instance, after quoting a passage from the French philosopher Blaise Pascal, he added, "Scarcely inferior in vivacity and power is the familiar passage of Paul." To place the insights of the apostle below those of the philosopher was an example of either sloppiness or bad theology, and was offensive in either case. Bushnell talked much about the Scriptures but cited them very little. For a person writing on the great scriptural themes of the person of Christ and the atonement, direct appeals to Scripture were strangely missing. The "great proof texts . . . teaching the cardinal doctrines of Christianity Dr. Bushnell has passed over in silence, as if they had no bearing on the momentous question." When a passage, such as 1 Corinthians 15 and its image of the subordination of the Son to the Father, seemed to call into question his modalistic Trinity, he was quick to dismiss it. "I will not go into a discussion of these remarkable words, for I do not care to open God's secrets before the time." He seemed to prefer his theories to the words of Scripture. All of these characteristics bespoke a writer who lacked the discipline of a true theologian.

In these criticisms one can hear the frustrations of professionally trained theologians in the face of Bushnell's new and radical insights. Where Bushnell saw the vision of the Spirit and a glimpse of a new order, his critics saw the revival of old heresies and the loss of important doctrines. Where Bushnell saw himself soaring like a poet or a seer blest, his critics saw a dilettante, voicing opinions and making judgments on the flimsiest of understandings. Where he saw himself to be a prophet, they saw him as a sloppy thinker unaware of the true implications of what he was proclaiming.

WHAT IS THEOLOGY?

To understand better what was at stake in the debate over Bushnell's *God in Christ* let us turn briefly to both one critic, Charles Hodge, and one defender, Amos Chesebrough, and let us look at how Bushnell appeared to Unitarian eyes. The contrast between these observers and their arguments reveals both spoken and implied issues.

Charles Hodge, professor of theology at Princeton Theological Seminary, was perhaps Bushnell's most thoughtful critic. Hodge and Bushnell were arguably the two greatest theological voices in mid-century America, but they could not have been more different. Bushnell was a Yankee pastor, always somehow on the outside of the theological community. Hodge taught at the very center of the Presbyterian world and was a major force in the Old School, or conservative, branch of that denomination. Bushnell was by nature an impulsive and imaginative thinker, at odds with plodding logical methodology. Before he had ever heard of the movement known as Romanticism, he had gravitated toward the intuitive, the organic, and the picturesque. Hodge seemed almost to have been weaned on logic. Scottish Common Sense philosophy secured both his view of the world and his religious convictions. The idea of intuitive inspiration as a foundation for knowledge was as foreign to him as would have been rejecting the Westminster Confession for the creed of Pius IV. If Bushnell approached the task of theology like an artist, Hodge was the consummate scientific technician. As if all this were not enough, from his student days in Germany Hodge had feared the subjective nature of the Romantic theology of men such as Schleiermacher. Few men could have been more different than the Presbyterian professor and the Yankee pastor.

Despite Hodge's reputation for logical analysis, however, one of the most impressive parts of his article in response to *God in Christ* was his perception of some of the underlying assumptions behind Bushnell's work. Hodge noted that Bushnell was far more successful in attacking the old theological system than he was in establishing a case for his new ideas. "It overturns but it does not erect." Such a failure doomed the work. "Men do not like to be houseless; much less do they like to have the doctrines which overhang and surround their souls as a dwelling and refuge, pulled to pieces, that they may sit sentimentally on the ruins." Bushnell offered little in the way of a constructive alternative. A second observation concerned his aptitudes. Bushnell was simply not the man to attempt the reconstruction of theology in such a grand way. He aimed at the stars but was technically hampered, so he could never achieve his goals. The theological issues were too complex for him, and he tended to jettison anything for which he saw no immediate purpose. But his discourses spoke more to his own theological limitations than they did to any failure of the old theology. His ambition did him in. "Machiavelli was accustomed to say, there are three classes of men: one who see things in their own light; another who see them when they are shown; and a third who cannot see them even then. We invite Dr. Bushnell to resume his place with us, in the second class. By a just judgement of God, those who uncalled aspire to the first, lapse into the third."

He went on to show that the work was marred not only by an inability to see subtleties but also by striking inconsistencies. As Hodge observed, Bushnell strove for boldness, innovation, and radical reconceptualization, but at the last his conservative nature would weigh in to thwart the thrust of his thought. The result was an intellectual mishmash. Thus, after rejecting the orthodox views on Trinity and atonement and seeming to establish the grounds for the Unitarian understandings, there appeared at the last minute an attempt to rescue the idea of Trinity and sacrifice. Consistency was thrown to the wayside in a desire to hold on to parts of the old belief. The same was true regarding Bushnell's alleged pantheism. Whatever fundamental errors there might be in Schleiermacher's attempt to revive the teaching of Sabellius, at least his writings were rigorously logical, Hodge noted.

"Schleiermacher's whole system rests on the doctrine that there is but one substance in the universe, which substance is God; and especially that the divine and human natures are identical." Accordingly he could with consistency speak of God emanating himself into the world, or of Christ having but one nature. Bushnell attempted to make use of the same language without adopting the pantheism that gave it coherence. "There is nothing in his book to intimate that he is really a Pantheist," Hodge noted, and this made *God in Christ* hopelessly confusing. "What therefore in Schleiermacher is consistent and imposing, is in Dr. Bushnell simply absurd. The system of the one is a Doric temple, and that of the other a heap of stones."

All of these observations hit their mark, particularly the recognition that Bushnell yoked innovation with a dogged conservatism. Hodge was also on solid ground as he carefully corrected some of the false renderings of traditional theological doctrines that Bushnell had set forth. But when he came to his foundational criticism of Bushnell's endeavor, Hodge was less persuasive. His fundamental criticism focused on two issues, one concerning epistemology and the other concerning the place of doctrine. *God in Christ*, argued Hodge, was fatally flawed in attempting to combine three antithetical tendencies: rationalism, mysticism, and the "new philosophy" of the Romantics. Rationalists weighed all doctrines on the scale of reason and dismissed those that did not make the grade. Mystics believed that truth could be communicated directly by God to the human soul. Romantics brought God and the soul together in a pantheistic unity. The collection of such opposite tendencies was for Hodge inherently grotesque. "The mystic Rationalist is very much like a Quaker dragoon," he snorted. Furthermore, taken in combination these approaches undercut the means by which God communicated with the world and replaced it with a dangerous error. If Bushnell's theory of language were true, the texts of Scripture could no longer be a source of sure communication. The imprecision of language would render the scriptural message similarly imprecise. But God did use the words of Scripture as his means of communicating to humanity. "All the operations of the Spirit are in connexion with the word," Hodge argued, "and the effects of his influence are always rational — i.e., they involve an intellectual apprehension of the truth, revealed in scriptures. The whole inward life, thus induced, is dependent on the written word and conformed to it." Truth, Hodge insisted, could come only through intellectual appropriation. Likewise, for Hodge, Bushnell dangerously elevated the place of Christian experience. The mystics and Romantics Bushnell appealed to differed on many particulars, but both groups appealed to the direct illumination of the soul. Such a belief in direct illumination was anathema to Hodge. Divine truth was never immediately intuited. The Holy Spirit did act immediately upon the soul at the moment of regeneration, but after that truth was intellectually mediated through Scripture.

Regarding the proper place of doctrine, Hodge was also critical. Bushnell had argued that experience preceded doctrine, and in some ways governed it. Doctrine was like the bark of a tree, which needed to grow if the tree were not to be strangled. For Hodge, however, doctrines were foundational. They were anchored in Scripture and beyond question. "Dr. Bushnell forgets that there are certain doctrines so settled by the faith of the church, that they are no longer open questions. They are finally adjudged and determined." Doctrine, far from being an attempt to intellectualize a more basic religious or spiritual experience, was rather the foundation of true Christianity.

Hodge painted his opposition to Bushnell so deftly that all could see the difference, but Hodge's stark epistemology was not to everyone's liking. His vision of religious truth was like a whitewashed Presbyterian church — plain, straightforward, and didactic, a proper receptacle for God's word. Bushnell's vision was more like a gothic cathedral where much of the communication had nothing to do with words. Some people preferred the gothic cathedral, even after being shown a proper whitewashed church, and Hodge's arguments, as satisfying as they were to those who already accepted his presuppositions, failed to move those who saw no inherent incompatibility in a rational critique of doctrine coupled with an openness to the Spirit.

Despite the avalanche of negative criticism, Bushnell was not without some defenders in print. A young Congregational minister, Amos C. Chesebrough, writing under the pseudonym "C. C.," attempted to turn the rhetorical tables on Bushnell's accusers. Bushnell's critics charged him with being largely ignorant of the fine points of theology, blithely tossing away carefully crafted distinctions merely because he saw no further use for them. The critics attacked Bushnell for his vague phrases and asked the question, "What does Dr. Bushnell mean?" Chesebrough argued that Bushnell's critics, like the king in the old story, had no clothes. Far from a univocal orthodoxy, the theological critics were themselves a hopelessly divided lot. He eagerly showed how New Haven differed from East Windsor and Bangor from Princeton when it came to describing where Bushnell had fallen into error. "Do they understand him?" he asked. He likewise twisted the knife on Bushnell's New England critics. Many of the schools represented by Bushnell's critics had themselves been charged with heresy in the recent past. Indeed, the whole New England theological tradition was of questionable orthodoxy from the perspective of Hodge's Princeton. Chesebrough wrote, "one thing is obvious, that the accusers of Dr. B[ushnell] on the point in question, have either never attended lectures at Princeton, or have departed sadly from the faith in which they had been indoctrinated." The great differences among his accusers indicated that the vaunted orthodox unity was more ephemeral than real. Just as Herod and Pilate united against Jesus, so too "a more modern alliance entered between the high Hopkinsians of New England and the Old School Presbyterians" united in trying to crush Bushnell.

C. C.'s pamphlet contained a second line of defense. Bushnell, he claimed, spoke for the common sense of believers in New England. Whatever errors he may have made, Bushnell was concerned with the fundamental questions of Christianity. A doctrine such as the Trinity was a practical truth, and as such it had great power, but the schools represented by Bushnell's critics were more interested in endless speculations about the theory behind the Trinity than in the Trinity itself. Theology had departed from the simplicity of Scripture, becoming rationalistic and dogmatic. This was the real meaning of Bushnell's call for placing Spirit over dogma. C. C. here took up the role of the plain man, pointing out the foibles and pretensions of the experts, and in doing so he touched an important cultural nerve in American life. If the theologians exhibited a spirit of scientific professionalism, C. C. offered the voice of the plain Christian. For the former theology needed to follow its own rules like any other science or profession, and in their eyes Bushnell was a violator who transgressed the rules. For the latter theology was something that always had to be checked by a spirit of common sense. It was all too easy for theologians to see themselves as an exclusive club and to use their position to strike down any challenges to their authority. Another of Bushnell's defenders made the same observation about his critics: "There is a tone of arrogant superiority assumed throughout — a feeling, almost visible, of — there is nothing to be learned here — that is the farthest possible from that of the patient, inquiring, receptive spirit which true criticism demands." The concerted attacks on Bushnell indicated that as a community the theologians felt threatened by *God in Christ*. There were realities that Bushnell as a pastor could see that theologians tied to their books could not. His errors were less important than his insights. Even when wrong, concluded C. C., he deserved to be heard.

There was one final group of critics who applauded Bushnell's work, the Unitarians. Both in America and in England they were Bushnell's strongest champions. Their support, however, was problematic.

Bushnell had good personal relations with many Unitarian clergy, and Cyrus Bartol of West Church, Boston, was during this time of controversy his closest clerical friend. These friends leapt to his defense. The Boston Unitarian journal, the *Christian Examiner*, spoke of the "freedom and freshness of thought" found in the volume, as well as its value in clearing away errors in the old theology. Although the reviewer found Bushnell's solutions problematic, he praised his willingness to go down new vistas. But surprisingly, the most positive reviews of *God in Christ* were found among British Unitarians, who interpreted it as a bold and radical assault upon traditional orthodoxy. The *Westminster Review* praised Bushnell's view of the atonement and contrasted it favorably with the theological conservatism of the Church of England. The radical newspaper *The Economist* reviewed it along with freethinker Francis Newman's *Phases of Faith*. *The Inquirer* of London offered perhaps the most positive review of the work on either side of the Atlantic, calling the volume "a very healthy and hopeful sign" and saying that it possessed a "certain scriptural freshness and fragrance." It lauded Bushnell for making "utter havoc with the orthodox doctrine of the trinity." It too saw the volume as transitional, but it saw it as a positive transition.

These Unitarian reviews were troubling to many of Bushnell's orthodox critics because they confirmed their own fears. Bushnell's work was primarily destructive in nature, attacking the old doctrines while failing to replace them with an adequate alternative. Furthermore, the fact that a Connecticut minister in good standing could be favorably cited by British radicals was disturbing. And as if this were not enough, when the radical book publisher John Chapman issued a British edition of *God in Christ,* he boldly advertised it along with works of D. F. Strauss, Francis Newman, Theodore Parker, and other radical authors. Such an association was scandalous, and it necessitated a response.

FUNDAMENTALLY ERRONEOUS?

These editorial critiques were undoubtedly painful to Bushnell, but of much greater seriousness were rumblings within the Congregational Church in Connecticut. Here as well objections to *God in Christ* were being heard. The semi-presbyterian polity of the Congregational Church in Connecticut was still governed by the Saybrook Platform, and its thirteenth article provided a mechanism for disciplining clergy. It claimed, "it is the duty of an [clerical] Association to receive an accusation against a pastor belonging to it, and to make provision for his trial before the Consociation." The clergy were to adjudicate whether the charge was valid, while the Consociation that contained both clergy and laity would be the judges. Bushnell's association was "Hartford Central," founded in 1843 for both demographical and theological reasons — Hartford had grown too large for a single association, and Yale-trained pastors, who made up the bulk of the clergy of the new association, found the conservatism of the East Windsor clergy irksome. So a new association was founded, and Bushnell was chosen as its first moderator. The clergy of Hartford Central would control his immediate fate. In June of 1849, Walter Clarke, of Hartford's South Church, introduced a resolution stating that since "Brother Bushnell has lately published a book entitled 'God in Christ' which is extensively believed and declared to contain doctrines inconsistent with some cardinal articles of the Christian faith," a committee be established to inquire whether his work was "fundamentally erroneous." Much of the furor that occurred over the next three years would be over what "fundamentally erroneous" in fact meant.

Together in consultation with Bushnell himself, the association selected five clergymen to evaluate the case: Noah Porter of

Farmington, Joel Hawes of Hartford, Charles B. McLean of Collins-
ville, Merrill Richardson of Terryville, and Clarke himself. Of the
members of the committee Hawes and Clarke were probable foes of
Bushnell, Richardson and McLean were friends, and Porter was the
swing vote. By late summer it had become clear that Porter had chosen
to side with Bushnell's allies, and by September the majority were
ready to offer a report that rejected initiating any legal process. The mi-
nority still criticized the book and stated that it contained if not fundamental errors, "serious and important errors." No agreement was
reached in September. Bushnell actively participated in this meeting,
defending and explaining himself.

In October reports were issued and the Association by a vote of
17 to 3 supported the majority report. This outcome has been traditionally interpreted as a great victory for Bushnell, but when the report is
viewed in its entirety it is at best a rather cool statement of support.
The report vindicated Bushnell but not *God in Christ*. At the request of
Lyman Beecher, Bushnell was asked to make a summary statement of
his beliefs concerning the doctrines of the Trinity, the atonement,
Christology, and justification by faith, and it was on the basis of this
statement that their decision rested. His statement on the Trinity was
typical of the responses he gave: "I start with the conception of the
One God," he wrote, "different I suppose, in no wise, from the one
substance or homoousion of the Church — which one God is developed to us, or becomes a subject of knowledge under the conditions of
a three-fold personality. I take the three, therefore, in their threeness . . .
only refusing to investigate their interior mystery." He also admitted
that some of his choice of language was "unhappy" and "not exactly
fitting." Such explanations convinced the majority of the Association
of the fundamental soundness of Bushnell's teachings. "In this statement he gives not his philosophical theories, as in various parts of his
book, but his views of the facts of the Gospel as he is accustomed to
present them in his preaching. . . . Now it is the latter . . . rather than
the former, which . . . we are mainly to regard, forbearing all questions
as to their consistency with each other."

Regarding the book itself, the clergy were dubious. In their statement they admitted that there were sections that did seem to be in conflict with orthodox theology. The book contained "dangerous errors"
and a number of its ideas concerning the Trinity and the atonement "if

followed out to their legitimate results would . . . lead to fundamental error." Indeed there were even passages that "when taken alone and understood according to the common use of language, are themselves fundamentally erroneous." But despite all of this the author himself was not in fundamental error.

To heap so much condemnation in a report that was in fact an acquittal is odd, and merits some observation. Clearly the members of the Hartford Central Association attempted to distance themselves from a very flawed and dangerous work of theology, but they stood by Bushnell. Their principle seemed to be a concern not to identify errors but to find an acceptable degree of orthodoxy within Bushnell's writings. Furthermore, they dismissed as irrelevant Bushnell's speculations (including, one should note, the entirety of the "Preliminary Dissertation on Language") and focused instead on practical questions that affected preaching. Why this lenience? Perhaps it was an acknowledgment of a principle Bushnell had stressed so strongly throughout his ministry — that there existed a greater truth or reality behind the web of words. The intuitive appreciation of the character of an individual, that sense of experiencing his or her soul, was the true touchstone of knowledge. Words at times helped in this perception, and at other times hurt, but they were always of a second order. It was for precisely this reason that Bushnell placed Spirit over dogma, because the former was more real. It appears as if Bushnell was ultimately judged by his fellow clergy according to this rule. They had known him to be a Christian pastor in a way that led them to dismiss the errors of his language. Thus his words were rejected as erroneous while his soul was accepted as true. One further factor perhaps played a role, namely, that those who knew him knew that he was by nature a tinkerer. He was always trying to improve things both great and small, and *God in Christ* was but an extreme example. At the time of his trials his daughter records him visiting friends in a nearby town who lived next door to an extraordinary house. She reported that his friends "found it difficult to get him into the house as he became instantly absorbed with inspecting another dwelling" and determining how it might be improved. She concluded, "having satisfied himself, finally, that the case was a hopeless one, he walked in remarking, 'There is no way for that man to improve his house unless he turns it bottom side up.'" His tinkering may have gone awry in the case of *God in Christ*, but his friends knew that it was his nature to do so.

In short, the munificence of Bushnell's character saved him. He was judged as a whole person. As one of his defenders was to explain, "we investigated the case of one intimately known, and with whom we have labored and prayed in building up the cause of Christ. We knew his manner of life and conversation, we were aware of his character and spirit." But the very nature of Bushnell's victory among his colleagues in Hartford Central planted the seeds of controversy. Persons who knew Bushnell more from his written works were and would continue to be less charitable. The conservative *Puritan Recorder* in its comments on the majority decision of the Hartford Central Association noted that Bushnell's friends considered him to be a "genius" and that gave him the right of indulgence. "He has become a sort of 'chartered libertine,'" it dryly observed, "and has acquired the right to do as he likes with impunity. He may therefore steal a horse from the pasture, where another man would have been hanged only for looking over the hedge." The conflict between those who judged Bushnell by his words and those who judged him by his character would divide the Congregational community for years.

CONTROVERSY IN CONNECTICUT

Other clerical associations found it hard to understand the action of Hartford Central, which seemed to fly in the face of the evidence. The major theological voices of New England had all condemned the book, yet these clerics acquitted their colleague. As if this were not enough, there was more than a touch of evasion in Hartford Central's explanations of its actions. As one member of the association admitted, "a great many things were said, proved, denied, affirmed, and guessed in our meetings, that would better be left unpublished." The decision by Hartford Central troubled many, but none more so than the clergy of Fairfield West Association. Even before Hartford Central had issued its opinion, Fairfield West petitioned the statewide General Association to take actions to protect the doctrines of the Trinity, the atonement, and the incarnation. Although the petition made no mention of Bushnell, the context was clear, and when the General Association at the time demurred, it noted that the district association had exclusive rights to institute Christian discipline. But early in 1850 the Fairfield

West clergy began their task anew. In late January they sent a remonstrance to the Hartford Central Association noting errors concerning a wide variety of doctrines in *God in Christ*. In their conclusion they claimed that the danger of the book was that while it kept some of the traditional vocabulary concerning the Trinity, redemption, justification by faith, and the atonement, the dogmas themselves were fundamentally changed, thus causing confusion. Upon receiving the document the clergy of Hartford Central refused to reopen the case, and made again the same arguments they had used earlier — that they were not giving sanction "to any peculiarities of Dr. Bushnell's scheme of doctrine," and that they put primary weight upon Bushnell's personal clarification of his teachings, not on the book itself.

This answer only infuriated the clergy of Fairfield West. For them the question was not about Bushnell as a person, but rather his teachings. And the teachings that concerned them were his publicly published works, not private statements he might have made to the clergy of his own association. They warned that if the errors of *God in Christ* were not condemned they would open the floodgates of error into their church. Indeed, Bushnell's ideas were already beginning to find favor among the young. The very careful and nuanced language of Hartford Central might protect their beloved colleague along with their own reputations, but it was allowing error to take root.

Many outside of the world of Connecticut Congregationalism agreed with Fairfield West. The *Princeton Review* applauded Bushnell's critics for demanding that Hartford Central retrace its steps and explain to skeptical outsiders how they had come to accept Bushnell's explanation, and how any such explanations could be reconciled with the published record. Unless the association made a clear statement the young and impressionable would be attracted to the ideas of "Schleiermacher, Morell, and Bushnell." The very theological reputation of Connecticut was at stake.

There was, as well, the unspoken question of prevarication. How could one reconcile the explanatory statements offered by Bushnell in his defense with the text of *God in Christ*? Bushnell had gladly admitted that he could confess to multiple creeds simultaneously; now he appeared to set forth two theologies, one in the book and the other to his accusers. Fairfield West was deeply suspicious of the elucidations. Bushnell's explanations formally retracted none of the ideas set forth in *God in Christ*; "the only difference is that in the communication, he has dealt in general terms, which in his book he has fully explained." His explanations were vague where the book had been specific. Regardless of whether this was a case of Bushnell shading his answers or of Hartford Central being unwilling to press him for clarification, it was clear that the full implications of the book were not being addressed.

The stage was now set for the General Association meeting of 1850. The association was to gather in Litchfield in June, and throughout the state Bushnell's opponents were busy mounting their case. One of Fairfield West's leaders was Lyman Atwater, pastor at Fairfield. Atwater, eleven years Bushnell's junior, showed a very different face of Connecticut Congregationalism. Like Bushnell he had graduated from Yale, and like him he had read the works of Coleridge. Coleridge, however, only made him more convinced of the importance of traditional orthodoxy. A conservative Calvinist, trained in philosophy, he was closely associated with the *Princeton Review* and reflected the conservatism of that journal. And, as with Charles Hodge, theology was for him the measure of all things. He liked Bushnell as a man and as a preacher but thought his theological works were wrongheaded. He and his clerical colleagues had written to each of the clerical associations of the state (Hartford Central excepted) asking them to evaluate Bushnell's volume. All rejected Bushnell's views and nine of the thirteen thought he should be brought to trial. Encouraged by this show of support Fairfield West offered a new memorial attacking the theological errors of *God in Christ* and claiming that since it was derived at least in part from a *Concio ad Clerum* to the entire clerical community of the state, it should be evaluated by the General Association. The book served as a judgment upon the theological life of the entire Congregational Church in Connecticut, and as such needed to be judged by all of the clergy of the General Association.

The question of action, however, involved a thicket of legal questions. According to the Saybrook Platform the district association was the body that had to recommend a trial. Was the action of Hartford Central a formal judicial action or only an evaluation by a group of ministers? If it were the former then it would have to be formally reversed before any further action could be taken. If it were simply the latter, however, the question became murkier. Then in theory Hartfield

Central could receive the charges made by others and authorize a trial based on them. Some in Hartford Central claimed this could be the case, although they refused to speculate how they themselves would evaluate any such charge. Finally, what could the General Association do? Would an action on its part be an attack upon Congregationalist polity, turning the statewide body into a court? These ecclesiastical questions were to some at least as troubling as Bushnell's alleged theological errors.

The General Association gathering did not begin well for Bushnell. Nathaniel Hewit, another Fairfield West leader, was chosen as moderator, and he duly offered prayers for "apostates" and "heretics." Fairfield West's memorial was received, and a committee of thirteen (representing all but one of the district associations) was established to report back to the Association. Many of Bushnell's sharpest critics were included in the thirteen, and it was later acknowledged that part of the report had been prepared in advance in New Haven. The report claimed legitimacy in addressing the concerns of Fairfield West by arguing that it was permissible for one association to question decisions made by another. The document declared that any district association could remonstrate the decision of another association on cases involving "the faith and purity of our churches." "We regard it as the duty of any Association," the proposed document continued, "receiving such a Remonstrance to reconsider the case in question, and if they do not see reason to bring charges themselves, to afford an opportunity for any person who may desire it to bring up the case for judicial investigation." No district association would be able to stonewall the concerns of others.

Bushnell and his allies responded by holding fast to the integrity of Congregational polity, arguing that the proposed change would bring about a centralized authority antithetical to the spirit of independence. Bushnell spoke forcefully in his own defense, praising the autonomy of the district associations. They functioned as a grand jury did in law — determining whether there was sufficient evidence for a trial. "If the deliberate decision of an association like this is not the final disposal of the case then you have persecution rather than judgement." A cleric would never be free from the pernicious charges of his critics and would constantly have to defend himself against charges.

The debate was intense, since both groups were convinced they were right. Bushnell was adamant in defending his orthodoxy. His discourses were attempts to improve a system that seemed to him to be breaking down. He saw no real difference between what he stated and the traditional faith, so he felt that he could affirm both traditional beliefs and his own new ideas. His opponents saw him as the carrier of a false theology that could infect the entire ecclesiastical body if not checked.

For two days the debate went on with the claims of theological rectitude being answered by a plea for Congregationalist integrity. In the end a compromise was worked out through an amendment offered by Bushnell himself: a district association that received a remonstrance asking it to reconsider a decision, "if they do not reverse their former action, [will] use their best endeavors to satisfy the complaining association in respect to their proceedings so complained of." In other words, another association would be guaranteed a full explanation, if not a reversal of the decision.

The General Association took another step as well. It affirmed the centrality of the doctrines in question. Here they admitted the force of Fairfield West's claim. "The General Association of the State of Connecticut do stand in peculiar relation to the subject," they explained, acknowledging that the address under consideration was a *Concio ad Clerum* and that it and the other two essays bound with it in Bushnell's volume were presented as "one harmonious system of doctrinal truth. It was therefore necessary for the Association to formally distance itself from any alleged errors therein and to affirm doctrinal truth. Using terminology borrowed from the long Westminster Catechism, traditional understandings of the doctrine of the Trinity and justification by faith were labeled fundamental articles of the faith. Thus, for example, the Association members clearly stated, "We believe that there are three persons in the Godhead — the Father, the Son, and the Holy Ghost — and that these three are one God, the same in substance, equal in power and glory." On the question of assigning error they carefully chose their words. "In respect to these [fundamental] views," they acknowledged, "the Fairfield West Association have stated (what is generally known) that these discourses have been extensively understood by divines to deny." However, as a body, the Association admitted that it did not "undertake to say whether the aforesaid doctrines are or are not denied in the book in question," but they were "fundamental articles of the Christian religion and the denial of them [is] heresy." The message of the General Association was clear: the errors alleged in *God in Christ* were to be condemned, and the traditional doctrines of the Trinity and atonement were affirmed. But no formal condemnation was to be issued against either the book or Bushnell himself.

With this, the second phase of Bushnell's ecclesiastical trials was over. He had been exonerated by his district association, and the General Association had declined to take the radical action called for by Fairfield West. His theology had been largely rejected, but he had not. Here, too, he was helped by the power his character wielded in personal confrontation. As one participant of the meeting confessed, they "proceeded carefully and earnestly, because they felt they were dealing with a man of God, though he might be a man of God in error." He could hope that the worst was past. After the June meeting, Lyman Atwater, deciding to evaluate Bushnell up close, spent two days with him in Hartford. As Bushnell wrote to a friend, Atwater went away, "if not satisfied . . . greatly quieted." In the spring of 1851, however, Bushnell decided to publish the explanations he had offered to the Hartford Central Association regarding the controversial doctrines of *God in Christ* in a new volume, *Christ in Theology*. The purpose of his new book, he explained, was not to "defend" his ideas but to "complete" them, and he noted that his earlier statement made up only half the material of the new volume.

CHRIST IN THEOLOGY

No volume of Bushnell's writings better reflects the strengths and weaknesses of his character than *Christ in Theology*. We see here the ultimate tinkerer — little concerned with theory, but greatly interested with results. In his introductory comments he admitted that only after publishing *God in Christ* did he begin to engage in a systematic study of the history of doctrine, and that he was amazed at what he had discovered. "I am so much nearer to real orthodoxy than I supposed," he proclaimed, "and . . . the New England theology, so called, is so much farther off." His admission was a confirmation of what many suspected. Bushnell's method, in the words of Orestes Brownson, was to have "read some, thought a little, felt much, imagined more." *God in Christ* was a work spun out of Bushnell's personal insights, and only after the fact did he examine the larger theological tradition. A survey of his notations also shows that his "examination" of the early church seemed to consist of the reading of a few articles on the Trinity that had been published earlier in *Bibliotheca Sacra*. But from this evidence he became convinced that he was closer to true orthodoxy than were his opponents.

Bushnell did make some attempts to meet his critics, particularly with regard to his views on language. Although he did not abandon the main outline of his teaching concerning language, he did modify it, both by offering further information and by refining certain points. In those refinements one can see the influence of his parishioner Henry M. Goodwin. Goodwin had penned an essay defending his pastor entitled "Thoughts, Words, and Things," which was far clearer and more tightly reasoned than the "Preliminary Dissertation" had been. Perhaps because of Goodwin, Bushnell jettisoned some of the extravagant claims of his earlier work, particularly those concerning the opaqueness of all intellectual language, and limited his focus to religious language. He wrote, "all religious truth . . . is and must be presented under conditions of form or analogy from the outward state." He also retreated somewhat on his disparagement of logic, admitting logic's value as a science but questioning how well it functioned in the realm of moral or religious philosophy. He used as his example of the limitations of logic his critic Orestes Brownson, who for logic's sake first became a Transcendentalist and then a Roman Catholic. "He is a man of infinite logic," he noted, "who holds premises by their forms without real insight." Again, Bushnell reiterated his belief in the superiority of the experience of the divine over logic when it came to religious belief.

On the main theological issues, Bushnell gave no ground. He refused, to begin with, any compromise on the question of the Trinity and adamantly held to his theory of an instrumental Trinity. Only an instrumental understanding based on revelation could be true to the scriptural record that spoke both of distinctions between the persons of the Godhead and of their interchangeability. He claimed that his theory was actually in line with the Council of Nicaea, which spoke of the Father and the Son being united in one substance *(homoousion)*, and that it was far more orthodox than the standard New England theory. Reiterating his rejection of the New England understanding, he proclaimed, "I frankly own to you that I accept no prevailing view of trinity now held in New England." The New England emphasis upon maintaining the distinctiveness of the persons of the Trinity led its theologians to fall into the heresy of tritheism, he argued. To combat this error, he refused to accept any theory that moved beyond the Trinity of revelation. Even though the General Association had adamantly affirmed that the tri-personality was rooted in the divine nature, he balked at affirmations that went beyond the clear message of Scripture, and refused to speculate on the relationship of the persons of the Godhead. "I am . . . protesting against all judgements and inferences that undertake to leap the gulf between us and the inscrutable mystery of God insisting that we stay by the Scripture and trust ourselves to *no* constructive reasoning on the subject."

He also defended his views on the person of Christ, proposing an "instrumental duality" concerning Christ's person. This would allow one to speak of both the humanity and divinity of Christ without having to theorize how the two natures were related. One could acknowledge the formal duality of Christ's nature while focusing on the unity of his personality. Such a theory, Bushnell claimed, not only avoided speculation but also offered a picture of Christ that could be effectively preached.

In addition, Bushnell defended his views on the work of Christ. Since there was no one view of the atonement set forth in Scripture, and since the church had never formally defined a theory, he felt free to advocate the one set forth in *God in Christ*. The objective view long cherished by the orthodox was untenable. "I come . . . to the conclusion that the objective view, in question, is not really held by competent theologians of any school, however, it may seem to be, in much of the language they employ." Recognizing that, he had attempted to salvage what could be retained of the old idea. In his Cambridge discourse he had addressed Unitarians who accepted only a subjective view of the work of Christ, and to them he had attempted to offer at least a modicum of the objective view through his altar imagery. "What I have called the subjective view of the atonement was the only one in which I could hope to find sympathy," he explained; "then the endeavor was, from this as a basis or first truth . . . to pass on to the objective view, which contains the substance of our orthodox formula, and carry a realization of that."

Throughout most of *Christ in Theology* Bushnell stood his ground, bloodied but unbowed. He argued that his view of Christ was essentially orthodox and defended his refusal to speculate on questions upon which Scripture was unclear. His view of the Trinity, he claimed, was closer to the Nicene teaching than were the views of his New England opponents, and since Scripture outlined no doctrine of atonement, his views on the matter were as good as any other. He summarized his method by concluding, "the main peculiarity of my exposition [is] that it proposes no single formula as containing the whole truth of the subject, but is chiefly occupied in showing how, or by what method of use, we may receive the true meaning and power of all the scripture language."

But if Bushnell was pugnacious in defending his theological formulations, he took great care in distancing himself from one of the charges made against him, that of pantheism. He went to great lengths to show how his views on the Trinity differed from those of Schleiermacher, and he adamantly maintained his devotion to a personal God. "There is no real security that God will be held as a person," he wrote, "save that a personal God is *wanted*. For if a World-God only is wanted, as the animal wants only a world to graze in, the mind will be as little likely to raise itself to any thing above the world, waiting to return its sympathies, and feed its longing after friendship." It was just such an emphasis upon sympathy and friendship that was so close to the heart of true religion for Bushnell. Doctrine was of the second order and could be debated or questioned, but the personal relationship between the believer and God had to be defended at all costs. The God of the philosopher no more stirred him than did the doctrines of the theologian. But the experience of the divine person was precious. Whereas in *God in Christ* he had felt free to yoke images from Eastern and Western religions, in this volume he pointedly divorced them. An impersonal God, such as that which lay at the heart of pantheism, was characterized as "the sleeping Brama of the East, or the pantheistic IT of the German schools." Bushnell made it clear that he had no sympathy for either, or, by implication, for the transcendentalist who combined the two. With the personal God of the Scriptures his loyalty lay.

REOPENING THE CONTROVERSY

Christ in Theology was in no sense an apology. Except for the question of pantheism Bushnell had largely stood his ground. He did not abandon his distinctive theological claims, nor did he tone down his criticism of the New England theological tradition. If anything, the critiques are ratcheted up. Indeed, he boasted that this second volume "was quite as heretical as the first [but] more adequately stated." Its publication prompted a new round of attacks from which his supporters found it difficult to defend him. The Hartford Central Association had carefully but surely distanced itself from the theology of *God in Christ,* claiming that it believed Bushnell's explanation of his theology showed him to be acceptably orthodox. Now in this new volume Bushnell seemed to be reiterating the bold claims of his earlier work. In the summer of 1850 the General Association had also sidestepped the issue by passing the modified resolution requiring that remonstrances be answered, and by passing a statement of fundamental beliefs. They had hoped that by this they could heal the wound, but *Christ in Theology* reopened it. In fact, Bushnell not only opened the wound but rubbed salt in it by claiming that his theory of the Trinity was more orthodox than that of the New England theological tradition. In his bold claims he baited his critics, but now his critics had tools by which to respond. If Bushnell in this new volume was teaching errors concerning the Trinity, the person of Christ, and soteriology, then the General Association was on record as having labeled such errors fundamental heresies.

Fairfield West had interpreted the decisions by the General Association in Litchfield far differently than had Bushnell's supporters. The latter had assumed that the General Association's refusal to take legal action closed the case. Fairfield West, in contrast, interpreted the actions of the General Association as clarifying how a continued attack on Bushnell and his theology could proceed. Making use of the modified resolution in the fall of 1850 they communicated to the Hartford Central Association a remonstrance for a formal explanation of both its opinion concerning Bushnell's orthodoxy vis-à-vis the fundamental doctrines established by the General Association and its decision not to proceed to a trial. Hartford Central put off answering until May of 1851. Finally, they claimed that these issues had already been discussed, and that further discussion would not be fruitful. They also claimed that the fundamental doctrines set forth by the General Association have "been so variously interpreted" that they could not be the basis for the evaluation for which Fairfield West asked. In effect, Fairfield West's request was dismissed as old business. Nevertheless, the clergy of Hartfield Central continued to distance themselves from Bushnell's writings. The Association's response included the following statement, laced with disclaimers and qualifications:

> While it is not known that there is a *single member*, the author himself excepted, who is *prepared to adopt or even commend* the views set forth in that publication, the majority are satisfied that it does not *substantially reject* the orthodox faith. *Analyzing* the doctrines in question, *reducing them* to their last elements, *throwing out* what may be termed the merely *incidental* or at least *non-essential parts*, and *inquiring* whether Dr. Bushnell's book, with *one passage set over against another*, with *due allowance for his somewhat peculiar views of language*, and with his *verbal and written explanations* of meaning, could be considered as denying the fundamental facts and significance of evangelical views, they have been brought to the decision against which you remonstrate. [emphasis added]

Defending Bushnell and his theology was no easy task, and although the Association stated that it would not reverse its decision, it also would not block an appeal directly to the Consociation for a trial.

With this, Fairfield West went for the kill. They appealed to the General Association and made their case. Against Hartford Central they claimed that the district association had made it clear that it would neither reverse its decision nor enter into a discussion of the several allegations presented in the communication. The former it could legitimately do, but the latter — the refusal to explain its action — violated the agreement hammered out in Litchfield in the summer of 1850. The Fairfield West contingent argued that by refusing to explain itself, Hartford Central was shielding a heretic, and they used *Christ in Theology* to raise anew the question of Bushnell's orthodoxy. "We do not find," they wrote, "that he has, in this second book, changed his position in any important particular, or so explained their meaning as to make them more consistent with the truth of the Gospel." Hartford Central's invitation to appeal directly to the Consociation was not a legal option under the Saybrook Platform. If Hartford Central would not reverse its opinion it should be rebuked for straying from the fundamental articles of the faith agreed upon in 1850.

In June of 1852 a bitter debate again marked the General Association, which was that year meeting in Danbury. Again the issue became for some the question of Bushnell's teachings and for others the integrity of Congregational polity. Bushnell's supporters attacked the idea of evaluating his theology when he was not present to defend it. Such would be the course of action of a "vigilante committee" rather than a body of Christian clergy. His critics again argued that the issue was the theology found in the two volumes, not Bushnell himself. "Why did Dr. Bushnell publish a book at all, if the readers cannot interpret it aright?" asked one exasperated speaker to the claim that he must accept Bushnell's own explanation of his meaning. "Why did he publish a second volume to expound the first if that is past comprehension also?" "Nine-tenths" of all who read the books agreed that they transgressed orthodoxy, including the radical press of Britain.

In the course of the heated debate a short incident occurred that reveals the high tensions of the time. For Bushnell's critics his defenders' strategy was just as odious as those who defended slavery. They, too, draped around them the sanctity of the law and used it to avoid addressing the morality of the issue. In response to this prevarication there had arisen the call for obedience to a higher law, in which the evil of slavery was condemned. Pushing the analogy one anti-Bushnell speaker continued, "Shall we be told that the human laws in the state must give way to the 'higher law of God' and is the decision of Hartford Central to be final? No we fall back upon our duty to God!" No, boomed back a supporter of Bushnell, "It is not 'Higher law' but 'Lynch law' which you advocate, and against which we protest!"

Again the General Association refused to act, stating that it was "not a legislative or judicial body, but a body for mutual consultation, advice, and brotherly love." There would be no redefinition of the role of the General Association. Congregational polity had again triumphed. The General Association refused to take on the role of the final court of appeal. The recommendation that was issued was wonderfully ambiguous. The Association urged that all obstacles, "whether real or supposed," be removed to allow "a full and fair investigation, according to our ecclesiastical rules," of the questions raised. Was this a rebuke to Fairfield West's attempt to bypass the Saybrook Platform or to Hartford Central's unwillingness to live up to the agreements of 1850?

The Bushnell controversy was very difficult for Bushnell's fellow Congregationalists because it was about a number of things, not only the case of Horace Bushnell. There was the question of church governance: Did Connecticut Congregationalists really want to go down the road of presbyterian polity, by which local decisions could be overturned at will by higher courts? Church trials had been a rare thing in Connecticut, particularly in contrast to its Presbyterian neighbors. Would they become common now, and if so how would that affect the cherished virtue of independence? That question, perhaps more than anything else, saved Bushnell. Despite the profound disagreement most Connecticut clergy felt toward his speculations, the majority could not commit themselves to theological censure.

Although the majority of Hartford Central's clergy continued to stand behind him as an individual, Bushnell's position was painful at best, precarious at worst. His clerical colleagues still showed no willingness to defend his theology and, indeed, invariably distanced themselves from it. Now they began distancing themselves from Bushnell himself and refused to exchange pulpits with him. His opponents both statewide and in his own association did not go away nor lessen their criticisms, and the prospect of continuing conflict stretched on indefinitely. Bushnell perhaps recognized that publishing *Christ in Theology* had been a strategic error. It converted no one, and it intensified the debate rather than quieting it. He took the radical action of withdrawing it from publication, and it remained out of print until published in a scholarly edition almost 140 years later. It remains to this day perhaps Bushnell's least-read published work.

Thus in late June of 1852, just after the close of the meeting of the General Association, North Church voted to remove itself from the Hartford North Consociation and to become an independent congregation. Such a break was not without precedent — there were twenty-nine other independent Congregational churches in Connecticut — but it was nonetheless a painful decision. Contemporaries claimed that the decision in no wise reflected any sense of loss of support within the Association for Bushnell. Perhaps.

What had begun immediately upon his return from Europe — Bushnell the tinkerer's great attempt to bring together the children of the Puritans — had ended in apparent failure. Unitarians and orthodox were no closer now than they had been before, and the orthodox seemed even more divided than they had been. The result, far from being a comprehensive unity, was even more division, seen most painfully in North Church's separation from its sister churches and Bushnell's alienation from his former clerical colleagues. As he confessed to a friend, "I seem to be now very much cut off from access to the public." It is ironic that the two Hartford clergy who befriended him represented traditions he had not always been kind to. "Dr. Murdoch," pastor of South Baptist Church, continued to exchange a pulpit with him, and perhaps Bushnell remembered some of the passages from *Views of Christian Nurture* that were so sharply critical of Baptist piety. The other friendly cleric was Thomas March Clark, the new rector of the Episcopal Christ Church. Clark, a broad-minded Episcopalian, shared Bushnell's love of music and interest in inquiry. He was perhaps the first person of that church that Bushnell had known and admired. After 1852, the strong anti-Episcopal flashes in his writings, so prevalent throughout the previous decade, subsided.

The controversy over *God in Christ* marked an end to one phase of Bushnell's ministry. Except for the topic of the atonement, he would not return in any formal way to the theological issues he had raised in these two works. A new concern for Christian experience would take their place. Likewise, his interest in comprehensive unity would shift. He became less interested in the narrow issue of reuniting the children of the Puritans and began to look at some of the broader implications of the issue of unity, particularly as the nation moved inevitably toward civil war.

One phase of Bushnell's career was closing. Another was about to open.

8 Nature and Supernature

TOWARD the end of his Andover address, "Dogma and Spirit," Bushnell described the sad state of the present-day church. In the apostolic age the regular occurrence of signs and wonders had kept the presence of the Spirit alive, and had held in check the encrustation of dogma, but now the Spirit seemed to be silent. The church had lost a sense of immediate inspiration, which "has caused a sad depression in our modern piety" and "cuts us off from the holy men of Scripture time." "A feeling is in us," he said, "that God is more remote, and . . . it is no longer permissible to realize the same graces, and expect the same intense union of the life with God." Bushnell found this understanding, this belief that such intense experiences no longer could occur, fundamentally false. The church was called toward an "intimacy of faith and love . . . between the church and God," and when such intimacy was brought about "there will be unfolded a style of piety wholly unknown, at present, in the world."

Bushnell's critique of the present life of the church and his vision for the future set a new tone for his personal and professional life. To recover the lost power of the earliest church became a decade-long quest for him and would result in the publication of one of his most important works, *Nature and the Supernatural*. In this quest he could be seen working out the implications of the experience he had undergone through the writings of Madame Guyon, and in *Nature and the Supernatural* he would offer a religious response to trends he saw emerging in both philosophy and science and present a positive corollary to his theory of language.

SEEKING HEALTH

But first there was the problem of health. The stress caused by the debate over *God in Christ* had exacerbated Bushnell's long-standing illness. In August of 1852, while on a country outing that he hoped would invigorate his health, he wrote his wife that he awoke one morning, on account of "a singular bit of coughing," only to discover that he had been coughing up blood. Throat problems were an occupational hazard for nineteenth-century clergy, particularly in New England. The strain of preaching and praying in barn-like buildings, and the additional combination of the frigid winter air and overheated churches, wreaked havoc on the throat. By the fall it became clear that Bushnell's problems were worse than the standard throat problems of clergy, however, and the quest for health began anew.

He first thought a western trip during the autumn of 1852 might help restore his strength. Again, as with his European trip, he would travel alone, but would correspond regularly with his family. His brother and sister-in-law resided at Fort Ripley on the Mississippi River in northern Minnesota, and he decided to visit them. Along the way he stopped at Oberlin, Ohio, to visit the famous evangelist Charles Grandison Finney and his wife. The two men had gotten to know each other when Finney had come to Hartford to preach in 1851, and, despite the obvious disagreements between the great revivalist and the great critic of revivalism, they got along well. In the period of Bushnell's isolation Finney seemed to sympathize with him instead of his opponents, and worked hard to bring about a rapprochement between Bushnell and his chief Hartford critic, Joel Hawes. The sympathy between Finney and Bushnell suggests that Bushnell was a more complicated figure than some of his biographers have painted. Both men were fascinated by the power of the Spirit, and each felt more comfortable speaking of religious experience than of fine points of doctrine. After Bushnell's death Finney wrote that although they disagreed on many points they nonetheless agreed "on their aims and burning desires and in their belief that Christians might claim and receive far higher blessings than were usually supposed to be any part of our earthly inheritance." In Finney, Bushnell saw a manifestation of that life of the Spirit that for him was the mark of true religion. "I find God with him," he explained, "and consciously receive nothing but good and genuine (he would say honest) impressions from him." He would later write testimonials for Finney when the latter visited England in 1860. Now, in 1852, he simply wrote his wife after his visit with the couple, "I had a most happy and blessed day here."

The trip as a whole, however, was not so enjoyable. The travel was arduous. As he wrote to his wife, "between hotels, and visitors, and mortal poundings, and sleepless nights, I can do nothing more than . . . tell you how fondly my heart turns back to find rest in you." The weather also took its toll. Winter so descended while he was at Fort Ripley that he referred to the place as the "North Pole." On his return trip he and his wagon driver almost lost their way in a blizzard and suffered mightily from the cold. He also feared that the Mississippi might freeze, which would compel him to return over land, a far more exhausting mode of travel.

But by December he was back in Hartford. Despite the difficulties, the trip seemed to revive him somewhat, and throughout 1853 and 1854 he busied himself with a variety of concerns. He defended himself at the General Association meeting of 1854 against still another attack on his defenders by Fairfield West. He also began labor on a project dear to him: the establishment of a great central park in Hartford, in a desolate spot then occupied by a few small factories, a garbage dump, and a pumping station for the new railroad. The park project reflected his long-standing interest in urban improvement. He later explained both the aesthetic and practical value of parks: "These varied spaces . . . will not only be so many breathing places, but will add immensely to the variety, vivacity, and impressive elegance of the city." In this endeavor he showed his political skills as well as his devotion to the city where he for so long served. The park would eventually be named Bushnell Park in his honor.

But his health began to fail again and in 1855 he decided that a southern voyage might serve him better than a Minnesotan winter. Another brother-in-law had invited him to California, but he decided instead upon a shorter trip to Cuba. Here, too, weather took its toll. The sea journey was rough, and the ship even had to endure a snowstorm while it crossed the Gulf Stream. But the weather began to cooperate by the time he landed, and just as the new experiences of Europe fascinated him and stimulated his observant eye, so too did his first experience of the tropics. Of the lush vegetation he encountered he admitted he could identify only turnips and Indian corn, but palm trees intrigued him. The palm tree "suffices to make a new landscape; for it shoots up indigenous . . . in tall pillars of wood some fifty to eighty feet high, and throws up on the top its magnificent tufts of feathers."

He was less impressed by the culture. As in his travels in Italy he found the lack of hygiene appalling. "My room, which is abundantly dirty, has no carpet, and, like all the other rooms of this island, has no window-glass; nothing but an immense two-barred shutter." Nor did he find the Sabbath customs of the natives very edifying. On one Sunday afternoon he watched as the mistress of the house not only did her usual labors but also flogged her servants with a bullwhip. "How different a place," he commented, "from that which God has heretofore given me in the quiet pulpit, among the devout people of God, on a well-kept New England Sabbath." Again, he wrote that Sundays reminded him of "heathendom." "Slavery and slaves; work, work all day and night; no church, no religion visible by any sign but the tithing."

An offer by an American living in Cuba, a Mr. Forbes, for Bushnell to take residence with him, improved Bushnell's physical lot. He could now write back about horseback riding, eating fresh vegetables, and enjoying the nectar of sugarcane. But none of these pleasures relieved a nagging trouble in his soul. The lack of religion in the society seemed like a sickness, which in turn reminded him of his own weakened state. He wrote that "I begin to think now that nothing will cure me but faith, a bath in the supernatural and healing grace of Christ, an inhalation of the Divine Spirit and his new-creating powers." Spirit had a power that environment lacked. Commenting upon the cold winter the people of New England were then undergoing, he wrote, "you have cold with a fire, we less cold with none." Throughout his stay he found paradoxically that while his general health seemed to improve, his throat ailment did not. He still coughed up blood. And without a voice he could not return to serve his faithful flock. He confessed as much in a letter to his congregation. "How great a struggle it costs me to write in this doubtful way, concerning the work of my life and the charge that for so long a time has been the burden of my affections and my prayers, I cannot tell you."

In April he left Cuba and headed back north, stopping in Savannah and Charleston along the way. He continued to reflect upon his health and see a connection between the religious truth he was wrestling with and his physical affliction. Writing to his wife he admitted he might never be a well man again, but he hoped that "I may somehow be able to add a closing part of my life which will be better than the part already fulfilled, and more significant as a contribution to the truth of Christ and the power of his Gospel; which if I do, what can it be but that my thinking, discovering, understanding life is concluded and consummated by a discerning of the way and power of faith."

By May he was home, still in doubtful health. A summer in the hills of Connecticut seemed to revive him somewhat, and he continued to labor on a work on the supernatural, but health concerns still plagued him. Finally in the winter of 1856 he decided to try the dry, warm climate of California. He planned to stay there between eight months and a year. The twenty-three-day boat trip was made easier by the completion of the Panama railroad, allowing travelers to cross the disease-laden isthmus in little more than three hours. Then it was on to the Bay Area in California.

California was no longer the gold-rush center it had been a few years earlier, but it still felt the effects of that time. The state was of course filled with a natural beauty that thrilled Bushnell, and he spoke enthusiastically about the flowers, the trees, and the natural vistas. He described a visit to Stockton Pass as "the nearest thing to a garden of Eden actually extant that I ever saw." But the destructiveness of "civilization" was also all too present. The process of mining for gold had destroyed the face of nature in many places. "The sides of almost every hill are gashed and torn, covered with rocks laid bare, and fresh earth of all colors . . . you could not imagine such devastation as a possible thing to be made in seven years by all the diggers in the world." The mess and destruction troubled his tidy New England soul. Nor was it only miners who scarred the landscape. A visit to the Giant Redwoods also showed humanity's destructive streak. Many of the trees were injured at their roots by fire, and there was worse. "That man, a living man, supposed to have a soul . . . should have cut down the biggest of all [the trees], and skinned the next, 'the Mother', one hundred and twenty feet upward from the ground — both sound as a rock at the heart and good for another thousand years of growth — oh, it surpasses all contempt!"

The new inhabitants' corrupting influences could be seen in social life as well. Bushnell was now able to witness up close the "barbarism" he had preached against a decade earlier. The political and legal situations were chaotic, and "Vigilance Committees" were needed to maintain some semblance of order. "It would be no surprise to me," he wrote, "to hear, almost any day, that fire and murder were loose in San Francisco, rank as in the days of Robespierre."

But there were voices on the other side. Bushnell was quickly introduced to some of the clergy of the area — many of them transplanted New Englanders. One was a college classmate and fellow Congregationalist, Henry Durant, who headed a small academy called the College of California. Through Durant, Bushnell met with a convention of Congregationalist and Presbyterian clergy whom he described as "fine-spirited, talented, and generally accomplished men." His contacts led him to be involved in the religious life of the area, and he was invited to preach at the installation of a new ministry at the First Congregationalist Church. The subject of his address was "Society and Religion: A Sermon for California," and in it he cast his Puritan Yankee eye on the new society.

The address reverberated with Connecticut Puritan themes, many from as long back as his Litchfield boyhood. "True religion," he explained, "including the pulpit and the church, is the only sufficient spring of civil order and happiness." Without religion the social order moved irredeemably back toward barbarism; with true religion even revolution could build and create. That was the difference, he went on, between Cromwell and the Jacobins of the French Revolution. "What was Cromwell's army but a grand prayer-meeting under marching orders?"

Some, he observed, might argue that this had been true in the past but was now no longer the case since the role of religion in enlightening the state ended with the separation of church and state. On the contrary, Bushnell argued, the formal institutional division of the two made the role of religion even more important. Alluding to the violence and political corruption he had witnessed during his stay he suggested, "when the social inventory of its history comes to be made up of patent ballot-boxes, pistols, bowie-knives, cork-screws, and coffins, interspersed here and there with a treatment of halter practice [i.e., lynching], it will be strange if some few do not suspect, that the state, separated from the church even more stringently needs religion." Just as the state was separate from family life yet dependent on its health, so too did the state depend upon the power of religion.

Others believed the health of the state depended only on the natural law of progress. Bushnell quickly dismissed such claims as "literary moonshine." If there was any law of history it was that of retrogression, as the fall of so many once-great civilizations attested. Christianity was a "supernatural power," and only the spirit of true religion checked the path of decline and allowed for advance. Where religion became corrupted (and here — in good New England fashion — he pointed to Spain and Mexico), the law of retrogression returned. Among those in decline he included, along with Spain and Mexico, the Dutch "boors of Southern Africa." "What indeed are these same boors but a race of modern barbarians under the name of John Calvin and the synod of Dort?" The people of California could not seek protection in any law of progress.

But they could in Christianity. By its transformation of the heart, said Bushnell, Christianity made government possible. It inculcated a respect for law, which allowed the law of conscience to replace public repression. Perhaps again thinking back to his boyhood, he added, "Thus, it was, that, previous to the influx of foreign immigration, crime was so great a rarity in some of our more Christian states, that a theft, robbery, or murder created even a streak of wonder." Christianity also offered the principle of industry. To a society of "gamblers, stock speculators, panders of vice, [and] brokers of the ballot box," it preached the law of righteous industry. It sanctified marriage and made the home the cradle of true morality. It offered the principle of public service, the idea that one should work for the greater good. One way it did so was by sanctifying the Sabbath and allowing its moral force to permeate the community. Here, too, Bushnell minced no words in his criticism of what he had found. "The people of California are determined, they say, to have laws executed, to have justice, personal security, and public order. You can have no such thing without a

Christian Sabbath." The California Sunday was a day "that corrupts more virtue, ruins more character, than all the other six days together!" In the cities work was suspended to make room for idleness and dissipation, while in the small towns Sunday was the great day of trade. Finally, he observed that Christianity brought a spirit of intelligence. Wherever it went it planted colleges. In his conclusion he said that California was being offered a choice. In the past it had been overridden by adventurers trying to extract wealth. The fruits of their labors were abundantly clear for all to see. But California need not continue down this path. Christianity offered a set of values and a vision that stressed community, education, law, and industry; and the people of California could choose to go down this path instead. Like John Winthrop on the *Arbella* in Boston harbor 24 years earlier, Bushnell offered a choice. Which would they follow?

Bushnell's sermon was a great success and a group of prominent civic leaders quickly had it published. It had, however, another immediate effect. His reference to true Christianity planting colleges energized the supporters of the College of California, and convinced them that the time was right to try to enlarge their meager institution. Despite its grand title, it was in reality but a small preparatory school in Oakland, begun in 1853 through actions taken by the Presbytery of San Francisco and the Congregational Association of California to establish a high school. In 1855 this institution changed its name to the College of California. The governors of the college invited Bushnell to accept the presidency of the institution and help it to become a true university.

Bushnell was flattered by the offer, and recognized that it had some attractions. The proposed university would be the type of institution Bushnell favored. Independent of any denominational identity, its board of trustees included representatives of all the leading Protestant communities, and it was proposed that sites be offered to all the churches on a public square in front of the institution, "allowing the students to attend on that form of worship preferred by their parents and guardians." Bushnell also shared the dream of the new institution, which hoped to become a center of literature and science, "a name clothed with associations as profoundly historical as Oxford or Padua, or Salamanca, or Heidelberg." Practical factors also weighed in. He found the climate of California conducive to his health. As he wrote back to his congregation, "I have ascertained . . . that I can live here in sufficient force to be useful. I may find that I cannot there [in Hartford]." But his loyalty to his old congregation was paramount. "I am a Christian pastor, holding a very peculiar relation to my flock," a flock loyal to him in his time of trial. If he could return and serve, he believed he must. But in the interim he offered his services to the school, and in particular he volunteered to scout out a site for the institution and to help raise an endowment.

Bushnell eagerly began his labors. If from the pulpit of First Congregational Church he sounded the voice of the old Puritan, as he surveyed the Bay Area searching for an appropriate site he was every bit the practical Yankee. No detail seemed to miss his eye: topography, vista, access to water, and even the possibility of getting the land for a fair price, all were duly noted. All around the Bay Area he traveled, taking notes. He recorded that at one point he feared being attacked by a grizzly bear, with only a small pocketknife to protect himself. He seemed from his letters home to enjoy himself immensely.

But his letters home recounted more than grizzly bears and pocketknives. A concern for the relationship between God and the world was never far from his thoughts. After regaling one reader with his wilderness exploits, he abruptly shifted topics. "Now to your catechism: Does God make direct revelations to men now? Did he of old, then why not now? Does not the personality of God imply it? In some sense I think it does, and that a kind of *latent* pantheism is a considerable ground of unbelief on the subject, which latent pantheism reaches farther than is commonly supposed." All during his years of travel seeking bodily health, he reflected and mused on the questions of the supernatural and God's relationship to the world. At one point in his California stay he heard a story which seemed to suggest that the heavens were not as silent as some thought. While in the Napa Valley he met a trapper named Captain Yount who told of an event six or seven years earlier. During a mid-winter night the trapper had a dream in which he saw a group of travelers caught in the snowy mountains, perishing from the elements. The dream seemed remarkably real. He awoke, yet when he fell back asleep the dream returned. The next morning he recounted the dream to a friend, who recognized the scene described as a spot in the Sierra Mountains by the Carson Valley Pass. Immediately the captain raised a party, and despite the incredulity of some, sought out the spot. There they found stranded travelers exactly as pictured in the dream. Another person, hearing the story along with Bushnell, corroborated its accuracy. "We Californians all know the facts, and the names of the families brought in, who now look on our venerable friend as a kind of savior." California would leave its mark on Bushnell.

Despite his labors he succeeded in neither of the tasks he undertook for the fledgling institution that would become the University of California. He proposed five sites, but none of them was finally chosen. Likewise, though he enthusiastically pushed the cause of the new university in a number of articles, his call for an endowment of $300,000 was not achieved. It was not all Bushnell's fault. The years of 1857-58, the period of his activity, coincided with the Great Panic of 1857, in which the northern economy suffered its greatest blow since the collapse of 1837. The eastern individuals, to whom he principally appealed, could not respond.

As he readied to return east in January of 1857 he could reflect that although he had not accomplished all he had hoped, he had done much. He had seen the threat of barbarism up close and had done his part to thwart it. He had experienced a haunting new land, and its memory would continue to be with him. He had achieved a certain modicum of health. And, finally, he had finished his reflections on the supernatural and was ready to make them public.

WHERE IS GOD IN THE WORLD?

Before discussing the work in which Bushnell published those reflections, however, it is helpful to have some background. The issue of the supernatural that had so captivated him for a number of years was complex and had a long history. His frequent lament that the present age lacked the immediate encounter with the Spirit recorded in the apostolic age was not original. Rather, it rested on an age-old question: what was the relation of the present life of the church to the world of the New Testament?

Key to this issue were the mighty acts of God. The Bible was filled with records of signs and wonders, usually called miracles. They accompanied the Israelites in the wilderness and the struggles of prophets such as Elijah, and they were particularly present in the ministry of Jesus. But whether or not they continued to be present in the life of the church was a point of controversy. Some parts of Scripture implied that miracles were to continue; for example, Jesus promised his followers that "He who believes in me will also do the works that I do, and greater works than these he will do." Other passages suggested the opposite; in 1 Corinthians 13 Paul suggested that the lesser gifts (such as miracles) would pass away.

Since the sixteenth century Protestants and Catholics had differed markedly over this question. Catholics saw the presence of miracles as a sign of holiness, and from the end of the tenth century miracles were a key element in cases of canonization. Their occurrence indicated sanctity in the case of individuals, and their presence testified to the faithfulness of the community. A true church manifested miracles. As one Catholic writer explained, "they cannot be among the adversaries of the true church and [show] that the true church is among us." Protestants took a very different position. Miracles, for them, witnessed to the authority of the Scriptures. Moses and the prophets performed miracles to show that their message was from God. Jesus was to be believed because he did works like no others. To the Roman Catholic taunt asking the Protestants where their miracles were, the reformer John Calvin could reply that Protestants needed no new miracles because they had no new revelation. When revelation was complete the signs and wonders departed. The age of miracles was limited and purposeful. Scripture was now the way God communicated to the faithful. This supposition lay behind Charles Hodge's bitter criticism of Bushnell's view of nonbiblical inspiration or illumination in *God in Christ*. Communication, for Hodge, came only through the Word.

The Protestant understanding had another important consequence: according to it, God no longer acted directly *upon* nature — that is, as a primary cause — but now worked *through* nature, as a secondary cause. Any divine action in the world could now be understood only as an act of providence. Providential actions were divine acts through the laws of nature. They could be acts of "general providence," blessings given to all through the ordering of nature, such as the gifts of food and sunlight; they could also be "special providences" directed to specific individuals. A piece of driftwood floating by a drowning man could rightfully be seen as an answer to a particular prayer, as could (at least among English Protestants) the storm that dispersed the Spanish Armada. But even here a providence never interrupted the regular course of nature. God worked through nature rather than interfering with it. All claims of later miracles, such as those made by Catholics, were dismissed out of hand. They arose from ignorance, superstition, priestly chicanery, or some combination of all three.

The Protestant belief that miracles occurred only in the distant past and Protestants' view of physical nature governed by natural law were a great boon for the developing scientific view of nature. A physical universe organized by law was a knowable and predictable universe, and throughout the eighteenth century English-speaking Protestants boasted of the close marriage between science and true Protestant Christianity. By Bushnell's day, however, the marriage was anything but happy. As knowledge of physical nature became clearer and clearer, the divine reality lying behind it became more and more problematic. To what degree was God necessary? Could the world not be understood in merely mechanical terms? Even more, if the scientific picture of the world was accurate, to what degree could one speak intelligibly of God ever intervening in the course of nature? In the middle of the eighteenth century the Scottish philosopher David Hume had called into question the credibility of miracles in general and the Protestant belief in ancient miracles in particular. Against the former he argued that the knowledge of the laws of nature was always more reliable than any claim that a law of nature had been broken by a miracle. Against the latter he observed that the historical evidence for modern miracle claims — one example he offered was a series of extraordinary healings in eighteenth-century France associated with the Abbé François de Pâris — was in fact much stronger than the evidence for any biblical miracle, yet Protestants rejected these modern claims out of hand. Were miracles then ever credible? Perhaps in response, out of Germany came new ways of interpreting the Bible that either explained away the miracles of Scripture or dismissed them as myth or legend. Finally, an even deeper question emerged: What did it mean to speak of the supernatural? What constituted the reality outside of nature?

It was in this context that interest in pantheism arose. Pantheism "solved" the problem of the relationship between God and nature by a bold reconceptualization. God was not outside of nature, but rather God and nature were one reality. Nature was alive with the divine breath. Early in the century the German theologian Friedrich Schleiermacher had taken up pantheism's cause to challenge the mechanistic model of reality fancied in the eighteenth century. God was not an external watchmaker, separate from the world, but was the very source of being. God and nature were united, meaning God was in the world, particularly in the human soul. The soul truly existed in God. The idea that the spirit of the divine permeated all became the message of the American Transcendentalists, particularly Ralph Waldo Emerson and Theodore Parker, and lay behind their attack on the traditional understanding of the miraculous. Because Christians erred in dividing God from the world they needed miracles to reintroduce him; once one had a true understanding of the relationship between God and the world miracles were unnecessary. "One mind is everywhere active," Emerson explained, "in each ray of the star, in each wavelet of the pool." The Christian view of miracle, he went on, was a "monster"; it rendered God's presence unnatural, "not one with the blowing clover and the falling rain." Parker was even more explicit in his criticism. He divided the religious world into three parts: "Naturalism" banned the divine from the world, turning the universe into a dead machine. "Supernaturalism" reduced the activity of God to ancient times. This condemned the modern age to possess but a tiny fraction of the divine power. The present generation, "born in the latter days and dotage of mankind . . . can only get light by raking amid the ashes of the past, and blowing its brands, now almost extinct." In contrast to both he offered the idea of a pantheistic "spiritualism" in which God was present in all reality.

The idea of pantheism was further stimulated by increasing knowledge of the religions of the East, particularly Hinduism. Hinduism taught that there was one all-pervasive deity, Brahman, that energized the whole universe and was present in all things. Brahman therefore Transcended any form of personhood. Like the pantheism espoused by the transcendentalists, Hinduism offered not a personal God who loved and willed and was spoken of in personal language, but rather a force or spirit present in all creation.

If intellectuals questioned the value of the supernatural or dabbled in pantheism, those on a more popular level found the supernatural alive and well. Despite the elaborate Protestant argument for an age of limited miracles and a reduction of divine action to providence, for many ordinary persons the age of wonders had not passed. Indeed, nineteenth-century America seemed at times awash with wonders. From the soil of New England Joseph Smith arose with his claim of new revelation and the recovery of lost religion. The Mormons found the supernatural very real and alive. Closer to Bushnell's Hartford was the rise of spiritualism.

In 1847-48 rumors had begun to fly in upstate New York that strange things were happening in the home of John D. Fox and his family. A strange rapping was heard in the house and two of Fox's daughters — Katherine (age twelve) and Margaret (age fourteen) — came to believe that the source of the sound was spirits of the deceased. By asking questions (in a yes or no format) they claimed they could communicate with the departed. The fame, or notoriety, of the two sisters quickly spread, and despite the controversy that surrounded it spiritualism clearly touched a nerve. The great question of what happened to the soul after death could now be answered, the spiritualists claimed; death was not followed by judgment, heaven, or hell but by continued existence.

Spiritualism attracted many, including Horace Greeley, publisher of the *New York Tribune*, but one of its most vocal supporters was Andrew Jackson Davis. Davis's religious experience had been very different from that of the typical American Puritan-Evangelical. Born in poverty, he had little formal education, developed an interest in clairvoyance early on, and in the 1840s claimed to have undergone an out-of-body experience and to have discovered the philosophy of Emanuel Swedenborg and its idea of multiple planes of spiritual reality. Davis combined his speculations with interest in spiritual communication, healing, and societal reform. He was popularized by another Swedenborgian (and former Presbyterian), George Bush, who wrote a column for the *New York Tribune*. When Davis heard of the rappings he became excited. He saw the experience of the Fox sisters as a testimony to his beliefs and strongly advocated their claims. As fate would have it his base of operations in the early 1850s was Hartford.

What to do with the supernatural became a pressing question by mid century. The old Protestant model of the limited age of miracles seemed to be out of date. But what alternative might replace it? Naturalism? Pantheism? Spiritualism?

As we have seen, much of *God in Christ* had been a criticism of dogmatic school theology in the name of religion. Bushnell's critics might focus on his views on the atonement, the Trinity, and language, but for Bushnell the fundamental issue was the reality of faith. So in the winter of 1851-52, as his opponents in Fairfield West piled up evidence against him for the next battle at the General Association, Bushnell had begun to speak on the question of the supernatural. He had been invited to give the Dudleien Lectures at Harvard later in 1852, but in December of 1851 he offered the first two of a series of four lectures on Christian revelation. The *Religious Herald* praised them for their thoughtfulness, particularly in the understanding of the supernatural they outlined. As Bushnell pointed out in the lectures, the very nature of the supernatural was will — not only divine will but human will itself. When will interrupted the course of nature, there one found a supernatural act. "Nature never furnished such a thing as gunpowder, or pulled a trigger," he explained. Hence the idea of supernatural activity in the world had to be conceived of far more broadly than it heretofore had been.

In the audience at that first lecture was Andrew Jackson Davis. He responded to it in a tract he entitled *The Approaching Crisis*. He lauded Bushnell for his willingness to take up the fundamental questions of the time. Referring to him as the "Martin Luther" of his age who called his orthodox brethren to a new set of ideas, he praised the boldness of *God in Christ*. Nevertheless, Bushnell's lectures on supernaturalism were, according to Davis, ultimately a failure. He noted that when all was cleared away Bushnell was ultimately a conservative. He wanted to show that miracles, the incarnation, redemption, special providence, and prayer were all consistent with the principles of nature. But he failed to address the fact that spiritualists had already reconciled these great truths by liberating them from their biblical anchor. Bushnell was a conservative because he would not jettison the Bible in favor of the "Christ Principle," which for spiritualists was the hidden metaphysical truth of Christianity. Being tied to the Bible he could not fairly evaluate the myriad of supernatural occurrences being set forth in spiritualism. For Davis the old religion was dying. Catholics attempted to maintain it by idealizing the saints, while Protestants tried to idealize the Bible, but both were ultimately failures.

Particularly in the latter part of his tract Davis focused less and less on Bushnell and more and more on his own teachings, but the issue he raised was real, and was in some ways the same issue raised by the conservative critics of *God in Christ*, albeit from the other end of the spectrum. Was it possible to pour the new wine of Bushnell's insights into the old wineskins of the inherited Scripture? Would it burst the old? Did not new ideas demand new wineskins?

All this preceded Bushnell's publication of *Nature and the Supernatural* in 1857. In his ideas on the supernatural Bushnell was playing the role of the Yankee Puritan even more boldly than in *God in Christ*, tinkering with traditionally accepted notions of revelation, nature, inspiration, and the supernatural in order to better anchor them in changing times. His agenda was adventurous. But would it be effective?

PUTTING GOD BACK IN THE WORLD

Nature and the Supernatural included all Bushnell's ruminations on the supernatural and related subjects and reflected many of the pastoral concerns he had been expressing for almost a decade. To have a sure experience of the reality of the supernatural was, Bushnell believed, the great need of the day. In a letter to his daughter he explained,

> We should most naturally expect that God would not hide himself from his creatures. . . . The infidels have said, 'If there be a God, why does he not show himself? Is there anything so important to man to know as God? Why, then, is this kept so ambiguous and dark, when other things are clear?' Are they not right, — that is, right so far as they assume the certainty that a living God will show himself the living God?

The volume also indirectly responded to other issues. Perhaps smarting from the earlier allegations of pantheism and his unasked-for association with religious radicals, Bushnell took specific aim against pantheism, D. F. Strauss, and Theodore Parker. Moreover, he recognized that the supernatural could not be divorced from the specific question of miracles but argued that older arguments had to be set aside in favor of new understandings.

Nature and the Supernatural can be divided into three sections: one that dealt with the theoretical question, one that dealt with the figure of Jesus, and one that addressed the question of post-biblical miracles. From the outset Bushnell acknowledged that the Christian faith found itself confronted with the great challenge of the "new infidelity" that attempted to strip it of its supernatural content. Not only skeptics and philosophers, but almost all aspects of modern life — business, medicine, politics — seemed to war against the idea of the supernatural. The great challenge for the church was to defend the reality of the supernatural. Here, however, it was hampered by a common misconception that had grown up about the supernatural. Earlier apologists had been so careful in protecting and isolating the supernatural that they had ironically succeeded in making it "too fantastic and ghostly to admit a possible defence." Bushnell preferred to cast a very broad net around the supernatural. He defined it, as he had earlier, as that which was not in the chain of natural cause and effect, or anything which acted upon cause and effect from without. The essence of the supernatural was will or freedom. He offered as an analogy the relationship between a ball and a child. The ball was like nature, passive and dumb, and completely dependent upon outside forces for its location and movement. The child was like a supernatural force, who through will (or, in this case, kick) influenced the ball and sent it in a trajectory that left to itself it would never have accomplished. The supernatural acted upon the natural in this same way; when it intervened in the course of the natural it endowed the latter with new thrust and direction. For Bushnell human beings as moral agents were in themselves supernatural beings and even such an action as the lifting up of an arm could be viewed as an example of a supernatural triumph of will over nature. The power of personality and character to move and affect and indeed even to change the course of nature and history testified to this supernatural basis.

Yet if human beings had the power to affect the natural, so even more did God. God, like humanity, when he chose could "kick" nature and give it a new force and direction. For evidence Bushnell appealed to the biological theory of the Harvard scientist Louis Agassiz, the leading American biologist during the time Bushnell composed *Nature and the Supernatural*. Agassiz's explanation for the development of species was a series of special creations accomplished by God; "whole realms of living creatures disappear again and again, to be succeeded by others fresh from the hand of God." These divine interventions within the course of nature, which changed the course of life, were the divine "kicks." Yet they were more than mere acts of will; they flowed from the divine nature. They were God's response to a fallen world and disordered humanity — a response that strove to produce what no mere law of nature could ever bring about. Supernatural interventions were part of the great goal of bringing forth the new creation.

The second part of *Nature and the Supernatural* focused on the figure of Jesus. For Bushnell, one recalls, all character was supernatural, yet the character of Jesus was qualitatively superior to that of any other human being. In this section Bushnell broke decisively with the old argument that tied Jesus' authority to his performance of miracles, arguing that it was through his character that Christ's true nature was revealed.

> He comes into the world full of all moral beauty, as God of physical [beauty]; and as God was not obliged to set himself to a course of aesthetic study, when he created the forms and landscapes of the world, so Christ comes to his rules, by no critical practice in words. . . . He does not dress up a moral picture and ask you to observe its beauty, he only tells you how to live; and the most beautiful characters the world has ever seen, have been those who received and lived his precepts without once conceiving their beauty.

The character of Christ revealed in the Gospels was the greatest of miracles, Bushnell argued. Through it one could see a living embodiment of the gospel message of love, moral beauty, and virtue. This claim would reverberate throughout a generation of Protestant liberals, and is often used to support Bushnell's appellation as father of American liberalism. But one should note that Bushnell, by linking Christ's authority to his character rather than to his miracles, far from rejecting biblical miracles in fact gave them new credence. Most immediately Bushnell argued that Jesus' character and moral beauty confirmed his miracles and established a moral distinction between his miracles and purported pagan and Roman Catholic miracles. True miracles had to be both physical (i.e., stemming from the intervention of a superhuman force within nature) and moral. But Bushnell went further, venturing to suggest a new understanding of the purpose of miracles in the divine economy. Their role lay not in validating revelation, but more properly in the practical certainty they offered of the reality of a transcendent God. As he noted, "There is no way to escape the faith of miracles and hold the faith of a personal God and Creator." They served for Bushnell as vivid reminders of the power of the supernatural and the limitations of the natural order.

Bushnell was singularly eloquent in his description of the personality of Jesus as the chief evidence of his supernatural nature. Chapter ten of *Nature and the Supernatural*, "The Character of Jesus Forbidding His Possible Classification with Men," quickly became the most heralded part of the volume and one of the best-known parts of Bushnell's entire corpus. It was later often reprinted as a separate volume. As one early commentator noted, "It has the finish of a classic, and by frequent republication has already become one."

The final section of the volume was also its most controversial. Bushnell's new understanding of the purpose of miracles led him to question the long-cherished Protestant rejection of post-biblical miracles. For him, the traditional position was fundamentally flawed, since, "If miracles are inherently incredible . . . nothing is gained by thrusting them back into remote ages of time." Hence in chapter fourteen of his work Bushnell set forth his claim that miracles, far from having been suspended, have occurred at all times in Christian history. Post-biblical miracles served the same function as biblical miracles in emphasizing the reality of a supernatural deity. Since they were "to lift the church out of the abysses of a mere second-hand religion, keeping it alive and open to the realities of God's immediate visitation," they were appropriate during any age.

Underlying Bushnell's claim was a fundamentally different picturing of sacred history than that usually employed by Protestant apologists. Instead of positing an apostolic age of miracles that stood in contradistinction to all that followed, Bushnell offered a dialectical understanding of the activity of the divine in sacred history. The Christian community historically fluctuated between periods of extreme rationalism, during which times God's role in the world was largely ignored, and periods of a hyper-supernaturalism — or "Corinthianism" — during which times miracles, signs, and wonders were sought after as ends in themselves. The propriety of miracles varied according to the age. During periods of oppressive rationalism God "break[s] forth in miracle and holy gifts, [to] let it be seen that he is still the living God, in the midst of his dead people." Conversely during times of excess, when the "sobriety of faith is lost in the gossip of credulity," miracles, signs, and wonders tended to decline. The dialectic, however, had been for some time interrupted by the increasingly rigid Protestant rejection of post-biblical miracles.

This rejection caused, in turn, two negative effects. One was that Protestant commentators were now forced to employ skeptical arguments in their rejection of modern miracles. He used as an example the debate that occurred over the manifestation of healings and glossolalia in Scotland in the 1830s. Protestant skeptics were forced to take "precisely the [same] ground as Mr. Hume, as respects the credibility of miracles performed now" — i.e., that any other explanation was more probable than the miraculous. A second negative effect was that Protestants' adamancy increasingly left them with only a secondhand religion that provided no outlet for the natural human craving for the supernatural. Perhaps with Andrew Jackson Davis in mind, Bushnell observed that modern individuals, with nowhere within the church to turn, had begun seeking the modern "sorcery" of animal magnetism, spiritualism, and ghosts.

Turning from the theoretical issue, Bushnell proceeded to offer a reassessment of several post-Reformation miracle claims. Reaching back to the seventeenth century, he looked favorably on John Howie's accounts of the Scottish covenanters' spiritual premonitions, divine judgments, and providential escapes. He was similarly positive concerning the healings recorded in George Fox's *Journal*, the charismatic gifts exhibited by the "French Prophets" in early-eighteenth-century England, and the healings associated with the Abbé Pâris, which Hume had described. All of these examples, according to Bushnell, possessed the proper combination of moral character and supernaturalism that merited classifying them as modern miracles.

Bushnell also displayed keen interest in the outbreaks of glossolalia and miraculous healings in Scotland in the early 1830s associated with the brothers James and George MacDonald. Indeed, Bushnell, the theoretician on language, seemed to find great significance in modern glossolalia:

> [T]here is . . . sublimity in this gift of tongues, as related to the great mystery of language; suggesting possibly, that all our tongues are from the Eternal Word, in souls; there being, in his intelligent nature as Word, millions doubtless of possible tongues, that are as real to him as the spoken tongues of the world.

Since all language was symbolic and proximate in meaning, Bushnell found nothing scandalous about this direct language of the Spirit. On the contrary, these outbursts, with the Spirit "playing the vocal organs of a man," demonstrated the power of the supernatural. The Eternal Spirit when it chose could overwhelm the limitations of human discourse just as easily as it overwhelmed the limitations of physical nature through miraculous healings.

Bushnell concluded his discussion by offering a series of present-day miracle accounts which he himself had gathered. He included the story of the dream that led to the rescue at the Carson Valley Pass as well as descriptions of further occurrences of glossolalia and healings. Lastly, Bushnell related an experience of his own in which an uneducated former slave with "a message from the Lord" gave him prophetic rebuke and direction. All of these occurrences, argued Bushnell, testified that miracles were as omnipresent in the modern era as they had ever been.

Bushnell's openness to modern miracles was viewed as a scandal at the time and was criticized soundly. Similarly, sympathetic students in later years have usually dismissed his interest in miracles as product of his unsophisticated philosophical categories. As one biographer explained, "a full doctrine of the divine immanence would have rendered needless many brilliant pages." We should nonetheless pause, however, before unqualifiedly accepting a picture of Bushnell as a frustrated liberal, condemned by his ignorance of divine immanence from ever realizing the true implications of his thought. For if Bushnell was here, as usual, not a logically rigorous thinker, we should not underestimate his sensitivity as a *religious* analyst. Bushnell's defense of modern miracles seems to have been no mere intellectual speculation but to have stemmed from an awareness of the religious state of his parishioners. This practical consideration is reflected in the final chapter of *Nature and the Supernatural*, where he hinted at the pastoral advantages of his view of miracles.

One advantage was the value of miracles in highlighting the reality of the divine and in serving as a continual reminder that the God worshiped in church was not some dead "metallic meteor" but a vital and active power. And, indeed, if the intellectual question of the second half of the nineteenth century was the reconciliation of the old Scripture and beliefs with the new learning, an important popular theme of religion during this period was the quest for the certainty of a transcendent reality or the vitality of the spiritual world. What evidence did modern believers have that God was real and personal? Throughout *Nature and the Supernatural* Bushnell argued that a religion that had lost its confidence that God acted in the course of history and nature would inevitably succumb to lassitude or to that "latent pantheism" he so sharply attacked. This belief lay behind his sharp critique of Emerson and Parker, for whom belief in an omnipresent spirit rendered embarrassing the idea of divine intervention that was immediate and personal. No matter how intellectually neat or interesting the pantheism of the Transcendentalists might be, Bushnell the pastor considered it religiously disastrous. Emerson had rescued the immanence of God through his pantheistic mysticism but had sacrificed God's active personality. Bushnell thus dismissed Emerson's transcendentalism as "Bramanism," which might delight the aesthetic impulse but had no transforming power. Immanence was not in itself enough; God must be present both in human character and in wonders such as glossolalia, premonitions, and healings. Bushnell's concern with miracles hence reflected his larger concern with the reality of the transcendent.

Another pastoral advantage, according to Bushnell, was that an emphasis upon miracles and the supernatural activities of God in the world could reinvigorate the Christian community. The theme he had raised in "Dogma and Spirit" was now placed in a very different context. Just as Christianity was suffering from a diet of secondhand experientialism, so too did it suffer from secondhand knowledge. Natural theology, which culled nature for evidences of religious truths while ignoring the great outpouring of supernatural "facts" such as "dreams, prophecies, premonitions, visions" and the like, had led even orthodox theology down the road to pantheism. Natural theology would never provide evidence for a supernatural deity since no God could be proven by an appeal to nature except the God of nature.

201

Only the personal activity of God in the world could reveal God's personhood.

Clearly then, Bushnell's interest in the miraculous was central to both his understanding of the relationship between God and the world and his reconstruction of Christian theology. In certain ways it can be seen as a counterbalance to his views on language, for if his famous theory of language challenged the reigning biblical basis of Protestant theology, his theory of miracles appears to offer a new foundation. Writing before the great liberal/conservative fission over biblical inerrancy Bushnell argued that the supernatural truth of the Gospels lay not in "verbal inspiration," "no point of infallibility . . . so as to prick and fasten each particular iota," but instead upon the person of Christ, the reality of his miracles, and the power of the supernatural. Indeed, the continuing of supernatural occurrences in the modern age could provide a new empirical basis for Christian understanding. Though no longer linked to revelation as they had been in the old schema, miracles nonetheless did still reveal a spiritual reality:

> Christ comes into the world from without, to bestow himself by a presentation. He is a new premise, that could not be reasoned, but must first be, and then can be received only by faith. When he is so received or appropriated, he is, of course, experienced or known by experiment; in that manner verified — he that believeth hath the witness in himself. The manner, therefore, of this divine experience, called faith, is strictly Baconian. And the result is an experimental knowledge of God, or an experimental acquaintance with God, in the reception of his supernatural communications.

Hence, Christians need never be ashamed of religious experience and view it as somehow lower than philosophical knowledge. On the contrary, for Bushnell it was essential. Christian understanding based on supernatural experientialism could provide for the present age a firm foundation, one equally open to the educated and uneducated, to the rich and the poor, and serve as a new basis for Christian unity.

RADICAL REFORMULATIONS

What does one make of Bushnell's discussion? It is clear that he rejected the Old Protestant view of miracles and proposed in its place a new experientialism. He was never completely clear, however, about the nature of this experience, and since his examples ran the gamut from dynamic personalities to miraculous healings he left himself open to alternative interpretations. Part of this unclarity stems from his style, which was always more evocative than precise, but it was also caused by his use of a number of ambiguous concepts to defend his view of the supernatural.

One vague concept was his definition of the supernatural as a force acting upon causality and his further analogical linking of human will and divine will as both being supernatural powers. Contemporaries recognized the novelty of this assertion, and its problems. "There is no difficulty in proving that there is a God if men are gods, that there are angels if men are angels, that the Bible is inspired if all great writers are inspired, or that the supernatural exists if we ourselves are supernatural." Through such an argument one could conclude that the human will was elevated to the level of the supernatural. Yet read from another perspective, Bushnell's analogy is open to a very different interpretation, particularly when one considers what it implied about the nature of the divine will, which was seen to have complete freedom to intervene in the natural. This freedom to intervene lay behind the interest in contemporary miracles.

Bushnell's argument turned upon another radical reformulation, the de facto abandonment of the distinction between primary and secondary causality. The Protestant rejection of post-biblical miracles rested, as we have seen, upon a careful distinction between the categories of miracle and providence. Both were from God, but miracles were acts of primary cause, while providential events were of secondary cause. An event in which God intervened in nature (such as in turning water into wine) was a miracle. An event in which God worked through nature (such as guiding a floating branch to a drowning mariner) was merely providential. That distinction between miracle and providence had been crucial for earlier Protestant writers. But Bushnell was willing to toss it aside. The fact of divine intervention, not the method, was for him the benchmark of the miraculous. Accordingly, he lumped together all manner of occurrences in his discussion, from the character of a person like Cromwell to the healings of the Abbé Pâris. All could serve as evidence of the reality of the higher realm. Underlying this entire discussion, moreover, was a very different understanding of evidence. A key part of the old Protestant position had been that testimony of miracles, in contrast to that of other acts of providence, had an objective authority. This distinction between the subjective witness of acts of providence and the objective authority of miracles is abandoned here. The evidential value of all Bushnell's miracles became to a large degree personal and subjective. Few others might be convinced by Bushnell's account of a "message from the Lord" delivered to him by a freed slave, but for Bushnell its reality was unshakable.

Personal surety rather than public testimony was, for Bushnell, the purpose of supernatural occurrences. And from this idea two widely differing conclusions were drawn. For some readers this blending of primary and secondary causality and Bushnell's subjectivizing of the supernatural effectively removed the question of miracles from public discussion, or at best made any discussion of the miraculous a subset of the larger question of personal religious experience. Others, however, saw Bushnell's recasting of the discussion as justification for a far greater interest in miracles than there had been for centuries. Both are possible readings.

God in Christ and *Nature and the Supernatural* can be seen as bookend volumes, complementing each other. Both were bold reconceptualizations of longstanding assumptions. If Bushnell had spoken in lofty terms about the importance of the former volume, he was no more modest about the latter, seeing it as a pebble tossed into the ocean, generating ever enlarging ripples. But he also feared that it, like the earlier book, might be in advance of the age. "My day has not yet come," he wrote, "and will not until after I am gone." The most important thing about these two volumes, however, is that taken together the two works reversed a three-hundred-year Protestant presupposition about religious authority and confidence. Since the middle of the sixteenth century Protestants (and particularly those of the Reformed tradition) had put more and more emphasis on Scripture. "Sola Scriptura" became for them the belief that through the Bible alone all true divine knowledge was received. Charles Hodge put the idea most bluntly: "The Bible is to the theologian," he explained, "what nature is to the man of science." Bushnell's theory of language called this assumption into question; the inexactitude of language meant that the Bible could no longer function in that way.

But what Bushnell took away with one hand in *God in Christ*, he restored with the other in *Nature and the Supernatural*. God and humanity were brought closer by, and knowledge of God could be gained through, the work of the Holy Spirit. Although there had been those in the Reformation and post-Reformation eras, such as George Fox and the early Quakers, who spoke of continuing revelation, they were usually dismissed by "proper theologians." For Bushnell, in the continuing of signs, wonders, and inspirations, God communicated to the world. In this way Bushnell prefigured the great Pentecostal revival of the twentieth century, which claimed that the charismatic gifts spoken of by Paul in 1 Corinthians and exercised in the early church were still available to the church. The present experience of God was what gave life to the historical communication; precisely because God continued to reveal himself at present one could be sure — contra a skeptic like Strauss — that he had already revealed himself in the pages of Scripture. Bushnell felt that the battleground between belief and unbelief in the modern age rested not in the past but in the present. If an assurance of divine action in the world could be secured in the present, the ancient revelations could rest easy. But if the divine action refused to be recognized in the present, then the record of the past would slowly but·surely ebb away.

PLEASING NO ONE

Was then Bushnell in *Nature and the Supernatural* the father of theological liberalism or of Pentecostalism? The difficulty with such a question is that there are elements of both present, and living as he did before the great divide he did not feel compelled to make a choice. To see how these two elements could blend together one must look at one final work of Bushnell's, the sermon "Christ Waiting to Find Room" from his collection *Christ and His Salvation.*

The sermon begins with an account of the nativity, with Mary and Joseph unable to find a place in the inn and forced to stay in the stable. But, said Bushnell, the failure to find a place for Jesus was not a problem only in the biblical era. He noted that the church was all too often like the inn in Bethlehem — preoccupied and crowded — so it commonly failed to receive Christ. The spiritual power Christ offered had never been taken up: Constantine in the fourth century offered worldly power but provided no place for the gifts of the Spirit. During the Middle Ages elaborate ceremonial engulfed the space Christ wanted for his own. But neither did the Reformation allow Christ truly to enter. The Reformers cluttered their minds and souls with dogmas. Such a line of argument — condemning both ceremonial and dogma — was to be expected from Bushnell, but he went on. Modern liberalism finally overthrew the old dogmas, but when "emancipated souls look for a new Christianity and a broader, worthier faith . . . the gospel vanishes even more strangely than before." The Holy Spirit becomes reduced to the laws of the soul, the "incarnation, the miracles . . . are stifled as extravagances," and a "new Christianity" emerges in which "nothing is left for a gospel but development, with a little human help from the very excellent person, Jesus." Modern liberalism found even less place for the power of the Spirit than had ceremonialism and dogmatism.

Against all of this he protested. What was wanted was neither dogma nor liberalism but that firsthand experience of the early generations. The power was still available and could be claimed. Sounding surprisingly like Charles Finney he claimed, "True there is no grace of Christ that will suddenly make us perfect; but there is a grace that will take away all conscious sinning, as long as we sufficiently believe." All of this would happen if believers allowed a place in their souls for Christ.

As is evident, on the level of doctrine, and particularly in his view of creeds, Bushnell contributed to the breaking up of the old theological order of New England. Yet in other ways he was a final flowering of a remarkably inclusive Christian imagination before theological divisions splintered the religious community at the end of the century. Bushnell sometimes sounds like a liberal or a proto-Pentecostal, or like a proponent of the Holiness movement, because ideas held by all of them were part of his understanding of the supernatural. Ironically, the reason *Nature and the Supernatural* did not have more impact was that it could not easily be appropriated by any of the later movements: Fundamentalists balked at his interest in glossolalia; Holiness-Pentecostals found his elevation of the human will to the level of the supernatural troubling; liberals were embarrassed by his interest in miracles. The work satisfied no one.

But *Nature and the Supernatural* was perhaps the most ambitious of Bushnell's works of theology. And it showed him at his Puritan best. Scholars have increasingly noted that despite the formal rejection of ecclesiastical miracles, there was in seventeenth-century Puritanism a fascination with wonder-working providence. Almost two hundred years earlier the Puritan minister Increase Mather, in *An Essay for the Recording of Illustrious Providences . . . Especially in New England,* had, like Bushnell, carefully collected the wonders and marvels that had occurred in New England to show that God was present among his people. Bushnell, in *Nature and the Supernatural,* tried to revive that sense of closeness.

Even though his tinkering was accepted by very few, he could look with satisfaction on his work. In it God and the world had been brought closer, God's personality was exalted, and the religious experience of humankind was uplifted. Though *Nature and the Supernatural* would be taken up only in parts, it would remain Bushnell's masterpiece.

9 Slavery, War, and Sacrifice

A NEW ENGLAND pastor in the mid nineteenth century was not a narrowly religious officer. The long tradition of the minister as leading citizen and active social figure, engaged in the larger social good, still held sway. The clergy's role was to highlight the great questions of the day, focusing concern upon not the immediate and political but the moral and foundational. Bushnell was no exception, and in the years following the publication of *Nature and the Supernatural* he found himself increasingly taking on this role as his ministry entered a new phase. Whether advancing universities or planning city parks, he regularly involved himself in the concerns of the greater community, and as a social commentator he would endeavor to help make sense of the great issues of the day, particularly those of slavery and the Civil War.

A MINISTRY AT LARGE

The flowering of Bushnell's broader pastoral focus coincided with the ending of his pastoral connection with North Church. For twenty-six years he had ministered to them and they had remained loyal to him, but his continuing throat problems made it clear that he could no longer serve as their full-time pastor. In April of 1859 he submitted his resignation and on July 3 he offered his "Parting Words." He assured his parishioners that he would continue to "prosecute . . . objects and themes of study that appear to me to have no secondary importance," but that his main ministry would now be through the pen. "I hope to support a fractional ministry by the press, when I cannot the full routine of the pastoral office."

Thus began what one biographer has called Bushnell's "Ministry at Large." Even with his new ministry, however, Bushnell could not forget his nagging health problems. After his resignation he traveled to Minnesota, which was then gaining a reputation as a spot salubrious to throat sufferers. There Bushnell fished, rode, "loafed," and occasionally preached. But the lack of a domestic life pained him. Eventually he was joined by his wife, which eased his growing sense of loneliness, but these were difficult months for the Bushnells. The separation from family and friends in the East was difficult. So too was determining what Bushnell's wider ministry might be and where it could be located. They considered a number of places, including even taking up farming in Minnesota, before deciding to return to Hartford. Mary Bushnell returned in the summer of 1860 to secure a residence. Bushnell decided to delay his final return and try the water cure at a spa at Clifton Springs, New York. He stayed there until the spring of 1861 and spent much of his time making plans for the future. His letters home reflected concerns for both his physical health and the nation as it lumbered toward division.

Finally he did return. One pleasant note was that he began to sense a warmer relationship with his fellow clergy. Throughout the 1850s his Congregationalist colleagues had continued to refuse to exchange pulpits, adding to the physical strain on him, since clergy exchanged pulpits to reuse sermons originally delivered to their home congregations. Upon Bushnell's return, however, the new pastor of Second Church Hartford, Edwin P. Parker, began to open his church to him. The young Parker had recently faced the fury of the Hartford Central conservatives, and his installation at Second Church had been publicly attacked. Parker saw Bushnell as a hero in the struggle for doctrinal flexibility and would become a good friend and later an early biographer. The vision of a ministry at large was slowly becoming clearer.

RECKONING WITH THE "PECULIAR INSTITUTION"

If Bushnell were a remarkably sensitive observer on questions of religion, often seeing below the surface and usually being a few steps
ahead of his listeners, the same could not be said for him as a social
critic. Here he was an amateur, strongly influenced by his regional culture. The influence of the Connecticut of his youth — with its tightly
knit, well-ordered community with the church at the center — shaped
his understanding of a good society. This predilection made him critical of many aspects of the society of the time and would eventually
contribute to his powerful analysis of the Civil War, but it would also
shape other opinions and judgments; and to those who do not share
his background some of these ideas can seem odd and jarring.

Nowhere is this predilection more clearly seen than in his reflections on the problem of slavery. Slavery was, of course, the great national issue during the middle decades of the nineteenth century. During the early decades of the century many hoped that the "peculiar
institution" could be ended gradually and painlessly by means of colonization, a system by which freed slaves were to be transported back
to Africa to establish a Christian commonwealth there. But by the late
1820s most admitted that colonization was a failure. Furthermore,
with the increased dependence on slavery by Southern cotton grow-
ers, slavery was becoming a key cause of sectional friction. In response
to the failure of colonization a far more intense abolitionist movement
emerged. Much of its moral fire was fueled by a shifting of categories.
It began to be argued that slavery was not merely a social and political
blot on the republic, but a sin. Indeed, it was an inherently sinful institution — a *malum in se,* to use the technical language of the time. Wherever a slave relationship existed — irrespective of the conditions and
meliorations — the relationship was sinful and the slave owner was as
much a sinner as if he were committing adultery. This led some abolitionists to call for the exclusion of slaveholders from communion, just
as any other notorious sinner would be excluded. In addition, since
the institution of slavery was inherently sinful it needed to be ended
immediately; just as the advocates of temperance called for total absti-
nence or the immediate rejection of all alcoholic beverages, so too did
critics of slavery begin to call for immediate emancipation. The gradu-
alism that colonization implied — along with its expectation that slave

owners would be remunerated for their losses — was cast aside, and the reinvigorated opponents of slavery called for a crusade against the institution.

The crusade of the abolitionists has been praised by later historians who have seen in the crusaders' heroic stance the stirring of the nation's conscience. To many at the time, however, particularly during the 1830s, these abolitionists were viewed as radical rabble-rousers, disturbing the peace of the nation out of a blind fanaticism. Slavery might not be a good institution, sober and conservative Northern commentators admitted, and one might wish that it did not exist, but it was deeply embedded in the culture of the Southern states. The actions of the abolitionists only inflamed Southern fears, making them even more defensive of their "peculiar institution," and threatened the unity of the nation.

Bushnell shared the attitudes of conservative Northerners on both slavery and abolition. Although he had touched on the issue in his first published sermon, "Crisis of the Church" (1835), he first fully addressed it in his 1839 *Discourse on the Slavery Question*. In the *Discourse* he posed two questions: was abolition a duty of Southern legislators, and what was the duty of Northerners? As a New Englander he shared his region's suspicions about the South and its folkways, including the institution of slavery, but the disruptive presence of abolitionists seemed to him the more pressing concern. He noted that anti-slavery sentiment was rising but that the abolitionists advocated measures with "which I have never been quite able to harmonize." Part of his problem with them was the violence of the rhetoric they used against slaveholders. Words such as "pirates" and "man-stealers" might gratify proponents of the *malum in se* argument but did little to clarify the issues at hand. Such rhetoric was "mere indiscriminate raving." Indeed, Southerners merited sympathy over their plight. "If there was ever a people on earth involved in crime, and yet deserved sympathy and gentleness at the hands of the good, it is the slave-holding portion of our country."

Nevertheless, slavery was an institution ultimately at odds with the spirit of the nation and the spirit of the age. All throughout the world the movement was toward a breaking up of old social structures and a free citizenry. Furthermore, as he had argued earlier, slavery had a destructive influence on republican character. Instead of inculcating a respect for the law, slavery taught the slave subservience and the master a violent willfulness, "strong and imperious passions and a general impatience of restraint." Slavery was clearly a corrupting element in national life.

In view of all this, Bushnell argued that its extinction was inevitable, even without the agitation of anti-slavery advocates. In the interim the institution needed to be reformed, and he singled out three particularly odious elements in American slavery. The first was the denial of family life. By not allowing slaves to marry, no true families could be formed, which resulted in "the cattle-state imported into humanity." The second was the lack of regard for the physical well-being of the slave with respect to life, limb, and chastity. Although technically there were laws on the books to protect slaves, they were virtually unenforceable since a slave could not testify in a court of law. Finally, Bushnell condemned the failure to recognize in the slave a moral or intellectual nature. "He exists for another; — in himself he is no man." Thus the citizenry of the nation needed to say to the South, "Establish among your slaves the family state, defend their bodies, do it in a way to satisfy God and humanity, and we ask no more." But, he added, when this finally happened, slavery would be doomed. Once slaves began to be treated as moral and intellectual creatures, Southerners would find it impossible to tolerate the condition of slavery "without sweeping away the whole institution down to the very roots." Slaves would become a free peasantry and their final emancipation would be a day of universal rejoicing.

With the ultimate demise of slavery assured, Bushnell argued, Northerners faced the present responsibility of continuing to exert a moral pressure without antagonizing the South. They must recognize Southern fears and assure Southerners that until slavery was finally extinguished Northerners would continue to honor the lawfulness of the institution and their obligation to support their Southern countrymen in the case of a slave revolt. Northerners must understand that slavery was an issue that Southerners themselves had to address. Congress could act to ban slavery from the District of Columbia, but that was all. One needed to allow the inevitable course of history to work its way. Anti-slavery activists, Bushnell believed, hurt the cause of emancipation. In their confrontational stance they alienated Southerners, erroneously believing that Southerners could be bullied to free their slaves in the same way temperance advocates bullied shop own-ers to ban the sale of alcohol. Such an attitude was not only ineffective but contrary to the spirit of the Gospel. "They . . . forget (as too many were doing, in temperance and other movements, just at that time) that it is not the spirit of Christianity to drive or put down, but, where it may be, to conciliate, draw, and lead." Anti-slavery advocates alien-ated not only Southerners but moderate Northerners as well. In their demand to exclude slaveholders from fellowship they divided churches, and in condemning as "dumb dogs" all sober and moderate clergy who would not take up their cause, they violated Christian charity. Many Northerners originally hopeful about colonization were now willing to consider other solutions, and there existed in the New England people a deep-seated dislike of slavery, which could provide the basis for a movement against it; but the presence of radical aboli-tionists kept a conservative opposition to slavery from emerging.

All of this was typical Northern conservative rhetoric, but unfor-tunately Bushnell did not stop here. He also offered some opinions on racial theory. Few things so separate modern sensibilities from earlier societies as attitudes toward racial theory. The demonic events of the twentieth century have aptly demonstrated how evil racial theory can be when acted upon, yet in the nineteenth century race theory was in the air, and Bushnell was always one to try on new ideas. He, like oth-ers of his era, often spoke of the vigor of the "Saxon race," and in his panegyrics to the Puritan founders of New England often spoke of their Saxon virtue. His observations from Europe and elsewhere showed that he had less respect for other races. Here in his *Discourse* he expressed little confidence in the eventual success of the freed blacks. Like others he saw the history of the American Indians as para-digmatic of what happened when different levels of civilization came into contact. "There is no example in history, where an uncultivated and barbarous stock has been elevated in the midst of a cultivated and civilized stock," he observed. Although there would be individual ex-ceptions, the African race in all probability would not flourish in a state of freedom. Their lot would be similar to that of the Irish, who were then beginning to arrive in great numbers. The Irish too were an example of the inevitable decline of a lesser race when it came in con-tact with a more advanced one. "It is not true . . . that they become an integral part of our nation to any considerable extent. They become ex-

213

tinct," unable to compete with the higher vigor and greater moral discipline of the native population. Such, Bushnell believed, would be the fate of blacks when slavery ended.

Few parts of Bushnell's writings sound more foreign to the modern reader than these early opinions on race, but they are not as alien to Bushnell's thinking as some have suggested. Indeed, we might note that they combined some of the intellectual weaknesses exhibited in his other writings. There is that sense of facile comprehensiveness, for example, that was always present in *God in Christ* — the confidence that the crucial questions dividing Unitarians and Trinitarians were slight and would disappear with just a little bit of linguistic tinkering. That same facile confidence underlies his view on slavery; slavery was not an inexorable national problem but would solve itself through the working out of the spirit of the age. It required no revolution or sacrifice, just a bit of tinkering. Bushnell's refusal to dirty himself with the real problem of slavery, as the abolitionists were doing, frustrated some. The Connecticut abolitionist politician Francis Gillette found Bushnell's stance annoying. He likened Bushnell's high-handed dismissal of the concerns of the abolitionists to a character in literature "who was too great a genius to be pleased with any thing, or to agree with any body." One sees here also that boldness (or foolishness) that led him to pick up theories and vigorously proclaim them without much reflection about their consequences. His having little firsthand experience with slaves didn't prevent him from offering up blunt theories about the future of their race. On questions of religion his deep, intuitive religious sense often counterbalanced these personality traits. On issues concerning the nation only experience would serve to temper his predilection.

But events of the ensuing decade did provide such a tempering. In the early 1840s his writings on slavery continued to display a sense of easy confidence that slavery would be ended through the moral progress of humanity, but by the middle of the decade he was beginning to have his doubts. The campaign for the annexation of Texas, and the debauching effect it had on the nation's political life, troubled him. If the Puritans were to his mind the source of the nation's solidity and law, their opponents, the advocates of the "bowie-knife society," seemed to be the chief proponents for the extension of slavery. Slavery was disturbing the health of the nation.

COUNSELING HIS COUNTRYMEN

The events of the 1850s made him even more convinced that the slave-holding South was taking aim at the liberties of the rest of the nation. He was dismayed by the Fugitive Slave Act, a key part of the Great Compromise of 1850 engineered by Henry Clay, which mandated that New England citizens be compelled to assist in the recapturing of escaped slaves. "There are things required in this abominable Fugitive Slave Law that I will not do," Bushnell wrote to one colleague, "not even to save the union." The Kansas-Nebraska Act of 1854, which repealed the Missouri Compromise's attempt to limit the extension of slavery, and opened up these two new territories to slavery under the principle of "popular sovereignty," was even more troubling. It resulted in a civil war in the Kansas territory between antislavery New England settlers and pro-slavery Southerners. Thousands of New Englanders flocked to the territory to ensure that it would enter the Union as a free state. The flamboyant minister, Henry Ward Beecher, raised money to arm them, giving to history the famous nickname for a Sharp's rifle — a "Beecher's Bible." Viewing the situation in Kansas during his California trip, Bushnell wrote back to another friend, "These are dark times. I could not read the Kansas news without throwing down the paper and waiting till next day." The nation seemed to be descending into chaos as a result of slavery.

It was the debate in Congress over the Kansas-Nebraska Bill, in fact, that had prompted Bushnell's next piece on slavery. *The Northern Iron* was delivered as a fast-day sermon in April of 1854 as the bill was being debated. The title came from the question posed in Jeremiah 15:12, "Shall iron break the northern iron and steel?" to which Bushnell offered a resounding "No!" The North would not break in the face of Southern aggression. He acknowledged that over the years the North had been divided and a united South had played upon the division. Southerners had been united in their defense of slavery, while Northern politicians had for decades compromised principles and connived with Southern interests, nowhere more so than in their support of the "confused obliquities called the compromise of 1850," which included the Fugitive Slave Act, and now in the proposed Kansas-Nebraska Act, which Bushnell disgustedly referred to as the "Nebraska Fetch." The actions of these Northern politicians sometimes revolted him and at other times deeply disturbed him. The willingness of Henry Clay to acquiesce to Southern interest came as no surprise. Bushnell described the former Senator from Kentucky as "that most accomplished party leader, or as some would say the sublimest demagogue the nation has seen," and his support of the Fugitive Slave Act merely confirmed his reputation. But the willingness of Daniel Webster, long seen as the champion of New England and the epitome of the principled politician, to support such an immoral piece of legislation deeply disturbed Bushnell. Northern political weakness had for years been played upon by the South, but the North's real strength, Bushnell believed, lay not in its politicians but in its free institutions. Free institutions would always triumph over unfree ones just as free labor would always triumph over slave labor. "All the currents of modern civilization are pouring, like a Mississippi, down upon the head of slavery."

At its core, Bushnell continued, Northern society was deeply steeped in moral values. Northerners were the children of those whom Washington had praised at Bunker Hill as being ready "to stand fire" for a cause, not counting the cost. Their equivocating politicians knew this and strove to keep the people in the dark concerning the true nature of slavery, all the while piously preaching a respect for the law. But as the Northern public's knowledge of slavery increased, so did its opposition to the institution. "They have been submitting to the Fugitive Slave Law and reading *Uncle Tom*['*s Cabin*] for comfort," Bushnell wrote. The latent anti-slavery sentiment of the North that he had spoken of a decade and a half earlier was now beginning to arise as the old "bugbear of abolition" was giving way to a "trumpet call of democracy." The time for compromising was coming to an end. He observed that Pontius Pilate was an early practitioner of compromise, a politician who acceded to the mob for the sake of peace. In the Kansas-Nebraska bill politicians were continuing to placate the mob by sacrificing principles. They "prepared us to crucify with a Nebraska after we had compounded in a Missouri." But the people of the North would have no more of it. A struggle of wills between the North and South was coming, and Bushnell had no doubt which side would triumph. He ended his tract by quoting Job 37:9, "out of the south comes the whirlwind and cold out of the north." The power of the South was like the whirlwind, violent but temporary. That of the North was like the cold, slow to rise but ultimately overwhelming.

Like other conservative New Englanders, Bushnell had by the mid 1850s come to fear Southern aggression more than abolitionist excess, and his anti-Southern rhetoric became more strident. Yet he continued to put his confidence in the course of history, believing that slavery would inevitably be overthrown in the natural course of events. One sees this attitude reflected in the last of his pre-Sumter writings on the question. *The Census and Slavery* was penned in November of 1860, soon after the election of Abraham Lincoln. As a candidate, Lincoln had pledged to prevent any further extension of slavery, and he had won election without garnering a single electoral vote from a slave state. His election created a political crisis, and the threat of secession by Southern states was again sounded.

The Census and Slavery reflected both confidence and caution. Bushnell noted that the growth of the Union had been nothing short of remarkable. In 1790 the nation possessed less than four million inhabitants. By 1850 it had twenty-three million, and at this rate by 1910 the population would be 138,000,000, making it the most powerful nation on earth. Such a providential growth, he argued, would have tremendous implications. A people whose numbers increased by such magnitude could never again be the same people simply enlarged; they inevitably become another people. "They . . . change their modes of culture and production, their polity, policy, character, public bearing, and the whole tenor, in fact, of their history." The great places of growth were the free states, and in the surging free state population Bushnell saw the final solution to the problem of slavery. The land between Missouri and California was considered nothing more than a vast desert, "a most arid, stony, sun-burnt, frost-bitten, God-forsaken country as there is in the world." Hence the only place to which the growing free state population could expand was the slave states. Soon large parts of the upper South, particularly Virginia and Missouri, would be occupied by a vast tide of land-hungry Northerners, just as the Indian lands had been occupied years before. Northerners would buy up plantations and divide them into small farms to be worked by free labor. Since free labor always outproduced slave labor, it meant that more and more land would be bought and possessed by free farmers. The land of the South would soon become too valuable for slavery. The vitality of this growing free population would ineluctably squeeze out the last vestiges of slavery over the succeeding decades. Talk of secession, then, was pointless; slavery was already doomed. "By no human possibility can such a proposed confederacy keep the institution alive for more than 75 or a hundred years — very short life for the halcyon age to be inaugurated." As the process advanced, the African race, he predicted, would largely disappear. Again he prophesied, "It will always be seen that the superior [race] lives the other down, and finally quite lives it away." With the future so clear, Americans did not have to take drastic actions to bring about the end of slavery, nor could they, if they hoped to remain united as one nation. "We are in no such relation to the question of a summary abolition, as the British people were, when they had to only carry the vote of a home parliament against it." But history was clear. Slavery was doomed. "He that holds the seven stars and Orion has it in his hands." All of the actions of extremists on both sides were futile in the face of this inevitability. All one had to do was wait for history to take its course. "Excuse me, if I do not strain the blood into my eyes, to push on causes that are going with a momentum of their own," he confessed. "The Almighty Himself has a silent campaign of inevitable doom against it, marching on the awful census tramp of south and north to push it forever away."

Despite his troubling racial attitudes, Bushnell's goal was in many ways worthy: he wanted to find a painless and easy solution to the crisis of union. The same pastor who had put so much faith in the law of growth — in the belief that God acted through slow but certain progress — now tried to find such a law of progress at work here. Surely, he rationalized, there was a way out. Surely one could think, imagine, or even tinker a bit to find a solution to the great issue that was dividing the nation.

But events did not play out as Bushnell hoped or expected. The strange twilight period from the election of Lincoln to his inauguration in March — in which first South Carolina and then the rest of the Deep South states voted to leave the Union, while President James Buchanan stood passively by — had a surreal quality. So much effort had been invested over the decades in keeping the nation together that the events of the winter of 1861 seemed hard to fathom. Bushnell confessed at the time to a friend, "these are really sad times for our poor country, such as I never expected my children to see." He, like so many others, hoped that a way might be worked out to make the government stronger, to have slavery "greatly moderated and weakened," while the nation might stay in peace. But the decision by Lincoln to re-inforce the federal garrison at Fort Sumter in Charleston harbor, and the South's decision to fire upon the fort, shocked many Northerners awake, including Bushnell. For twenty years he had predicted the inevitable ending of slavery through the natural course of history, but now the nation was divided and blood was beginning to be shed. What was one to make of it?

INTERPRETING THE WAR

The war had an effect on Bushnell much like that of his great religious experience of 1848. It pulled him out of the facileness to which he often succumbed and replaced it with a much greater appreciation for the power of God in the world. The shock of war also convinced Bushnell that the crisis facing the nation was far deeper than he had earlier imagined. Slavery was of course a major factor, but it was not so much the cause of the crisis as the occasion. The true cause lay in the structure of the nation itself. In addressing the question of the war Bushnell drew on his New England roots, but in the end offered his own distinct understanding of the war's meaning.

Nothing more revealed to Northerners the magnitude of the war than the debacle of the Battle of Bull Run. There, in July of 1861, a barely trained Union army attempted to squash the Confederacy in its infancy. Scores of civilians, complete with their picnic baskets, traveled out from Washington to see the spectacle, imagining the battle to be like some great sporting event. The death, carnage, and confusion — not to mention the defeated Northern soldiers' inglorious retreat — made it very clear that warfare was a serious and deadly activity. Bushnell used the Battle of Bull Run as the occasion for his first reflection on the war, provocatively entitled *Reverses Needed*.

Adversity killed only where there was weakness, he explained; real vigor was tested by adversity and emerged from it stronger. In this sense the war was a test of the nation's health. But the war would not only test the strength of the nation but also help determine the true nature of its soul. The reason the war came, he continued, was that the American nation rested on an ambivalent foundation. There emerged at the time of the Revolution two competing understandings concerning the true foundation of government. For the advocates of independence in New England true government rested on divine will. The Revolution was a defense of organic societies that had been planted over a century earlier. The revolutionaries in the South, in contrast, propounded Thomas Jefferson's belief that true government had to rest upon the consent of the governed. Sixty years earlier, the old Federalist "Pope" Timothy Dwight had warned about the fundamental dichotomy between the holy commonwealths of New England and the speculations of "the infidel" Thomas Jefferson; now Bushnell resounded the same warning. "On one side, we have had the sense of a historic and morally binding authority, freedom sanctified by law and law by God himself," he noted. "[O]n the other we have not so much been obeying as speculating, drawing out our theories from points back of all history — theories of compacts, consentings, reserved rights, sovereignty of the people and the like — til finally we have speculated almost every thing away, and find that actually nothing is left."

A nation not rooted in the specificity of history and grounded in God had no basis for authority. If one followed the "glittering generalities" of Jefferson, one could never have a final authority, for nothing that was of merely human origin could ever bind the consciences of other human beings. If the nation were created by humans, Bushnell argued, it could be sundered by them as well. The nullification principle of South Carolina's John C. Calhoun — which claimed that a state had the right to reject any federal law it chose — was merely the logical conclusion of Jefferson's Declaration of Independence.

The war provided a test to see which vision would prevail.

In conclusion Bushnell argued that if the nation were truly valuable, then it was worth sacrificing for. No quick solution would work. If the war were to end tomorrow, the problem would remain. All would eagerly retreat to the pre-war compromises, leaving unresolved the fundamental issue. Reverses were necessary to instruct the Northern people as to why the war had come about, and to steel their will to carry it to its logical conclusion.

He returned to these themes later in the war in his address "Popular Government by Divine Right." The war, he noted, made people realize that the great error of the founding generation was the attempt to rest sovereignty on some abstract principle. The recent decision to place the phrase "in God we trust" on the nation's currency was token of the belated recognition that without God there could be no government. The war was furthermore the occasion of a great national maturation. America had been founded only a few decades earlier, and a nation was never truly complete at such a young age. Only through history, struggle, and suffering could the moral power of the nation be advanced and the national reality set. Again he observed how anomalous was the nation's founding: "New England and Virginia, Puritan church order and the doctrine of the French Encyclopedia, fused happily together in the language of Mr. Jefferson." The ambivalent origins of the nation had led it into a series of crises. The first great crisis emerged during the struggle for independence. The Revolution, properly understood, was an outgrowth of the colonial experience and of the slow maturation of deeply held principles. At the time, however, some adopted "the political theories of Rousseau and other French infidel writers" to make sense of the clash between the motherland and her colonies. The second great crisis occurred during the period of the Articles of Confederation and resulted in the framing of the Constitution, through which the different states became one. A sense of nationality began to emerge, and state loyalties began to subside. But the old division reappeared under the guise of states' rights, whose proponents saw the nation again to be only a collection of states. The third crisis led to the war. During the course of the conflict the Union slowly learned that God was the ultimate source of all authority. Americans thought they had created a nation and written a Constitution, but they were merely responding to that which God had already planted. "He is Founder before the founders, training both them and us, and building in the Constitution before it is produced without." The war was providing for the final abandonment of the "atheistic philosophy" of human sovereignty.

God brought the war, therefore, to make America truly a nation. But even more, Bushnell wrote in 1864, God, in the war, was offering an answer to the slavery question. Like others, Bushnell had to reflect upon the course of events — of a war that began merely to save the Union, without any intent of addressing the issue of slavery, but had providentially become a war to end the institution. Slavery was ending, wrote Bushnell. "I say not how it should go, but go it must; nay it is already broken to the fall, [even] if we touch it by no civil action

221

whatever. . . . There was never a funeral where the mourners were so many and so happy." The false principles that had protected slavery had given way. "The demoralizations are all stopped, and we feel it in us to be true for liberty and right, true for the law, and the good great government as God has given us."

The crisis of war forced Bushnell to think deeply about what constituted a nation and what held it together, and his social observations paralleled some of his earlier theological reflections. One recalls that his rejection of revivalism had led him to consider the true nature of the church. The church, he had argued, was not a collection of converted individuals, held together in a voluntary society, but a covenanted or organic community. It was a community that no given generation created, but rather each participated in. So, likewise, was the true state. Like the church it rested in God's will, and also like the church it was knit together not by rational assent but by deeper forces, most particularly the power of loyalty. Loyalty, he acknowledged, was a term not usually used in an American context. It smacked of feudalism or an aristocratic state in which individuals were connected through particular moral promises to other individuals. "It supposes," he explained, "some kind of hereditary magistracy, such as belongs in other nations to royal and princely orders." Indeed, while traveling in Europe decades earlier he himself had pooh-poohed the English fixation on loyalty, and proudly noted that the American nation rested not upon loyalty but law. But now in the crisis caused by secession he became convinced of the importance of loyalty. It stood on the same footing as patriotism, honor, and bravery — it was a moral and indeed a religious virtue. And it was loyalty that made a nation one. Loyalty was a high virtue of character that governed the heart. Law was a far lower concern. It merely constrained actions.

Lying behind Bushnell's discussion of loyalty lay a particular crisis that had emerged as a result of the war. The government had begun to exercise powers, such as confiscation and the suspension of the writ of habeas corpus, that it had never previously exercised. Opponents of the war effort used the law as a basis for criticizing the nation's policies. They proudly affirmed the Constitution "as it was" and condemned as illegal many of Lincoln's war policies. The law was superior to the nation, they argued, and it would be better for the nation to perish than for the law to be transgressed. Indeed, they used the law to define the limits of loyalty. No one could be commanded to a greater degree of loyalty than the law dictated.

"The Doctrine of Loyalty," another of Bushnell's great war essays, addressed the relation of law to loyalty. According to Bushnell, the relationship between law and loyalty was precisely the reverse of the claim that law prescribed or limited loyalty. Rather, loyalty undergirded society, and with it society's laws. The elevation of law over loyalty was as dangerous as the principle of popular sovereignty, since it robbed the nation of any moral power. In ordinary times the chaining of loyalty by law might be tolerated, but the great national crisis showed that the country could not survive without the deeper motivation of loyalty. A nation was like a family in that it was held together by forces greater than individual choice: "Government, like marriage, is either a finality, a state of supreme order that suffers no other even to be thought of, or else it is nothing." Law could not tap this great moral reservoir. It dealt only with things external, not with things of the heart and character. It could not speak against dishonesty, but could only prosecute actions like theft and perjury. It required only the minimum of acceptance, and this minimum was usually framed in negatives — you could not murder, you could not steal — but did not address what a positive obligation ought to be. Law was prudential, not heroic. A true society needed to be grounded on loyalty because only through loyalty could those sacrifices be offered up that ensured the nation's survival:

> The supreme law requires not one of the duties that are so genuinely great and true in loyalty; to volunteer body and life for the country, to stand fast when leaders are incompetent and armies reel away in panic before the foe; to send off to the field, as bravely consenting women do, husbands, sons and brothers, the props and protectors of home . . . the supreme law requires not one of these, nor in fact any thing else that belongs to a loyal and great soul's devotion.

In this regard there was a relationship between loyalty and religion; "we may even speak of loyalty as the religion of our political nature." Loyal citizens offered their lives for the same reason the Christian martyr offered hers — because their devotion was greater than any concern for personal well-being. "We do not commonly speak of those who give up their lives on the battle-fields of their country as dying by martyrdom. And yet it is the martyrdom of loyalty into which they freely gave their bodies and knowingly consented to the sacrifice."

Bushnell continued to ponder the issue of sacrifice. Shortly after the war's end Yale College asked him to speak at the school's commencement to honor those sons of Yale who had fallen in the war. These youths had been the flower of New England; they had been the great souls Bushnell had previously praised, and included men such as the lionized novelist Thomas Winthrop and Bushnell's own parishioner, Henry W. Camp, a great scholar and athlete who was cut down leading a charge outside of Richmond in 1864. Why, many asked, was all this suffering necessary? Why was so much blood shed?

"Our Obligation to the Dead," Bushnell's Yale address, focused on the meaning of sacrifice. It would have been all too easy, said Bushnell, particularly in the victorious North, to focus on the survivors and shower them with their richly deserved heroes' welcome, but it was with the dead that the real meaning of the war was found. The war was but one great chapter in the law of sacrifice: "According to the true economy of the world, so many of its grandest and most noble benefits have and are to have a tragic origin, and to come only as outgrowths of blood." The law of God taught that only through the shedding of blood could greatness be accomplished. "God could not plan a Peace-Society world, to live in the sweet amenities, and grow great and happy by simply thriving and feeding." Through the blood shed in the war a new chapter had opened up for the nation. Before the great carnage the various states had simply been "kenneled under the Constitution and not reconciled," but now a unity had been cemented, one much deeper than that of law.

The sacrifice of the dead had opened to all a new consciousness, continued Bushnell. "We are not the same people that we were, and never can be again." "The pitch of [our] life is raised. . . . [We] perceive what it is to have a country and a public devotion." Before the war, Americans did not have a true historical consciousness. For Bushnell, a true sense of history rested upon the recognition that God was in charge of history, and demanded a giving up of self-will and self-centeredness. Now through the suffering and shedding of blood Americans had finally learned this and had gained a historical consciousness. "So much worth and character were never sacrificed in a human war before. And by this mournful offering we have bought a really stupendous chapter of history." The blood shed by the fallen was vicariously shed for the entire nation. It sealed God's call to the nation.

"Our Obligation to the Dead" is at the same time one of the most moving and one of the most troubling of Bushnell's works. In it he discovered a great and solemn meaning in the national tragedy; in the words of one historian, "Bushnell could rejoice in the war just as, and because, he could call the day of crucifixion a 'good' Friday." Yet there are points in the essay — such as when he spoke of how the war's suffering would serve to improve the nation's literature and oratory — when the reader is left wondering how much Bushnell really fathomed the pain and suffering the war generated. It is important to note, however, that for Bushnell the binding power of sacrifice included both black and white Americans. Part of the obligation to the dead was to eliminate every vestige of slavery. "We did not begin the war to extirpate slavery; but the war itself took hold of slavery on the way." The living had an obligation to ensure that the black code and all the other laws that impeded emancipation be eliminated. And at the end of his address Bushnell acknowledged that the blood that transformed the nation had been shed by black soldiers as well as white. "I remember the massacre of Fort Pillow. I remember the fatal assault on Fort Wagner and the gallant Shaw sleeping there in the pile of his black followers. I remember the bloody fight and victory on the James, where the ground itself was black with dead. And there is a debt of honor here!" The sacrifice of the black Northern troops was part of the expiation of the nation, and, accordingly, blacks must have a place in the cleansed nation. And one might hope that part of what the blood washed away in Bushnell's case was the all too easy racial theorizing he had so often indulged in. If the war led to the jettisoning of abstract theory in favor of organic community, could it also lead Bushnell to advocate a more racially inclusive community than he had previously favored?

One sees hints of a new racial attitude in Bushnell's last significant writing on race, his 1868 essay "Distinctions of Color," which was later included in *Moral Uses of Dark Things*. Although the essay is still troublesome to modern sensibilities, it shows a marked shift from his pre-war views on race. Gone are his predictions about the ultimate demise of the African race in America. Likewise, rather than associating himself with those who claimed that Africans traced their origins to a non-Adamic source, he maintained the unity of the human race in Adam. A modern reader can find many disturbing phrases in Bushnell's essay, and he still shared many of the racialist presuppositions of his (white) contemporaries, but the thrust of the essay concerned the *positive* value of racial distinctions, and two of his observations bear mentioning. The first entailed an appreciation for the full integrity of humanity. It was all too easy, he argued, to attribute humanity only to those who were like us and to dehumanize others, but this (as the nation had learned) could not be done.

> The distinctions of color and race will sometimes strike us for the moment, with such force that we seem to be stunned or confounded, and so, and for so long a time, the sense of common unity is quite driven out of us; but our next thought strikes through the casement of color and body into the *men*, and the word by a ring of eternity and true moral significance, more distinctly pronounced than we could ever get for it under any one given type or color.

Racial diversity highlighted the unity of humanity. The other observation dealt with the course of history. Just as God in the course of the Civil War had taken the history of the nation into his own hands, so too might he now be taking up the question of the races. If so, the future might augur not the deterioration of the African race but its remarkable advance. The spirit of Christianity was a spirit of inversion. God was continually making the weak things of the world confound the mighty. Hence there might come in the future a "sublime inversion of order" that had never before been seen or imagined. "I refer of course to the possible consummation of our gospel by the uplifting and spiritual new birth of the African race." They were for Bushnell the "true Nazarenes and Galileans" of the world. Despite their present lack of culture they possessed a deep capacity for faith. And just as God had used the lowly in the past, so might he raise up the African race in the future. God was in charge; thus all things were possible.

THE MEANING OF SACRIFICE

As might be expected, Bushnell's reflections on sacrifice and atonement were not confined to the affairs of the nation, and an extended examination of the atonement would constitute his last great theological endeavor. As early as 1859, in a letter to a friend, he had written that he had begun to think of how the doctrine of the atonement might be conceived so as to be better able to express its power to the world. As had been the case with some of his other writings, his thoughts on the atonement flowed from a perceived spiritual discovery concerning the nature of God's love and Christian discipleship. While he was staying at Clifton Springs, seeking physical health, he wrote his wife and announced, "now . . . I lay hold of and appropriate the general culminating fact of God's vicarious character in goodness, and mine to be accomplished in Christ as a follower." The volume he eventually published, *The Vicarious Sacrifice, Grounded in Principles of Universal Obligation*, appeared in 1866, and elaborated on a number of themes found in his earlier writings on the atonement. He continued to reject any penal view of the atonement, and, indeed, was very explicit in his criticisms of Anselm. The sacrifice of Christ was not offered to pay any debt, but flowed from his being. It was an essential part of his nature.

In this work one also finds Bushnell's long-standing suspicion of dogma. His goal was not to set forth a doctrine of the atonement but principally to set forth a portrait of "the Christ whom so many centuries of discipleship have been so visibly longing and groping after." Again and again he attacked the idea of preaching a system of doctrine. Systems were artificial and missed the real power of the gospel. The center of the Christian life should be Christ himself: fulfilling the love principle in his willing sacrifice, demonstrating in his own obedience to God's will an everlasting obedience to the law, "doing honor to God's retributive justice by subjecting himself to all the corporate evils it brings upon the human state," and in all of these things setting forth the righteousness of God, so as to prepare humanity for the gospel message of true justification. All of these actions were part of the gospel picture of Jesus and should occupy center stage in the presentation of Christ's message.

Bushnell also returned to his long-standing interest in the altar imagery of Scripture as a way of understanding sacrifice. Such imagery, so long as it was not interpreted literally, had an important function; in fact, it was the best organizing metaphor for understanding the mystery of Christ's saving work. The imagery provided an objective language for expressing the gospel. Objective imagery was important because it shifted the focus from the sinner to Christ's objective act. When one began by focusing solely on Christ's wonderful character it was all too easy to end up focusing on the human experience of the character of Christ. In such a shift the great drama of salvation was lost. As Bushnell explained,

> It was going to be a great fault in the use, of that the disciple, looking for a power on his character, would keep himself too entirely in the attitude of consciousness, or voluntary self application. He would be hanging round each fact and scene, to get some eloquent moving effect from it. And he would study not only how to get impressions, but, almost ere he was aware of it, to make them. Just here accordingly it was that the Scripture symbols, and especially those of the altar service, were to come to our aid, putting us into a use of the gospel so entirely objective, as to scarcely suffer a recoil on our consciousness at all.

Through the altar imagery God caused human beings to get out of themselves and their own preoccupations and to become aware instead of the free state of faith and love that was provided by Christ. As he had tried to do in *God in Christ,* Bushnell strove in *The Vicarious Sacrifice* to rescue the power of the altar imagery simultaneously from those who wanted to interpret it literally and turn it into the foundation of a penal system and from those who wanted to do away with it altogether in favor of a general moral vision.

A number of elements stand out in the work. As the title suggests, the principle of vicarious sacrifice is presented as a principle of universal obligation. "Love is a principle essentially vicarious in its own nature," he explained, "identifying the subject with others, so as to suffer their adversities and pains, and taking on itself the burden of their evils." The mother, the patriot, and the friend were all reflective of the willingness to sacrifice because of the impulse to love. Here lies an argument parallel to that which stood behind *Nature and the Supernatural,* namely, the connectedness between divine and human action.

In his earlier work on the supernatural Bushnell had suggested that in the will's interruption of the course of nature one found the essence of the supernatural, and that this supernatural activity was present with both God and humanity. In this most recent work, he claimed that virtue and love led to sacrifice. The power of love was such that the lover would do anything for the sake of the beloved. Both God and humanity participated in vicarious sacrifice because both possessed the power to love. The principle of vicarious sacrifice linked all loving creatures. "As Christ is here discovered in vicarious sacrifice, so all good beings, God in the Old Testament before Christ, the Holy Spirit in the times of Christ, and the good created minds both before and after, are and are to be in accord with Christ, enduring the same kind of sacrifice."

A second element, echoed in the above reference to the sacrifice of the patriot, was the impact of the Civil War on Bushnell's thinking. The events of the four years of struggle reverberate in numerous places in the volume, but are quite explicit in two places. In describing the moral message of Christ he noted, "No life becomes a power, until we somehow get the clue of it," and argued that in the death of Christ, Christ's most inward nature was revealed. Without his death the depths of his greatness could never have been known. But, Bushnell continued, such a process of revelation only after death was not unique to the gospel. The same was true about President Lincoln. "I send these sheets to the press, when our great nation is dissolving, as it were, in its tears of mourning, for the great and true Father whom the assassins of law and liberty have sent on his way to the grave." This despite the fact that during the dark days of the war many had doubted Lincoln's decisions and his abilities. Even when the tide had begun to turn, the great multitude hesitated in their praise. "A certain grotesqueness and over-simplicity . . . kept off still the first impression of his dignity, and suffered us to only half believe." But his tragic death at the very moment of triumph added a new point of view. "The great name now of Abraham Lincoln emerges complete, a power of blessing on mankind, and a bond of homage in the feeling of his country forever." The interrelationship between Christ's sacrificial death and the death of Lincoln haunted Bushnell, as it did many in the North.

A second Civil War reference concerned the question of the sanctity of law. The death of Christ, Bushnell explained, far from making the law inconsequential, gave to it a new majesty. Christ's death magnified the law by enthroning it in love, "organizing in it a kingdom worthy of its breadth, beneficence, dignity, and all-encompassing order." To illustrate this point he again chose an event from recent history — the immense sacrifice of blood and treasure poured out during the war. Failure was prophesied but the nation sacrificed to save the integrity of its institutions and to establish the broken order of the law. "No composition could be endured, or even thought of, that did not settle us in obedience and pacify us in the sovereignty of law. . . . The victory we sighed for, and the salvation we sought, were summed up in the victory and salvation of law."

Still another distinctive point was a continuing interest in healing. One biographer succinctly summarizes as the thesis of the volume, "Christ's object is the healing of souls. He is to be God's moral power in working such a soul-cure. His life and sacrifice are what he does to become this saving power." But the healing of Jesus was not limited to a soul-cure. During his earthly ministry Christ's power was manifested in signs of healing. "It is only when the GREAT HEALER dies, that we look to find his cross a deed of power." The gift of healing, Bushnell said, had continued. He expressed great interest in the enigmatic passage in the Epistle of James that urged the sick to call upon the elders to pray for them and claimed that "the prayer of faith shall save the sick." Concerning this passage, the same Bushnell who had but a few years earlier shown so much interest in supernatural power explained, "It will not be understood, of course, that the prayer of faith is pledged to restore all sick, but only that it will restore as many sick as can have the prayer of faith given, or allowed; for God will not help any to pray in faith for such as he will not restore." The promise of Christ was sure and involved physical transformation as well as spiritual.

Finally, there was a surprising hardness in a number of places in the *Vicarious Sacrifice* which was rarely found in Bushnell's earlier writings on the atonement. He still emphasized the great loving nature of God and saw love as the great motivation in the ministry of Jesus. "Christ came just because the law that he had been in from eternity sent him, and his incarnate appearing was but the necessary outcoming in time of God's eternal love." Love and sacrifice were intricately interconnected. But this did not mitigate that God also judged and punished. "There must be no delicacy here," he explained, "as if God's love and vicarious ministry of Jesus were too softly good, to do any so rugged and severe thing as to punish." He urged that the nature of divine punishment and Christ's role as the future judge of the world be faithfully declared. The God of the Bible was a just God and finally a God of judgment, but when his justice is lost and he becomes merely a "beautiful God," his power over sin will be diminished. Bushnell continually hammered on the theme that judgment was a necessary part of the Christian message, and indeed worked hand in hand with divine love. He noted that there was a deep and subtle reason both why divine judgment and future punishment were originally instituted and why they held such a prominent place in the message of Christ himself. "By these tremendous severities alone of God, could men be made to feel the cutting edge of principle enough to have it really get into their love and make it a principled love. Otherwise it would have no moral quality at all, but . . . would be only a brazen forwardness of approving such a God as meets their liking; a God without terrors, concerned to get them into happiness, either with or without principles."

Where this new appreciation for the sternness of God came from one cannot know. Perhaps the destructiveness of the Civil War reminded him of the harshness of the world. Perhaps it came from the reflections of a man now in his sixties who had suffered decades of illness, who now viewed the world in far more sober terms than had the younger man who authored *Christian Nurture*. But few devotees of Bushnell would have anticipated a line such as the one quoted above. And students of American religion cannot help but observe the eerie parallels between it and H. Richard Niebuhr's famous declamation of nineteenth-century theological liberalism, "a God without wrath brought men without sin into a kingdom without judgement through the ministration of a Christ without a cross."

"I AM GROWING OLD"

The more somber parts of *The Vicarious Sacrifice* did not go unnoticed. Though Bushnell was still criticized for his liberal tendencies by reviewers such as Alvah Hovey and William W. Andrews, the more tell-ing criticism now began to come from Unitarian reviewers. In the *Christian Examiner,* James Freeman Clarke characterized Bushnell as writing a book for the benefit of those benighted few who still doubted God's friendliness to humanity and chastised him for still clinging to the idea of a judgmental God. "We object, *toto coelo,* to his doctrine of eternal punishment, which seems to us as weak as it is false." The *North American Review* was even more pointed in its criticisms. The reviewer found Bushnell's core argument, that all love was vicarious, far-fetched. Dismissing the idea, the reviewer wrote that according to Bushnell "we have only to scrutinize our own hearts [to discover] that we ourselves — like the *bourgeois gentilhomme* who was surprised to find that he had been talking prose all his life without knowing it — are also, in our degree, vicarious lovers, and entitled to the dignity of that repute." He went to great lengths to demonstrate that the idea of a vicarious sacrifice made no sense, and that Bushnell's grand attempt at divine-human analogy was an embarrassing failure. But even more cutting was his suggestion of why Bushnell had chosen such a tack. "On the question of the vicarious nature of Christ's suffering, it is well known that he has for some years felt a divided mind, being more or less heterodox in heart, but more or less orthodox in head. He sits psychically upon the stool sanctified by the late Dr. Channing, but his carnal part refuses to budge from that consecrated by the Church's gray fathers." Bushnell suffered from an impulse both to follow in the footsteps of Channing and to remain loyal to the older language. The result was his bending of words such as "vicarious" and "sacrifice" in an unnatural way in an attempt to satisfy both. Quoting an old proverb, the reviewer said of Bushnell that he "runs with the hare and chases with the hounds."

As younger theological minds began to contemplate the difficulty of reconciling eternal damnation with a God of love, and began ever so tentatively to think in terms of universal salvation, Bushnell unabashedly continued to defend the idea of sacrifice and a final judgment. Solutions that had seemed so daring in the 1840s, by the 1860s seemed out of date. No longer was he pictured as a heretic; to some he was almost a has-been. Like so many others, Horace Bushnell found himself being labeled a radical in his youth and a conservative in his later years without having significantly modified his ideas.

In the spring of 1866, soon after *The Vicarious Sacrifice* was published, Bushnell had the chance to travel south. During the war he had followed events closely; the battle reports he read in the papers were like puzzles, and his Yankee sense of tinkering and figuring often led him to devise strategies other than those chosen by the Union generals in the field. He therefore took the opportunity on his trip south to tour many of the battlefields he had so often read about. Gettysburg left him in awe. "Oh what a grandeur hangs over that sacred valley and town, where the fires of a true devotion to the country's life burnt with a vigor so glorious!" He also toured Richmond and Petersburg. Perhaps remembering the reports of Abraham Lincoln's triumphal entrance into Richmond but a year earlier, during which crowds of freed slaves surrounded Lincoln with their adulation, he wrote to his wife with pleasure that while in Richmond he had visited the great "African church."

All of the places that had so concerned him, where such sacrifice had been offered, he could now see. But during his journey he admitted he was now an old man. "This is my birthday, and the loss that I have made in my hearing admonishes me more than ever that I am growing old."

The experiences of the war transformed America, and the nation would never be the same. Some old questions were finally put to rest, but new ones soon began to be heard. Bushnell was able to explain to his countrymen how the war had affected the nation, and how it would bring forth new understandings. But Bushnell, himself, was very much part of the old order. He understood the tensions and questions, the hopes and fears, of the pre-war world. Whether he would be able to make sense of the post-war world remained to be seen.

10 Holding the Faith in a Strange Land

THE LAST decade of Bushnell's life would find him doing much that he had always done. He would continue to write regularly, and preach when he could. He would continue to speak out on a myriad of issues. He would continue to be curious about almost everything that came his way. In short, he would continue to be Horace Bushnell. But during these years his distinctive habits of mind, along with the predispositions that had always kept him so close to his community, no longer did so. Rather than illuminating the world around him, they began to show how much things were beginning to change, and how on so many levels the world was very different from what it had been during his active ministry. Like many that are fortunate enough to be blessed with long life, Bushnell ultimately became an emblem of a passing era.

A NEW WORLD

It is perhaps a truism to note that the world is constantly changing, and it is an even greater truism that the older a person becomes the more aware she is of the changes. But it was not simply age that caused Bushnell to reflect upon the great difference between the world of post-war America and that of his early years of ministry, much less that of his homespun youth. The rate of change in the decades after the Civil War was mind-boggling. Henry Adams famously wrote that in all areas of learning, with the possible exception of mathematics, a young man coming of age in 1854 was intellectually closer to the year 1 than to the year 1900. And it was not only in the field of learning that things were changing so rapidly. Another writer confessed, "The eight years in America from 1860 to 1868 uprooted institutions that were centuries old, changed the politics of a people, transformed the social life of half the country, and wrought so profoundly upon the national character that the influences cannot be measured short of two or three generations." These forces may not have been created by the war, but they were intensified by it.

All this could be seen within the city of Hartford itself. The town of slightly more than ten thousand inhabitants where Bushnell had begun his ministry had become by 1870 a city four times that size, and one poised for a period of even more rapid growth that would see its size double again by century's end. But it was not merely a question of size. By 1871 Hartford had been able to secure the honor of being the sole capital of the state (wresting co-capital status from New Haven). The building of the new capitol involved severe political wrangling, cost overruns, and such faulty construction that the dome tower collapsed while being built. If it did not also entail the bribery and corruption becoming endemic in the new American cities, then it was clearly the exception and not the rule. Hartford resident Samuel Clemens (better known as Mark Twain) would co-author a book with Charles Dudley Warner in 1873, entitled *The Gilded Age,* that recorded the decline in civic virtue during the post-war era. Furthermore, industry had dethroned commerce as the chief source of wealth. By 1870 half the working population was employed in the several hundred factories that now peppered the city. The war had been a great boon to the Colt Gun factory, which had turned out massive numbers of weapons for the Union cause. A far more complex class structure emerged in the industrial city than had been the case decades earlier. Finally, the pluralistic nature of the city was now a foregone conclusion. In the 1830s Bushnell had predicted that the new Irish immigrants would pass away. In the 1840s he and others had hoped they might be converted to what he considered true biblical Christianity. In the 1850s nativist organizations had hoped to marginalize their influence. But none of these hopes bore fruit. The Catholic community was now part of the permanent landscape of a city like Hartford. The valor of Irish Catholic soldiers during the war became the stuff of legend, and in turn made the new immigrants as much a part of the new nation as any others. Eight thousand Irish citizens served in the Connecticut forces during the war, and Hartford contributed its share. The all-Irish Ninth Connecticut Volunteers was particularly noteworthy for its service. It would not be for many years that the site of Jonathan Edwards's homestead would be bought by children of the new immigrants, and a Polish National Catholic Church built on it, but the signs that the Puritan-Congregationalist hegemony was lapsing were there for all to see.

The war did not intensify social forces only but cultural ones as well, and these too would change profoundly the world Bushnell had known. The war catalyzed a movement toward professionalization. A concern for professionalization was of course on the rise throughout the nineteenth century, particularly in America. As the English visitor James Bryce observed, "In a country where there is no titled class, no landed class, no military class, the chief distinction which popular sentiment can lay hold of as raising of one set of persons above another is the character of their occupation, the degree of culture it implies, the extent to which it gives them an honourable prominence." Professionalization entailed specialization and credentialing. Already by 1870 there were more institutions in America offering bachelor degrees, more medical schools, and more law schools than in all of Europe. The war had convinced observant Northerners that their cause had succeeded because of the higher levels of education and organization found in the North. The Army of the Potomac, not to mention the vast industrial system that supplied it, depended on levels of organization and management never before imagined. Such organization required trained individuals and rational planning. The decades after the war would see this movement toward professionalization increase as doctors, lawyers, teachers, and others established systems of organized education and bodies for credentialing. The societal watchword was *rational planning*. Through such planning one could create a fundamentally better world. The poet-physician Oliver Wendell Holmes, who like Bushnell represented a passing era, could only exclaim, "Statistics have tabulated everything — population, growth, wealth, crime, disease. We have shaded maps showing the geographical distribution of larceny and suicide. Analysis and classification have been at work upon all tangible and visible objects."

The movement toward professionalization was a great blow to Bushnell's world. Bushnell had been the preeminent Yankee tinkerer. Armed simply with a native ingenuity, the tinkerer was a generalist or amateur, a jack-of-all-trades, and the simple criterion of success was whether he or she solved the problem. Bushnell had brought his proclivity for tinkering to a whole variety of tasks and issues during his lifetime. Whether building stone walls when a child or writing on subjects as diverse as theology, language theory, race, child development, and city planning as he aged, he offered his opinion on almost everything. With the possible exception of theology, however, he had no professional expertise in any of these areas. He offered his opinions simply from his position as a Christian pastor, and his success in gaining the public's ear indicated that the opinion of a generalist mattered. Part of the role of a Christian pastor like Bushnell was to be (to use an anachronistic phrase) a public intellectual. Professionalization suggested, however, that only credentialed persons could speak authoritatively on issues. Linguistics was a specialized discipline, and serious opinions needed to be restricted to people with professional credentials. As we shall see, in the realm of theology there emerged a lack of patience with Bushnell's style of theology. The increasing emphasis on the role of the expert would make the world far less hospitable to tinkering amateurs like Bushnell than had been the Connecticut of Bushnell's youth.

THE SHADOW OF DARWIN

One sees this cultural trend at work in two areas that had been dear to Bushnell: the relation of science to religion, and the religious life of the children of the Puritans. The cooperative relation between science and religion had been a great concern for many during the first half of the nineteenth century, and both clergy and scientists had recognized that they must present a common front. Thus clergy looked at the careful design of the world and saw in it evidence for the existence of a wise and benevolent God, while scientists described their work as "doxological" and claimed that in discovering the order of the universe they were unearthing the very thoughts of God in creation. By mid century this neat marriage had begun to fray, and Bushnell realized the issue needed to be revisited. Throughout the decades of the 1850s he labored hard to clarify a relationship between the natural and the supernatural that would respect both the concerns of scientists and the idea of a personal God active in the world. It was his concern for the latter that caused him to reject the pantheistic solution offered by Emerson and the other Transcendentalists. He had eagerly embraced Harvard scientist Louis Agassiz's idea of multiple successive creations. This could explain the fossil records then being unearthed, and it suggested that in each individual species one saw the handprint of God. In Bushnell's *Nature and the Supernatural* both order and will co-existed in the universe. But only a year after the publication of that volume Charles Darwin published his *On the Origin of Species*, which proposed a very different way of seeing the world. Gone was any necessity à la Agassiz for positing a systematic creation of each individual species. Species evolved over time from simple to complex through the wholly natural force of natural selection. God was no longer necessary to explain the world, and was absent from Darwin's work except for a brief reference in the conclusion. All change in nature came from natural uniform forces of nature. The natural had vanquished the supernatural.

The triumph of Darwinism can be seen as a chapter in the triumph of professionalization within the scientific community. Previously scientists were viewed as important members of a broader culture, whose responsibility it was to support that culture. An earlier doxological scientist, such as Benjamin Silliman, who had taught Bushnell chemistry at Yale, would have seen himself as a devout Christian, a responsible scientist, and an important figure in Yale's task of shaping young men in morality and character. Each role was essential, and Silliman's employment at Yale depended on his carrying out all three. In that sense no academic discipline was independent. Each had a responsibility to uphold the cultural good. The professionalization of science, which coincided with the triumph of Darwinism, emphasized that the scientific endeavor was an autonomous venue of enquiry. Scientists were responsible to their professional peers, not to that larger matrix of authorities that had informed a man like Silliman. By bracketing questions of religion, morality, and culture, the scientist could study the world of nature as it truly was. The result would be the liberation of science from its earlier restraints and an advance in knowledge unlike anything the world had seen before.

Such a picture of the world was alien to Bushnell. It was true that he loved studying the world to see how it worked. In an address before the Sheffield Scientific School at Yale he spoke of the need for studying the world as it was and not simply as it was presented in books. "It will be found that the teaching of science in mere class-lessons, apart from experiment by the pupil, where it is possible, and apart from all uses of application, is the very worst method as respect the distinctness and real intelligence of the impressions given." Bushnell was sympathetic to the scientific quest — but not if it meant jettisoning the supernatural. Darwin had announced that matter and energy were all that existed in nature. Far from elevating the truly organic aspect of nature — which for Bushnell involved matter and spirit working in harmony — Darwin reduced all to the material. He eliminated the divine will from the cosmos even more completely than had the pantheists whom Bushnell had earlier attacked. Darwin claimed to understand the universe as it was, but did so by the principle of exclusion rather than by inclusion. Bushnell by his very nature was a synthesizer. As his daughter wisely observed of him, "He had no unrelated facts." All for him worked together — nature and supernature, law and will, religion and science. He said of Darwin's theory, "When it is proved, if it must be the fact, we may well enough learn to live without religion." Later students of Bushnell have blushed over this line and have usually apologetically explained that he really did not know Darwin. But they have missed the thrust of his observation. Bushnell had always maintained that any meaningful description of Christianity had to have a place for a personal God actively involved in the world. A personal, active deity was something Darwin and his nineteenth-century followers would not allow. Many religious figures made their peace with Darwin as the century progressed and as the scientific community was drawn into his camp by following the lead of the pantheists and claiming that spirit lay behind all matter. But many who did so abandoned the category of the supernatural and deemed divine intervention in the world an antiquated concept. Such a path Bushnell would not follow.

If Darwin was changing the world of science he was also making an impact on the field of theology, one that would change the religious milieu of the children of the Puritans. One recalls that Bushnell had spent much energy trying to restore the lost unity among New England Congregationalists and Unitarians. We have seen how much his great works of the 1840s — "Christian Comprehensiveness," *Christian Nurture,* and *God in Christ* — were concerned with repairing this breach. He had been encouraged by the initial Unitarian rejection of the radicalism of the Transcendentalists and had found a sympathetic ear in Unitarian pastors like Cyrus Bartol, who stood by him when he was attacked by his orthodox critics. But the history of New England Unitarianism in the decades following was not so congenial to Bushnell's outlook. Throughout the early 1860s a number of younger Unitarians had begun to argue that to address truly the challenges of modernity found in such ideas as Darwinism, old beliefs had to be radically reassessed. The new science called into question the meaning of revelation. The young Francis Ellingwood Abbot was a case in point. While at Harvard College he fell under the sway of Professor Frederic Dan Huntington, who preached an "evangelical Unitarianism" that saw Unitarianism as the purest form of Christianity. Abbot studied for the ministry, but while doing so, his contact with the new science led him to doubts. There could be no specific Christian claims since all had to be buttressed by the authority of revelation and "there can be no such thing as an authority superior to our own individual reason." Reason, particularly when aided by a rigorous metaphysical and scientific philosophy, could attest to the authority of religion but not to any of the unique claims about Jesus.

Thus Abbot was led out of Christianity and toward a commitment to "Free Religion." Others came to this rejection of Christianity, many of them through the study of the religions of the world, and the result was a great intra-Unitarian debate over whether or not Unitarianism should remain a Christian religion. At the Unitarian convention in Syracuse in 1868 the representatives debated over whether Unitarianism should discard any specifically Christian identification. The radicals were defeated in the short run but would eventually reshape Unitarianism. In the interim they founded in 1868 a Free Religious Association, the goal of which was to "promote the interests of pure religion, to encourage the scientific study of theology, and to increase fellowship in the spirit." Among the association's supporters was Cyrus Bartol, Bushnell's old friend. Bushnell was troubled by this turn of events. It seemed so out of keeping with the future he had predicted in which Trinitarians and Unitarians would be united in the spiritual power of the gospel. He was on the whole charitable to Bartol himself. "I dreaded what you might be going to say," he wrote to his friend after receiving a publication from him, "for I had heard so much of the new radicalism, that I expected a kind of half apostasy from yourself." Instead, Bushnell was relieved by what he found. Nonetheless, he found the tone of the work troublesome; "you pronounce the negatives a little stronger and a little more antagonistically."

He reserved his full censure for the young Abbot. Abbot had been making a name for himself as one of the leading anti-Christian radicals, and because of this found churches shunning him as he sought pastoral employment. In 1867 he wrote to Bushnell, whom he had never met, seeking his assistance in finding an academic appointment. Abbot and Bushnell represented two very different eras — Bushnell was a Romantic enamored by the power yet limitations of words, while Abbot was a scientific theist who passionately believed that through rigorous scientific philosophy one could firmly establish religious claims. Bushnell's response to Abbot highlighted these differences. Abbot did not really understand what religion was all about, he said. Abbot believed that religion rested on key irrefutable propositions, but in this he was mistaken:

> You assume that *opinion* . . . is going to be the final *science,* and so the end of all debate; whereas I look upon opinion as a kind of clatter that can settle nothing. Faith is a much higher, more explorative way of knowledge here than opinion, and cannot be ignored as the summit faculty of souls. . . . Faith has nothing to do with propositions; opinion with nothing else. Thus, when I believe in God, it is the act of one being committing himself in trust to another being, and in that trust getting immediate knowledge and consciousness of him.

The common ground that once undergirded the separated children of the Puritans seemed to have ebbed away.

OLD THEMES REVISITED

In this new world Bushnell remained the Puritan Yankee tinkerer, and during the last decade of his life he penned three works that show his continuing interest in theology, the social order, and the power of the Spirit.

It seemed as if no sooner had he finished the *Vicarious Sacrifice* than he set about improving it. In *Forgiveness and Law,* published in 1874, Bushnell offered to the public his third distinct rendering of the doctrine of the atonement. In *God in Christ,* one recalls, he had focused on the objective/subjective distinction in understanding the work of Christ. In *The Vicarious Sacrifice,* he was concerned with the meaning of sacrifice. In this latest work he chose to emphasize still a different theme, the work of Christ as true propitiation. "I asserted a propitiation before," he admitted, "but accounted for the word as one by which the disciple objectivizes his own feelings, conceiving that God himself is representatively mitigated or become propitious, because he is himself inwardly reconciled to God. Instead of this, I now assert a real propitiation of God, finding it in evidence from the propitiation we instinctively make ourselves, when we heartily forgive." As before, his work rested upon a grand analogy between the moral nature of humans and that of God. True forgiveness involved a sympathy with the wrongdoing party that entailed taking up his nature and, further, suffering through that nature. In this way Christ reconciled God to humanity, fulfilling the eternal law of propitiation.

Bushnell's theory seems to have had very little influence at the time — since many of his liberal-leaning Congregational brethren were moving toward a lessened emphasis on the sacrificial nature of Christ's death — and it has had precious little influence since. Likewise, despite the fact that one writer has deemed *Forgiveness and Law* Bushnell's most important book, few if any have followed his path of rethinking the meaning of atonement while holding fast to the biblical imagery. Bushnell's writings on this subject do, however, demonstrate his tinkering character. He was always fidgeting with his ideas, never satisfied, always willing to try something new. Unlike the "typical" theologian, who attempted to carve out firm doctrines, Bushnell always had about him the spirit of the Yankee, a readiness to invent a contraption to solve a given problem. Bushnell's real interest was in the intense, trusting relationship between the believer and a personal God; all formulas used to explain that were secondary, functional at best.

Another work of the period that showed Bushnell to be still the Yankee Puritan was *Women's Suffrage: The Reform Against Nature.* It was, at least posthumously, his most scandalous book. In it, Bushnell addressed a topic then beginning to attract wide discussion. An organized movement to gain the vote for women emerged out of the Seneca Falls conference of 1848, which had met "to discuss the social, civil, and religious rights of women." From its beginning the suffrage movement was linked to other antebellum reform movements, including the anti-slavery and temperance campaigns, though it had the popular support of neither. Immediately after the war the cause was quickened by the campaign to pass the Fifteenth Amendment, which guaranteed to the freed slaves the right to vote. Advocates of the vote for women made use of the same expansive rhetoric as the proponents of the vote for former slaves, rhetoric anchored in the language of the Declaration of Independence. In 1867 campaigns were launched in New York and New Jersey to extend suffrage to women, though both endeavors failed.

In his discussion of this issue, Bushnell displayed a number of themes and concerns that permeated his long ministry, and his arguments, if not always persuasive, are reflective of the world of Horace Bushnell. To begin with, one finds in *Women's Suffrage* Bushnell's overwhelming confidence in "organic" progress. Institutions and cultures prospered when they directed themselves in accordance with the plan of nature. One such organic advance was the gradually increasing role of women in society. He noted that women were often abused in primitive societies, and that even in his own society they had been legally proscribed concerning property rights and employment. Likewise, access to education had been limited. But the course of progress was toward elimination of these barriers and an increased social role for women. Bushnell particularly applauded the growth of co-education. He admitted that he had been at first suspicious of mixing men and women in education, but his experience at Oberlin College had converted him. He particularly lauded the effect of co-education on the moral life of the collegiate. Perhaps reflecting on his own memories of Yale, he wrote, "the ancient, traditional, hell-state of college life, and all the immense ruin of character propagated by the club-law of a stringently male or monastic association, was totally escaped and put away," as a result of co-education. He predicted that this progress would only continue. Women would eventually become professors of "languages, of botany, of moral science, and not improperly, of the exact mathematics." They would begin to have a role in other professions such as medicine, law, and theology. Such was the course of nature.

But here came another of Bushnell's familiar themes. There were other types of social change that would be contrary to nature, and they would bring about not advance but decay. Bushnell, like many others of his age, held that male and female natures were different but complementary. Women could be involved in the law but not in trials, because "she is not wicked enough." The same law of nature also proscribed their activity in the ministry. Significantly, Bushnell put far more weight on arguments limiting women's ministry that were drawn from an understanding of human nature than he did on those drawn from Scripture. In response to the famous (or infamous) injunction of the apostle Paul about women's role in church and home, he noted that "If Paul had been well married . . . I think he would have learned some things about women which, in fact, he never did learn." But nature did shape women's roles. Their spiritual gifts made them adept at "quickening and edifying the Spirit," but they lacked the gift of administration. Hence ministration rather than administration was their true natural role.

All these notions prepared the way for his discussion of women's suffrage. Women's participation in political life was for Bushnell a clear contradiction of their natural role. The political world was an arena of vulgarity, corruption, and force. He had been preaching against its evils for decades. Yet now the moral purity of women was in danger of being drowned by it. Who was to blame for such a suggestion? The student of Bushnell's earlier writings on slavery will be amused to discover that the villains were his old *bêtes noires* — abolitionists and secessionists. Bushnell may have become reconciled to abolition, but he still harbored suspicions over the radical spirit of the abolitionists themselves. That same radical spirit was here at work, but now divorced from the social good of emancipation. "Many persons who mistook their ground, in opposing the abolition of slavery, are naturally shy, under this new question, of being caught again, and are half ready to leap into the gulf into what is called the emancipation of women, before they can distinctly see the bottom of it." The abolitionist language of emancipation was now being used to advance the cause of votes for women.

If the abolitionists were one group in error, the blame could also be placed on the line of thought beginning with Voltaire and Rousseau, running through Jefferson, and ending in John C. Calhoun. The Enlightenment writers thought they could create a world to their own liking; "they betook themselves mentally to the woods and began to envy the people of the woods." They created the idea of government by the consent of the governed and the notion of abstract rights. They led Calhoun into "his miserably delusive state-rights sophism," which led to the bloody Civil War. But the same principle was at work in the claim that there was a universal "equal right to vote." "Bitterly have we paid for this very cheap imposture of philosophy, in our late dreadful war of rebellion, and now it is to be seen, whether it may plunge us again down this other, deeper gulf of women's suffrage."

Thankfully Bushnell spared us any prophesying about some great feminist bombardment of Congress that would parallel the Confederate firing on Fort Sumter, but to the elderly Bushnell both secessionists and suffragettes were one in their errors. He spent much of the volume highlighting the deleterious effects of the reform in question. Not only were the errors linked but so too were the solutions. To avoid the power of the mob and the destructive assertion of one inalienable right after another, it was necessary to reassert the true nature of authority, and that was the authority of God. Obligation came from above and not from below. Christianity rightfully taught that the world was shaped by obligation and not by abstract rights. The nation needed to be taught the ways of true religion if it was to regain social clarity, but Bushnell feared that the nation was becoming less and less religious. Hospitals and schools were abandoning their religious and spiritual functions for want of workers. Here, he noted, one saw how a wrongheaded reform could have terrible social consequences. These occupations were the real area of progress for women. "Here are ministrations, teachings, offices, and magistracies of mercy without number, all a great deal worthier and higher than any that our women can hope to obtain at the polls, but they do not see it." If the women of America took up this challenge, which was theirs according to the true course of nature, the moral fiber of the nation would be strengthened.

Many who shared Bushnell's view of separate spheres for men and women, such as the editors of *The Nation*, did not believe that such a view precluded votes for women, and the truth was that *Women's Suffrage* revealed more about its aging author than it contributed to the issue at hand. Few if any new ideas can be found in the volume. It confirms the image of Bushnell as at heart a conservative child of New England Puritanism, progressive up to a point, but convinced that there was a set order of things that needed to be preserved at all costs. As one great Bushnell scholar has noted, while Bushnell was extremely astute on pre-war issues, "with post–Civil War problems — urbanism, industrialism, immigration, evolution, and scientific method — [he] was less able to cope." And to this list we might add suffrage. Nevertheless, one who has followed the long course of Bushnell's life cannot but smile when noticing that he chose to end his essay by invoking again the figure of Madame Guyon. The same female writer who had most profoundly affected him years earlier was now invoked as a true role model for women.

It is also worth noting that even on a subject such as this, Bushnell could not refrain from tinkering. Throughout his long career he had claimed many competencies — theologian, philosopher, student of language, social analyst, and urban planner among them — but here he tried his hand at dating and courtship. Some women remained unmarried, he wrote, because there was a class of men who could never muster the nerve to initiate a relationship. This could be corrected. "The present iron-clad modesty, which is simply ridiculous in either party, might be so far mitigated as to let feeling feel its way, and carry on its own courtship." Likewise women should be encouraged to abandon the practice of expecting to be "married into condition," that is, to a man who had already established his fortune. "Our young men are getting the impression now, and a good right to it is given them, that they cannot marry till they have good condition to offer." With just the right amount of tinkering, Bushnell was convinced that the marriage process could be improved.

One final work that dealt with earlier themes was Bushnell's last work, "Inspiration by the Holy Spirit," of which only a few fragments were ever completed. It reflected his long-standing interest in the power of the Spirit in the life of the church.

He began the work by noting that "inspirableness," or the facility for inspiration, was the supreme faculty of human beings. It opened them Godward. But Christian inspiration was unlike general inspiration in that it involved the work of a personal Spirit. Again he had little patience with pantheism and its understanding of inspiration as the influence of the universal spirit on the individual soul. The Christian Spirit was not a mere influence; it acted. "A carpenter makes a tight joint by making it, and not by an influence on the timber. In like manner a power that can inwardly configure a soul to God, and conjoin it by living adaptations with his inmost nature, must be divinely personal itself, working more directly and less vaguely than by any mere influence."

The fragments of the work, like many of Bushnell's other writings, include themes and ideas found both in later liberalism and in Pentecostalism. At times he spoke of the power of inspiration very much as later liberal writers would, and, in one of the few occasions he had anything good to say about the Sage of Concord, he praised Emerson's essay "The Oversoul" as a model of the working of the spirit of inspiration. "Inspiration" includes passages brimming with cloudy reasoning and uplifting rhetoric that one could easily imagine coming from the mouth of some late-nineteenth-century liberal "Prince of the Pulpit" such as Phillips Brooks. (For example, "The Holy Spirit carries the heart of God with him, and the heart of God is universal. . . . To say that he ministers the love of God puts him in a like paternal relation to all mind, even as gravity to all matter.") In addition, Bushnell's claim that the power of inspiration was universal but fallible fitted comfortably into a liberal model. In the middle of the piece, however, Bushnell's interest in glossolalia returned. Speaking in tongues, he observed, "shows the Spirit making discourse and playing out intelligence in words, a living proof that he is at the seat of intelligence within. So here again the Spirit is got more nearly incarnated in that he is seen to be the occupant, if not of body, yet of mind." The same fascination with the phenomenon of divine language that one saw in *Nature and the Supernatural* returned as well. God's language overcame the limitations of human language. And this fascination with the power of the Spirit led Bushnell to push his enquiry even further. Years earlier he had confidently written that the Christian process was one of growth rather than of revolution. Yet now, at the end of his years, the author of *Christian Nurture* could reflect on the dramatic outpouring of the Holy Spirit at Pentecost. It was a common assertion that such works of spiritual power had long since passed, and were never to return. "Men, it is said, are not to be converted in this sudden, almost indecorous, way hereafter, but more gradually, in a sacramental fashion." "All these and other like questions will be discussed hereafter," he promised, "when we come to speak of miracles and supernatural manifestations, and are therefore passed for the present."

He was never to complete that discussion. All we have is a brief sketch and outline of his projected work, and in the last point of the last division one finds simply, "All inspirations are supernatural. Whether miracles go with them? Have they ceased? Will they ever cease?" In light of *Nature and the Supernatural* one can perhaps assume that Bushnell's answers would have been "yes" to the first question and "no" to the next two. Here as earlier Bushnell found himself striving to straddle two worlds that were quickly moving apart. Already while he was writing his last work some Protestants, led by Charles Cullis in Boston, began to claim again the power of supernatural healing promised in the Bible. Just a few years after Bushnell had penned these words other Protestants, such as Charles A. Briggs at Union Theological Seminary, began to reconceptualize what was meant by biblical inspiration. Briggs and others used phrases similar to Bushnell's assertion that all inspiration was supernatural, but for them the purpose of such an assertion was to limit any qualitatively distinctive supernatural element in biblical inspiration. They wanted to make the Spirit less immediate to the prophets and apostles, no more present than it is now. For Bushnell such language had the reverse purpose. It served to elevate the role of the Spirit in the present life of the church. The Spirit is present now as it was then. Few in the years that followed would accept Bushnell's unique view of the supernatural and the Spirit, but he was always willing to offer it, even in this last unfinished work.

AT THE END A CHRISTIAN SOUL

If Bushnell's later years reflected many themes and interests that had been common throughout his life, one new factor was the interest in Bushnell and his work by a number of younger men. Edwin P. Parker had welcomed him to the ministerial circle of Hartford upon his return to the city in 1861. Another man influenced by Bushnell was Washington Gladden, a young Congregational cleric. Having suffered a nervous disorder while serving in a church in Brooklyn, Gladden in 1862 retired to the more restful surroundings of Morrisania in the (then still rural) Bronx. He was close enough to New York, however, to frequent the Astor Library, where he discovered the writings of Bushnell. He was first attracted to his sermons, but someone suggested that he read *God in Christ.* As an old man he later reflected on that volume: The "Dissertation on Language" gave to him "a new sense of the nature of the instrument which I was trying to use," and convinced him of the futility of the dogmatic method. He found the treatises themselves even more powerful. "I found an emancipation proclamation which delivered me at once from the bondage of an immoral theology." The vision of God he found there, centered on love and compassion, thrilled him. Bushnell's real heresy, he explained, was "the unfaltering belief that God is just."

He quickly adopted some of Bushnell's themes into his own preaching, and he strove to rescue Bushnell's reputation from the attacks of critics. He had his chance in 1867. A Congregationalist ministerial candidate from Illinois had just been denied ordination by his association for expressing sympathy with Bushnell's views on the atonement. In response, Gladden published in the *Independent,* a leading Congregationalist weekly newspaper of its day, an article entitled "Are Dr. Bushnell's Views Heretical?" He defended Bushnell's recasting of the question of the atonement from an objective or penal model to a subjective or ethical one. "I set forth . . . in a brief article, the substance of Dr. Bushnell's teaching, and expressly committed myself to it, declaring that if this was heresy, I desired to be counted among the heretics," Gladden later wrote. On account of the article he had the chance to meet Bushnell, and he called his subsequent friendship with him "one of the most stimulating I have known." He would later ask Bushnell to preach the installation sermon for him when he was called to a church in North Adams, Massachusetts. Bushnell's effort, "The Gospel of the Face," is generally considered one of his finest sermons.

Gladden helped popularize many of the new theological trends and would gain great fame as a vigorous proponent of the Social Gospel in the latter part of the century. Another person who would emerge as a leading theologian and who became attracted to Bushnell as a young minister was Theodore Thornton Munger. Munger, who had close connections with both New Haven and Yale College, had encountered Bushnell even earlier. He and a friend had been present in 1852 when Bushnell delivered his address "Religious Music" to mark the twenty-fifth anniversary of the Beethoven Society at Yale, which Bushnell as a student had helped to organize. The effect of the address was dramatic. The friend — Andrew Dickson White, who would become the first president of Cornell University — later described the experience: "[It] carried us both off our feet as indeed it did a great number of our fellows." It was not until Munger was ordained, however, that he encountered Bushnell's theological writings, which challenged the Taylorism that he had been taught at Yale. Bushnell's view of the relation of the human soul to God stirred Munger greatly. He confessed to a friend that Bushnell had a unique ability for presenting the meaning of the gospel in a way that touched the deepest facts of human existence. He also took to heart a criticism Bushnell made of his preaching. In 1863 Munger had delivered a series of sermons while "candidating" for Bushnell's old pulpit. Bushnell wrote to the young minister praising him for the sermons' contents but faulting him for their overblown style. "Are you not too nearly a literary gentleman in your habit — not enough an apostle? . . . Preaching is the grandest of all works when the apostolic ring and movement are in it."

Munger, too, early on took up the challenge of rescuing Bushnell from his opponents. Writing to a friend he noted that the old minister needed his defenders. "Who is there to say anything in defense of Dr. Bushnell's new book [Christ in Theology]?" he pleaded. "Unitarians will appropriate the negative side, but who will show or say, that Dr. B. is orthodox and may have place in the true church?" Munger would eventually write the first (and still the best) systematic account of Bushnell's thought.

Both of these men were part of a new generation of clergy. Gladden's language about Bushnell offering an "emancipation proclamation" in theology was not casually chosen. To them, the great travail of the nation, seen most dramatically in the crisis of union but also perhaps in the many challenges facing the post-war nation, called for a fresh start. Left on the field of battle were not only men and equipment but ideas and understandings that had failed to measure up to the crisis of the day. Bushnell, the champion of freedom in the antebellum church, became a heroic figure for young clergy seeking a similar freedom. He was the Moses who had led the promised people out of slavery.

But it was not merely the younger men who started to appreciate Bushnell anew. As age mellowed him the spirituality of his personality and the great depths of his soul became even more apparent. As one acquaintance noted, the granite roughness of his youth disappeared as he aged except where it formed a part of his strength of character, and in its place "the tenderness, the sweetness, the bearing and forbearing strength of his nature came to their perfection." One episode that occurred at a meeting of the Hartford Central Association gives some hint of Bushnell's character. An elderly Bushnell had been appointed to read a sermon. Speaking to his clerical brethren, who had stood with him during his time of trial two decades earlier, he said in a quiet voice, "Brethren, I am going to read to you what is probably the last sermon I shall write." He had chosen as his topic "Our Relation to Christ in the Future Life." As he proceeded with his reading the audience sensed that he was speaking not in terms of conjecture but almost as if he were peering through the veil that separated this life from the next. A quiet fell on the room, and when he had finished no one dared to speak. Bushnell insisted, calling on one minister to comment — "tell us what you think of it," he said. The man began, "Dr. Bushnell tells us that this — is — his — last — sermon," and then stopped to weep. The rest of the clergy present joined in the tears. One person wrote later that it reminded him of the apostle Paul's parting with the Ephesian elders in Acts 20. "Then we knew how we loved him, and what an unspeakable, irreparable loss would be for us, — that departure that was evidently nigh at hand." The power of Bushnell's soul had not only carried him through his time of trial, it had convinced those around him that it was a more reliable testimony than the words of his books. Now, near death, it glowed more brightly.

By the winter of 1875, Bushnell seemed to be on the very verge of losing the long battle with illness that he had been waging for over thirty years. When asked, "How is your health to-day?" he would note, "my very common answer is that I have no health." He would fail, and then recover a bit, but always be weaker. When still another illness befell him in 1876, his wife and daughters could but watch. A pious death was expected of a good Victorian Christian, and Bushnell didn't disappoint. One night he awoke from his sleep and exclaimed, "Oh, God is a wonderful Being!" His daughter, sitting next to him, tried to comfort him and asked if he felt God's presence. "Yes, in a certain sense he is with me," he said, pausing, "and I have no doubt that he is with me in a sense I do not imagine. I account it one of the greatest felicities to have a nature capable of such changes." Then he rested. Finally, out of his weakness he spoke: "we are all going home together; and I say the Lord be with you — and in grace — and peace — and love — and that is the way I have come along home."

Bushnell "came along home" early in the morning of February 17, 1876. His death was noted across the nation. From California, Theodore Thornton Munger (who had traveled there, like Bushnell, in search of health) delivered and then later published a "Commemorative to Dr. Bushnell." In New York, the *Christian Union* also noted his death. The writer observed that Bushnell was by no means a popular figure because of the complexity of his thought, but that his influence was nonetheless widespread. "There are thousands of men and women who never heard the name of Dr. Bushnell who yet have received a strong impress from him from preachers and teachers who had drunk directly from his thought." The writer also touched on the true source of Bushnell's power, which lay not in the power of his logic, nor in the beauty of his prose, though both were present. "Higher than all these is the power everywhere present of a heart on fire with love and with longing for the divine life. The adverse theologian may read to criticize . . . but if the Christian be in him stronger than the theologian, he will be drawn at every page into sympathy with the emotion and the moral purpose, however they may dissent from the intellectual statement."

In Hartford his death occasioned four columns of obituary notice in the local paper. His successor in what was now called the Park Street Church remembered him in a funeral oration for the originality of his thought, the beauty of his voice, and the magnetism of his personality. He had left his mark on his adopted city. Just two days before he died the Common Council of Hartford had voted to name in his honor the park that Bushnell worked so hard to establish. When Bushnell heard the news he smiled. He had always foresworn the idea of having a statue erected in his honor, tersely saying he would prefer later generations to ask why there was no statue for him than for them to ask why there was one. But a park was something different. It was organic. It was alive. It could change.

A QUESTIONABLE LEGACY

Other memorials were more ambiguous. To the younger, more progressive clergy of New England, Bushnell came to be seen as the great liberator, the man who had set the children of the Puritans free from the bondage of John Calvin. Within a decade after Bushnell's death, a new theological movement emerged within New England Congregationalism based at Andover Seminary, calling itself the New Theology or "Progressive Orthodoxy." Its followers strove to finish the task of liberating New England theology as well as to bring about a rapprochement between Christianity and the new science of evolution. They would largely transform American Congregationalism, and by century's end had made it the most liberal Protestant denomination. Their labors were so successful that in 1908 Andover Seminary — created a century earlier to be an orthodox bastion against the heresies of Harvard — moved to Cambridge and merged with its historic rival. The proponents of the New Theology looked to Bushnell for inspiration. As one historian of the movement wrote, "Bushnell was in some respects almost as truly the father of the later constructive development of American theology as was Jonathan Edwards of the earlier." Hence, soon after his death Bushnell became enthroned as father of American theological liberalism. Theodore Thornton Munger, who from his pulpit in United Church, New Haven, was himself an important representative of the New Theology, penned *Horace Bushnell: Preacher and Theologian* to memorialize this picture of Bushnell. A Centenary Edition of his writings was issued to commemorate the hundredth anniversary of his birth, and these volumes bear strong physical resemblance to contemporary editions of the collected works of

Ralph Waldo Emerson and Theodore Parker. They were printed almost as if intended to sit upon a bookshelf together, testifying to the triumphant liberal New England faith.

But it was never an easy adoption. Some parts of Bushnell's thought, like his Sabellianism, were quietly shelved. The new theological interest focused on Christ's full humanity, not the question of the nature of the Godhead that had so interested Bushnell. Although these admirers appreciated his attacks upon the penal or objective view of the atonement, few took up his positive views. We have already seen how writers who might praise him in general found serious fault with his views on miracles and final judgment. Almost every positive aspect of the theology he had set forth was rejected.

Why then the attraction? He was of course a noted figure, and if one were in search of a founding figure, he was perhaps the best. Even more, they recognized that Bushnell's real contribution to them was negative. He was the liberator. He had broken the hegemony of the old orthodoxy. Like the critics of Bushnell's own time, his younger admirers knew that Bushnell was far more successful in destroying the old than in replacing it with a new. If he was Moses, he was more the one who led the people out of captivity than the one who led them to the promised land. Another image younger writers used to refer to Bushnell was that of a pioneer. As one noted, "he hewed a path — rough but not blind — into the realm of the spirit to which [our] age is slowly opening its eyes." The pioneers opened the wilderness, but left few lasting physical marks. It was the task of later settlers to build and grow and replace the rude cabins and mud trails of the pioneers with fine buildings and great highways. The pioneer was not a builder but an explorer. Such was the case with Bushnell. His "buildings" were replaced by more carefully crafted studies and treatises, but his courage of exploration would be always remembered.

Two other factors may help explain the paradox of Bushnell being elevated as a symbol while being dismissed as a theologian in the years immediately following his death. The one work of Bushnell's that did continue to be read (and indeed has been regularly back in print for over a century) was *Christian Nurture*. But it was not the edition of 1847. In 1860 he had published an expanded version of the work, with the cantankerous but revealing parts about Episcopalians and Unitarians carefully removed, and this became the handbook of the Christian education movement. At the time of the centennial observation of Bushnell's birth one admirer could write, "of all of Dr. Bushnell's writings, those on Christian Nurture were most convincing and therefore most influential." Later figures saw Bushnell as a genius in his ideas of child development and the role of the family in true nurture. *Christian Nurture* was "an epoch making book," wrote Luther Weigle, longtime dean of Yale Divinity School. Particularly in the early twentieth century, as Protestant Christian education moved from standardized lessons with a biblical base to a system that emphasized the stages of moral development in the child, Bushnell's volume was viewed as prophetic. He became the source for the idea that successful religious education must be related to the psychological state of the developing child. To what degree such a reading of *Christian Nurture* was accurate, particularly if one read it in the light of Bushnell's larger corpus, is of course another question. But to a progressive era, Bushnell was the morning star of progress.

One final factor was the disjunctive nature of Bushnell's writings, which permitted him to be interpreted in many different ways. *Christian Nurture* was a very different book from *God in Christ*. Both were different from *Nature and the Supernatural*. One of his strongest traits as a writer was his suggestiveness. His explications sometimes failed but there were always parts of even his most problematic writings that could inspire a reader. Yet this very suggestiveness contributed to the disjunctive interpretations of him. It is ironic that a person who has in the twentieth century been almost always compared with the German theologian Friedrich Schleiermacher was in the late nineteenth century more often compared with Albrecht Ritschl. But this should not be surprising. Bushnell's interest in religious experience does remind one of Schleiermacher, while his rejection of metaphysics and his Trinitarian writings remind one of Ritschl. One can see in Bushnell what one wants to see. The same irony can be seen in the changing reputation of his "Dissertation on Language" over the years. Throughout the end of the nineteenth century the "Dissertation" was considered a failed endeavor. When Williston Walker, writing in the famous eleventh edition of the *Encyclopaedia Britannica*, catalogued Bushnell's accomplishments, the "Dissertation" was relegated to a brief parenthetical observation. It was only rediscovered in the mid twentieth century by literary critics and theologians. The recognition of important parallels between Transcendentalists and other representatives of the "American Renaissance" in the mid nineteenth century and European writers of the "Symbolist" school led eventually to a reassessment of Bushnell's theory of language. Scholars such as Charles Feidelson began to see in it parallels with uses of language in other New England writers, and Bushnell began to be praised for the suggestiveness of his theory. "There is a striking modernity," Feidelson announced, "in Bushnell's conception of a literature that frankly relies on 'antagonistic figures, paradoxes, and contrarious representations.'" Theologians began to reassess it as well during the post-war period when the reigning neo-orthodoxy took a linguistic turn. Even some philosophers, particularly those interested in general semantics, began to take up Bushnell's theory of language. But in all these cases the "Dissertation" took on a life of its own, separate from the rest of *God in Christ*, not to mention the larger Bushnell corpus.

Bushnell reflected a brief era in American Protestant theology in which the professional or academic model of theology had lost its dominance of the field. He was the pastor-theologian *par excellence*, a man whose theology flowed from his experience with his people. He was also deeply reflective of the Romantic spirit that enjoyed great popularity in the middle decades of the century. For Bushnell, the theologian was the seer blessed, looking into his soul for inspiration just as the poet did. Much of Bushnell's interest in language was part of a poet's awareness of the strength but limitations of language. From all of these perspectives he offered his criticism of the crabbed New England theology he had been taught in New Haven. But already by the time of his death the world of theology was beginning to change. The New Theology of Andover was decidedly an academic theology. It was part of the drive toward professionalization. Another speaker at the centennial of Bushnell's birth confessed, "Dr. Bushnell was not a theologian, in the sense in which that other great son of Connecticut, Jonathan Edwards, was a theologian. He had no desire to be. . . . He had a poet's fire of imagination, and a prophet's perception of the reality of God." The poet's imagination, however, was a weak foundation for academic theology.

Theology in late-nineteenth-century America was heading not toward poetry but toward science. In making peace with Darwin many theologians also attempted to lay claim to the new scientific method. Theology, they believed, could be as rigorously scientific as any other profession. The idea of evolution became the chosen tool for evaluating old beliefs and promoting the new. Religious thought, like everything else, evolved over time, and one could look at the roots of troublesome doctrines to offer a natural explanation of why they emerged and how they might be changed. As Theodore Thornton Munger explained, once evolution could be used in this way, theologians had no need for Bushnell's theory of language. The problem was not with the imprecision of words but with the limitations of certain historical doctrines. When the late-nineteenth-century American liberal theologian A. V. G. Allen revisited the question of the atonement in his book *The Continuity of Christian Thought* he did so through the vehicle of history, not language. By the beginning of the century many of Bushnell's professed heirs were questioning whether he could even be considered a theologian. George A. Gordon, himself a pastor-theologian at South Church Boston, though complimentary of many aspects of Bushnell's legacy, admitted,

> He has been an obstacle in the way of theological science. He identified the science of theology and the non-sensuous; he thought that all presentation of spiritual ideas must be, in the nature of the case, poetry. He did not see that poetry creates images for particular cases with a universal suggestiveness, while science presents through its symbol the universal idea from the heart of particulars.

Bushnell could offer no foundation for a new theological science.

ALWAYS THE PURITAN YANKEE

Later generations of scholars have tried to reinterpret Bushnell in their own images, but it has been the goal here to try to see him in light of his own time. He was very much a product of his New England background — both Puritan and Yankee. He was the product of a tinkering tradition in an age where tinkering was still an honorable occupation. He was doggedly loyal to the values of his home state at a time when a national character was still being formed. Even in his failings he reflected the New England of his age.

What was most significant about Bushnell was his concern with connecting things. He had, to repeat his daughter's observation, "no unrelated facts." A later era that accepted specialization also accepted division. Pastoring was one thing, planning parks another, speculating on language was still a third. A young man or woman had to decide in which of these areas he or she would specialize. But Bushnell lived in an era before a person had to make such choices. He wrote on such a myriad of topics and concerns because they all interested him and because he felt them to be important not only for himself but also for his fellow churchmen and countrymen. He wanted to hold all those things together and fought the idea of division. It has been said that a person is fundamentally changed when she lives in a town where she can see neither its beginning nor its end. She is robbed of the possibility of seeing her home in its entirety and possesses only a fragmentary vision of it. Bushnell knew the truth of this observation — particularly as it relates to one's larger world. The preacher's calling was to set forth God's rules for the sound ordering of body, soul, and community, and Bushnell's small Connecticut town made sense because all was in view: society was ordered around the village green with the church, town hall, and school holding its center. He truly believed that it was necessary to see in its totality the new world of the middle decades of the century in order to make sense of it. At the same time, however, it had to be viewed in a new way. In that sense he was always the Yankee, tinkering to make the vision clearer. He would tinker with language, with doctrine, and with ideas. He never rested from attempting to improve the world around him. But he never doubted that through that tinkering the vision would be the same: a personal God, whom human beings personally approached, and who, through his Spirit, was in contact with men and women, leading them in the path of truth, and grounding their families, communities, and nation. The world would always for Bushnell reflect those basic truths he had gleaned in Litchfield long ago. He would live and die a Puritan.

A Note on Sources

THE PRESENT study is largely based upon fresh readings of the writings of Horace Bushnell and his contemporaries. Because of this, whenever it may not be clear to the reader where the appropriate Bushnell text is to be found, I have indicated its location in the note on sources. For students interested in the precise citations, annotated copies of this manuscript have been deposited at the Burke Library of Union Theological Seminary, Columbia University, St. Mark's Library of the General Theological Seminary, and the library of the Yale Divinity School.

GENERAL RESOURCES

The student of Horace Bushnell finds himself or herself awash in secondary literature, inundated by a vast corpus of printed works, yet with relatively few private papers. Yale University (both its main library and the Divinity School library) contain the great bulk of Bushnell's unpublished works. For other manuscript sources the reader should consult the bibliography of Robert L. Edwards, *Of Singular Genius, of Singular Grace: A Biography of Horace Bushnell* (Cleveland: Pilgrim Press, 1992). Bibliographies of his printed works are found in three separate volumes: Henry Barrett Learned's compilation in Horace Bushnell, *The Spirit of Man: Sermons and Selections,* ed. Mary Bushnell Cheney (New York: Charles Scribner's Sons, 1903), William Alexander Johnson, *Nature and the Supernatural in the Theology of Horace Bushnell* (Lund: C. W. K. Gleerup, 1963), and James O. Duke, *Horace Bushnell on the Vitality of Biblical Language* (Chico, Calif.: Scholars Press, 1984). Duke also includes a comprehensive bibliography of secondary literature up to the time of the volume's publication.

On the life of Bushnell no student can avoid beginning with Mary B. Cheney, *Life and Letters of Horace Bushnell* (New York: Harper and Bros., 1880). She sets forth the basic narrative of Bushnell's life, as well as providing the vast bulk of his extant correspondence. Theodore T. Munger, *Horace Bushnell: Preacher and Theologian* (Boston: Houghton Mifflin, 1899), is not only a solid biography but is also still the best introduction to Bushnell's thought. In the 1950s, Barbara M. Cross, *Horace Bushnell: Minister to a Changing America* (Chicago: University of Chicago Press, 1958), knocked Bushnell off the liberal pedestal on which he had been placed, casting him instead as the spiritual precursor of the suburban minister of the 1950s. The last full biography is Robert L. Edwards, *Of Singular Genius, of Singular Grace: A Biography of Horace Bushnell* (Cleveland: Pilgrim Press, 1992). The work, while not placing Bushnell in a new framework, fills in some of the details of his life.

Almost every study of American theology has touched on Bushnell. Frank Hugh Foster, *A Genetic History of the New England Theology* (Chicago: University of Chicago Press, 1907), considered him in the context of the passing of the New England Theology, and returned to Bushnell in *The Modern Movement in American Theology: Sketches in the History of American Protestant Thought from the Civil War to the World War* (New York: Fleming H. Revell, 1939), in which he saw Bushnell as an early exponent of the modern movement. During the heyday of Protestant theological liberalism Bushnell was regularly evoked as a pioneer. See, for example, John W. Buckham, *Progressive Religious Thought in America: A Survey of the Enlarging Pilgrim Faith* (Boston: Houghton Mifflin, 1919). Another example is the particularly insightful *Bushnell Centenary: Minutes of the General Association of Connecticut at the One-Hundred and Ninety-Third Annual Meeting . . .* (Hartford: Hartford Press, 1902). Representative short studies of this period include George B.

Stevens, "Horace Bushnell and Albrecht Ritschl: A Comparison," *American Journal of Theology* 6 (1902): 35-56, and Luther A. Weigle, "The Christian Ideal of Family Life as Expounded in Horace Bushnell's 'Christian Nurture'," *Religious Education* 19 (1924): 47-57. Bushnell is also treated in historical studies of this era of American theology. See, for example, Kenneth Cauthen, *The Impact of American Religious Liberalism* (New York: Harper and Row, 1962), and William R. Hutchison, *The Modernist Impulse in American Protestantism* (Cambridge, Mass.: Harvard University Press, 1976). Following the Second World War Bushnell continued to be identified with liberalism, but also began to be yoked (by both theological and literary critics) to Transcendentalism. See, for example, the writings of Sydney Ahlstrom on Bushnell, particularly his discussions in *A Religious History of the American People* (New Haven: Yale University Press, 1972), and his "Horace Bushnell," in *A Handbook of Christian Theologians*, ed. Dean G. Peerman and Martin E. Marty (Cleveland: World, 1965); see also Charles Feidelson, *Symbolism and American Literature* (Chicago: University of Chicago Press, 1953); and R. W. B. Lewis, *The American Adam: Innocence, Tragedy, and Tradition in the Nineteenth Century* (Chicago: University of Chicago Press, 1955).

In the forty plus years since 1960 Bushnell has been treated by a myriad of scholars. Indeed, the nature of this scholarship — both in quantity and quality — makes any writer pause in enumerating "significant" contributions for fear of falling into the sin of omission. Some more specialized studies will be noted later in this essay, but among the most important are H. Shelton Smith ed., *Horace Bushnell* (New York: Oxford University Press, 1965), who focuses on the theme of comprehensiveness; Conrad Cherry, *Nature and Religious Imagination from Edwards to Bushnell* (Philadelphia: Fortress, 1980), who takes up the theme of organicism; Daniel Walker Howe, "The Social Science of Horace Bushnell," *Journal of American History* 70 (1983): 305-22, who argues for the coherence of Bushnell's thought; Donald A. Crosby, *Horace Bushnell's Theory of Language: In the Context of Other Nineteenth-Century Philosophies of Language* (The Hague: Mouton, 1975), Philip F. Gura, *The Wisdom of Words: Language, Theology, and Literature in the New England Renaissance* (Middletown, Conn.: Wesleyan University Press, 1981), James O. Duke, *Horace Bushnell on the Vitality of Biblical Language* (Chico, Calif.: Scholars Press, 1984), and David L. Smith, *Symbolism and Growth: The Religious Thought of Horace Bushnell* (Chico, Calif.: Scholars

Press, 1981), all of whom treat aspects of Bushnell's use of language; Ann Douglas, *The "Feminization" of American Culture* (New York: Alfred A. Knopf, 1977), who addresses some of the negative aspects of the liberal tradition; Daniel Walker Howe, *Making the American Self: Jonathan Edwards to Abraham Lincoln* (Cambridge, Mass.: Harvard University Press, 1997), David W. Haddorf, *Dependence and Freedom: The Moral Thought of Horace Bushnell* (Lanham, Md.: University Press of America, 1994), and Lee J. Makowski, *Horace Bushnell on Christian Character Development* (Lanham, Md.: University Press of America, 1999), each of whom treat Bushnell's interest in moral character; Bruce M. Stephens, *The Prism of Time and Eternity: Images of Christ in American Protestant Thought from Jonathan Edwards to Horace Bushnell* (Lanham, Md.: Scarecrow Press, 1996), who focuses on Christology; and Howard A. Barnes, *Horace Bushnell and the Virtuous Republic* (Metuchen, N.J.: Scarecrow Press, 1991), who treats Bushnell's social thought.

CHAPTER ONE

"The Age of Homespun" can be most conveniently found in Horace Bushnell, *Work and Play; or Literary Varieties* (New York: Charles Scribner's Sons, 1864).

The world of Bushnell's youth was far different from the world in which he spent his active career. Contemporary accounts of early-nineteenth-century Connecticut society include Timothy Dwight, *Travels in New England and New York*, 4 vols. (New Haven: T. Dwight, 1821); and Benjamin Trumbull, *A Complete History of Connecticut, Civil and Ecclesiastical . . .*, 2 vols. (New Haven: Maltby, Goldsmith, 1818). On a more anecdotal level, see Lyman Beecher, *The Autobiography, Correspondence, etc. of Lyman Beecher, D.D.*, ed. Charles Beecher, 2 vols. (New York: Harper and Bros., 1864); and S. G. Goodrich, *Recollections of a Lifetime . . .*, 2 vols. (New York: Miller, Orton, and Mulligan, 1859). The notorious Samuel Peters, *General History of Connecticut . . .* (New York: D. Appleton and Co., 1877), in which the term "blue law" may well have been coined, offers a very different picture of the Nutmeg State. For an understanding of the world of provincial Litchfield, see Arthur Goodenough, *The Clergy of Litchfield County* (n.p.: Litchfield County

University Club, 1909); Charles Shepherd Phelps, *Rural Life in Litchfield County* (Norfolk, Conn.: The Litchfield County University Club, 1917); and Alain C. White et al., *The History of the Town of Litchfield, Connecticut, 1720-1920* (Litchfield: Enquirer Print, 1920).

For an understanding of the political world of the commonwealth, see Albert Carlos Bates, *The Charter of Connecticut: A Study* (Hartford: Connecticut Historical Society, 1932); Robert J. Taylor, *Colonial Connecticut: A History* (Millwood, N.Y.: KTO Press, 1979); Alexander Johnston, *Connecticut: A Study of a Commonwealth-Democracy* (Boston: Houghton Mifflin, 1887); Richard L. Bushman, *From Puritan to Yankee: Character and Social Order in Connecticut, 1690-1765* (New York: W. W. Norton and Co., 1970); Oscar Zeichner, *Connecticut's Years of Controversy, 1750-1776* (Chapel Hill, N.C.: University of North Carolina Press, 1949); Bruce C. Daniels, *The Connecticut Town: Growth and Development, 1635-1790* (Middletown: Wesleyan University Press, 1979); Jackson Turner Main, *Society and Economy in Colonial Connecticut* (Princeton: Princeton University Press, 1985); Richard J. Purcell, *Connecticut in Transition: 1775-1818* (1918; reprint, Middletown, Conn.: Wesleyan University Press, 1963); and Jarvis Means Morse, *A Neglected Period of Connecticut's History, 1818-1850* (New Haven: Yale University Press, 1933). Richard L. Bushman, *The Refinement of America: Persons, Houses, Cities* (New York: Vintage Books, 1993), is an insightful cultural discussion of the transformation of New England life during these years.

No one can hope to track the world of New England clergy without the help of three multivolume reference works: William B. Sprague, *Annals of the American Pulpit . . .* , 9 vols. (New York: Robert Carter and Bros., 1857-69), offers irreplaceable biographies of colonial and early national clergy. Franklin B. Dexter, *Biographical Sketches of the Graduates of Yale College with Annuals of the College History*, 6 vols. (New York: Henry Holt, 1885-1912), and John L. Sibley [continued by Clifford K. Shipton], *Biographical Sketches of Those Who Attended Harvard College*, 14 vols. (Boston: Massachusetts Historical Society, 1873-1968), are both invaluable resources. On other aspects of the religious world of Bushnell's youth see Ola Elizabeth Winslow, *Meetinghouse Hill: 1630-1783* (New York: Macmillan Publishing Co., 1952); Leonard Bacon, *The Genesis of the New England Churches* (New York: Harper and Bros., 1874); Williston Walker, *The Creeds and Platforms of Congregation-*

alism, with an introduction by Douglas Horton (Boston: Pilgrim Press, 1960); Leonard Bacon et al., *Contributions to the Ecclesiastical History of Connecticut* . . . (New Haven: William L. Kingsley, 1861); David W. Kling, *A Field of Divine Wonders: The New Divinity and Village Revivals in Northwestern Connecticut, 1792-1822* (University Park: Pennsylvania State University Press, 1993); M. Louise Greene, *The Development of Religious Liberty in Connecticut* (Boston: Houghton Mifflin, 1905); and Jarvis Means Morse, *The Rise of Liberalism in Connecticut, 1828-1850* (New Haven: Tercentenary Commission of the State of Connecticut, 1933).

On the musical tradition in New England, see George Hood, *A History of Music in New England: With Biographical Sketches of Reformers and Psalmists* (Boston: Wilkins, Carter, and Co., 1846); and Percy A. Scholes, *The Puritans and Music in England and New England: A Contribution to the Cultural History of Two Nations* (London: Oxford University Press, 1934).

Finally, on the question of Puritanism and "Yankeedom," in addition to the Bushman volume cited above *(From Puritan to Yankee),* see Richard S. Dunn, *Puritans and Yankees: The Winthrop Dynasty of New England, 1630-1717* (Princeton: Princeton University Press, 1962); George M. Dutcher, *Connecticut's Tercentenary: A Retrospect of Three Centuries of Self Government and Steady Habits* (New Haven: Yale University Press, 1934); Chard Powers Smith, *Yankees and God* (New York: Hermitage House, 1954); and Michel Chevalier, *Society, Manners and Politics in the United States: Being a Series of Letters on North America* (Boston: Weeks, Jordan and Co., 1839). Christopher Collier, "Steady Habits Considered and Reconsidered," *Connecticut Review* 5 (1972): 28-37, offers some bibliographical suggestions for the discussion of the veracity of the label "land of steady habits."

CHAPTER TWO

"Natural Science and Moral Philosophy" is found in the archives of the Yale Divinity School Library.

The standard history of the city of New Haven is still Rollin C. Osterweis, *Three Centuries of New Haven, 1638-1938* (New Haven: Yale University Press, 1953). Contemporary descriptions of the city can be found in Daniel Haskel and J. Calvin Smith, *A Complete Descriptive and Statistical Gazetteer of the United States of America* . . . (New York: Sherman and Smith, 1843); and S. G. Goodrich, *Recollections of a Lifetime* . . . , 2 vols. (New York: Miller, Orton, and Mulligan, 1859). Yale College has never lacked for people eager to tell its story. See Ebenezer Baldwin, *Annals of Yale College from Its Foundation, A.D. 1701, to the Year 1838* (New Haven: Benjamin and William Noyes, 1841); Frank Bowditch Dexter, *Sketch of the History of Yale University* (New York: Henry Holt and Co., 1887); Clarence Deming, *Yale Yesterday* (New Haven: Yale University Press, 1915); and Reuben A. Holden, *Yale: A Pictorial History* (New Haven: Yale University Press, 1967). On the religious life of Yale see: Ralph Henry Gabriel, *Religion and Learning at Yale: The Church of Christ in the College and University, 1757-1957* (New Haven: Yale University Press, 1958); and James B. Reynolds et al., *Two Centuries of Christian Activity at Yale* (New York: G. P. Putnam's Sons, 1901). On the Divinity School see Roland H. Bainton, *Yale and the Ministry: A History of Education for the Christian Ministry at Yale from the Founding in 1701* (New York: Harper and Bros., 1957); and *Eighth General Catalogue of the Yale Divinity School: Centennial Issue, 1822-1922* (New Haven: published by the University, 1922).

On the theological issues that divided the children of the Puritans, see Frank Lambert, *Inventing the "Great Awakening"* (Princeton: Princeton University Press, 1999); Edmund S. Morgan, *The Gentle Puritan: A Life of Ezra Stiles, 1727-1795* (New Haven: Yale University Press, 1962); Michael J. Crawford, *Seasons of Grace: Colonial New England's Revival Tradition in Its British Context* (New York: Oxford University Press, 1991); Allen C. Guelzo, *Edwards on the Will: A Century of American Theological Debate* (Middletown, Conn.: Wesleyan University Press, 1989); Bruce Kuklick, *Churchmen and Philosophers: From Jonathan Edwards to John Dewey* (New Haven: Yale University Press, 1985); Nathan O. Hatch and Harry S. Stout, eds., *Jonathan Edwards and the American Experience* (New York: Oxford University Press, 1988); Joseph A. Conforti, *Jonathan Edwards, Religious Tradition, and American Culture* (Chapel Hill, N.C.: University of North Carolina Press, 1995); Charles R. Keller, *The Second Great Awakening in Connecticut* (New Haven: Yale University Press, 1942); Richard D. Shiels, "The Second Great Awakening in Connecticut: Critique of the Traditional Interpretation," *Church History* 49 (1980): 401-15; also Shiels' dissertation, "The Connecticut Clergy in the Second Great Awakening" (Ph.D. diss., Boston University, 1977); Richard Birdsall, "The Second Great Awakening and the New England Social Order," *Church History* 39 (1970): 345-64; Joseph A. Conforti, *Samuel Hopkins and the New Divinity Movement: Calvinism, the Congregational Ministry and Reform in New England Between the Great Awakenings* (Grand Rapids: Christian University Press, 1981); Robert C. Whittemore, *The Transformation of New England Theology* (New York: Peter Lang, 1987); Earl A. Pope, *New England Calvinism and the Disruption of the Presbyterian Church* (New York: Garland Publishing Inc., 1987); Paul K. Conkin, *The Uneasy Center: Reformed Christianity in Antebellum America* (Chapel Hill, N.C.: The University of North Carolina Press, 1995); Leonard Woods, *History of the Andover Theological Seminary* (Boston: James R. Osgood and Co., 1885); and Sidney Earl Mead, *Nathaniel William Taylor, 1786-1858: A Connecticut Liberal* (Chicago: University of Chicago Press, 1942); as well as a number of the works cited in the last chapter.

There are a number of works on the Unitarians and Episcopalians during this era. On the Unitarians see John Corrigan, *The Hidden Balance: Religion and Social Theories of Charles Chauncy and Jonathan Mayhew* (Cambridge: Cambridge University Press, 1987); as well as his *The Prism of Piety: Catholick Congregational Clergy at the Beginning of the Enlightenment* (New York: Oxford University Press, 1991); Conrad Wright, *The Beginning of Unitarianism in America* (Boston: Starr King Press, 1955); Wright's *The Liberal Christians: Essays on American Unitarian History* (Boston: Beacon Press, 1970); Daniel Walker Howe, *The Unitarian Conscience: Harvard Moral Philosophy, 1805-1861* (Cambridge, Mass.: Harvard University Press, 1970); and George Edward Ellis, *A Half-Century of the Unitarian Controversy . . .* (Boston: Crosby, Nichols, and Co., 1857). The literature is not as complete on the Episcopalians. Samuel Peters, *General History of Connecticut . . .* (New York: D. Appleton and Co., 1877), is a Tory Anglican history. See, too, E. Edwards Beardsley, *Life and Correspondence of Samuel Johnson, D.D.* (New York: Hurd and Houghton, 1874); E. Edwards Beardsley, *The History of the Episcopal Church in Connecticut*, 2 vols. (New York: Hurd and Houghton, 1866); Nelson R. Burr, *The Story of the Diocese of Connecticut: A New Branch of the Vine* (Hartford: Church Missions Publishing Co., 1962). For an account of an influential Episcopal laywoman, see Gordon S. Haight, *Mrs. Sigourney: The Sweet Singer of Hartford* (New Haven: Yale University Press, 1930).

Bertram Wyatt-Brown, *Lewis Tappan and the Evangelical War Against Slavery* (Cleveland: Press of Case Western Reserve University, 1969), provides some choice details about Bushnell's days in New York that have eluded other biographers. Finally, for two works Bushnell studied while at Yale, one of which he rejected and the other accepted, see William Paley, *The Principles of Moral and Political Philosophy*, 2 vols. (Boston: Printed for John West, 1801); and Josiah W. Gibbs, *Philological Studies: With English Illustrations* (New Haven: Durrie and Peck, 1857).

CHAPTER THREE

Bushnell's address to the Andover Love of Inquiry Society is found in the archives of the Yale Divinity School Library. A typed transcript is included in David S. Steward, "Horace Bushnell and Contemporary Christian Education: A Study of Revelation and Nurture" (Ph.D. diss., Yale University, 1966). *Sermons for the New Life* (New York: Charles Scribner's Sons, 1858) contains many examples of early Bushnell sermons, including those cited in this chapter. "Taste and Fashion" is found in the *New Englander* 1 (1843): 153-68. "Review of the Errors of the Times" is found in the *New Englander* 2 (1844): 143-75.

A detailed contemporary description of the city of Hartford about the time of the beginning of Bushnell's ministry is found in Daniel Haskel and J. Calvin Smith, *A Complete Descriptive and Statistical Gazetteer of the United States of America* . . . (New York: Sherman and Smith, 1843). There exist a number of contemporary accounts by foreign visitors that offer a sense of place. See Una Pope-Hennessy, ed., *The Aristocratic Journey: Being the Outspoken Letters of Mrs. Basil Hall* . . . (New York: G. P. Putnam's Sons, 1931); John Robert Godley, *Letters from America*, 2 vols. (London: J. Murray, 1844); and James Stuart, *Three Years in North America*, 2 vols. (New York: J. and J. Harper, 1833). For reflections by native residents, see Increase N. Tarbox, ed., *Diary of Thomas Robbins, D.D., 1796-1854* (Boston: Thomas Todd, 1887); and Edward A. Lawrence, *The Life of the Rev. Joel Hawes, D.D.* . . . (Hartford: Hammersley and Co., 1873). Histories of the city include J. Hammond Trumbull, ed., *The Memorial History of Hartford County, Connecticut, 1633-1884*, 2 vols. (Boston: Edward L. Osgood, 1886); Helen Post Chapman, *My Hartford of the Nineteenth Century* (Hartford: Edward Valentine Mitchell, 1928); Ellsworth Strong Grant and Marion Hepburn, *The City of Hartford, 1784-1984: An Illustrated History* ([Hartford]: Connecticut Historical Society, 1986); and Willis I. Twitchell, ed., *Hartford in History* (Hartford: Press of the Plimpton Mfg. Co., 1899).

On aspects of the religious scene, see George Leon Walker, *History of the First Church in Hartford, 1633-1883* (Hartford: Brown and Gross, 1884); *A Brief History of the Formation of the North Church, in Hartford, Ct., Together with . . . a Form of Covenant* (Hartford, 1832); Stanley B. Weld, *The History of Immanuel Church, 1824-1967* (Hartford: Connecticut Printers, 1968); and Robert L. Edwards, "Portrait of a People — Horace Bushnell's Hartford Congregation," in *Studies of the Church in History: Essays Honoring Robert S. Paul on His Sixty-Fifth Birthday*, ed. Horton Davies (Alison Park, Pa.: Pickwick Publications, 1983). On the question of church architecture, in addition to Richard Bushman's *The Refinement of America: Persons, Houses, Cities* (New York: Vintage Books, 1993), the reader should consult Peter Benes, ed., *New England Meeting House and Church, 1630-1850* (Boston: Boston University, [1980]); and Gretchen Townsend Buggelin, "Elegance and Sensibility in the Calvinist Tradition: The First Congregational Church of Hartford, Connecticut," in *Seeing Beyond the Word: Visual Arts and the Calvinist Tradition*, ed. Paul Corby Finney (Grand Rapids: William B. Eerdmans, 1999).

Bushnell was noted for being both a pastor and a preacher. Both responsibilities were in transition during this period. On preaching, see Lewis O. Brastow, *Representative Modern Preachers* (New York: Macmillan Publishing Co., 1904); Ernest Trice Thompson, *Changing Emphases in American Preaching* (Philadelphia: Westminster Press, 1943); and Lee J. Makowski, *Horace Bushnell on Christian Character Development* (Lanham, Md.: University Press of America, 1999). On ministry, see Daniel Dulany Addison, *The Clergy in American Life and Letters* (New York: Macmillan Publishing Co., 1900); Edwin D. Mead, *Horace Bushnell: The Citizen* (Boston: Congregationalist Bookstore, 1900); Gordon Arthur Riegler, *The Socialization of the New England Clergy, 1800-1860* (Greenfield, Ohio: The Greenfield Printing and Publishing Co., 1945); Donald M. Scott, *From Office to Profession: The New England Ministry, 1750-1850* (Philadelphia: University of Pennsylvania Press, 1978); and Richard Rabinowitz, *The Spiritual Self in Everyday Life: The Transformation of Personal Religious Experience in Nineteenth-Century*

New England (Boston: Northeastern University Press, 1989). Although this study has not overly emphasized the Bushnell-Coleridge connection, others have. See Mildred Kitto Billings, "The Theology of Horace Bushnell Considered in Relation to That of Samuel Taylor Coleridge" (Ph.D. diss., University of Chicago, 1959). See also Claude Welch, *Protestant Thought in the Nineteenth Century*, Vol. 1: *1799-1870* (New Haven: Yale University Press, 1972), for one scholar's placing of Bushnell into the larger theological framework.

An under-explored aspect of Bushnell's ministry was his active role in religious disputation. On the "Episcopal controversy" see *Contributions to the History of Christ Church, Hartford*, 2 vols. (Hartford: Belknap and Warfield, 1845-1908); "Catholicus," *A Letter to Dr. Bushnell of Hartford, on the Rationalistic, Socinian, and Infidel Tendency of Certain Passages in His Address Before the Alumni of Yale College* (Hartford: Henry S. Parsons, 1843); Thomas C. Brownell, *Errors of the Times . . .* (Hartford: Case, Tiffany and Co., 1843); and Alonzo B. Chapin, *New-Englandism Not the Religion of the Bible . . .* (Hartford: Henry S. Parsons, 1844). For historical background for this dispute, see Robert Bruce Mullin, *Episcopal Vision/American Reality: High Church Theology and Social Thought in Evangelical America* (New Haven: Yale University Press, 1986).

CHAPTER FOUR

Bushnell's European Travel Diary is the great untapped resource in Bushnell scholarship. Although it is written in his almost indecipherable handwriting, it contains insights and observations found nowhere else. The diary is found in the archives of the Yale Divinity School Library. The "Letter to His Holiness Pope Gregory XVI" is reprinted in *Building Eras in Religion* (New York: Charles Scribner's Sons, 1910).

Marie Hansen-Taylor and Horace E. Scudder, eds., *Life and Letters of Bayard Taylor*, 2 vols. (Boston: Houghton Mifflin, 1885); and Albert H. Smyth, *Bayard Taylor* (Boston: Houghton Mifflin, 1896), offer some details concerning Bushnell's trans-Atlantic crossing.

On the religious condition of Britain at the time, see Frances Knight, *The Nineteenth-Century Church and English Society* (Cambridge:

Cambridge University Press, 1995); Richard Brown, *Church and State in Modern Britain, 1700-1850* (London: Routledge, 1991); and Owen Chadwick, *The Victorian Church,* 2 vols. (London: Adam and Charles Black, 1966-70). For the religious world of continental Europe, see Hugh McLeod, *Religion and the People of Western Europe, 1789-1970* (New York: Oxford University Press, 1981); Nigel Aston, ed., *Religious Change in Europe, 1650-1914* (Oxford: Clarendon Press, 1997); Hugh McLeod, ed., *European Religion in the Age of the Great Cities, 1830-1930* (London: Routledge, 1995); Owen Chadwick, *The Secularization of the European Mind in the Nineteenth Century* (Cambridge: Cambridge University Press, 1975); and René Rémond, *Religion and Society in Modern Europe,* trans. Antonia Nevill (Oxford: Blackwell Publishers, 1999).

The controversy over the state of the American church, to which Bushnell alludes, is recorded in the *Congregational Magazine* [London] 9 (April 1845). The Evangelical Alliance was a much discussed issue on both sides of the Atlantic. See Richard Whately, *Thoughts on the Proposed Evangelical Alliance* (London: B. Fellowes, 1846); Leonard Bacon and E. N. Kirk, *The Christian Alliance: Addresses . . .* (New York: S. W. Benedict, 1845); and Thomas Chalmers, *The Evangelical Alliance* (Edinburgh: Oliver and Boyd, 1846). For historical background to the movement, see Philip D. Jordan, *The Evangelical Alliance for the United States of America, 1847-1900: Ecumenism, Identity, and the Religion of the Republic* (New York: The Edwin Mellon Press, 1982).

On contemporary interest in the German "Reformation," see "The German Anti-Papal Movement," *New Englander* 5 (1847): 282-305. On issues of anti-Catholicism, see Ray Allen Billington, *The Protestant Crusade, 1800-1860: A Study of the Origins of American Nativism* (New York: Macmillan Publishing Co., 1938); and Carleton Mabee, *The American Leonardo: A Life of Samuel F. B. Morse* (New York: Alfred A. Knopf, 1943).

The two most important works of the philosopher John Morell during this period are *The Philosophy of Religion* (New York: D. Appleton and Co., 1849); and *An Historical and Critical View of the Speculative Philosophy of Europe in the Nineteenth Century* (New York: Robert Carter, 1848). On Morell, see Robert Theobald, *Memorials of John Daniel Morell* (London: Stewart, 1891).   •

CHAPTER FIVE

Both "Day of Roads" and "Barbarism the First Danger" are reprinted in *Work and Play; or Literary Varieties* (New York: Charles Scribner's Sons, 1864). "Christian Comprehensiveness" is reprinted in *Building Eras in Religion* (New York: Charles Scribner's Sons, 1910). It is also found in H. Shelton Smith, ed., *Horace Bushnell* (New York: Oxford University Press, 1965), but the anti-Anglican passages have been edited. On the theme of comprehensiveness, see also Irving Henry Bartlett, "Bushnell, Cousin, and Comprehensive Christianity," *Journal of Religion* 37 (1957): 99-104.

On the question of revivalism in antebellum America, see William Sprague, *Lectures on Revivals of Religion*, 2nd ed. (New York: Daniel Appleton and Co., 1833); Robert Baird, *Religion in America* (New York: Harper and Bros., 1856); and Calvin Colton, *History and Character of American Revivals* (London: Frederick Westley and A. H. Davis, 1832). For critics, see Daniel Walker Howe, *The Unitarian Conscience: Harvard Moral Philosophy, 1805-1861* (Cambridge, Mass.: Harvard University Press, 1970); Sydney E. Ahlstrom and Jonathan S. Carey, eds., *An American Reformation: A Documentary History of Unitarian Christianity* (Middletown, Conn.: Wesleyan University Press, 1985); Calvin Colton, *Thoughts on the Religious State of the Country: With Reasons for Preferring Episcopacy* (New York: Harper and Bros., 1836); John Henry Hopkins, *The Primitive Church, Compared with the Protestant Episcopal Church of the Present Day . . .* (Burlington, Vt.: Smith and Harrington, 1835); and John W. Nevin, *The Anxious Bench*, 2nd ed. (Chambersburg, Pa.: Printed at the Publication Office of the German Reformed Church, 1844). Nevin, along with Bushnell, was perhaps revivalism's most famous critic. On Nevin see Glenn A. Hewitt, *Regeneration and Morality: A Study of Charles Finney, Charles Hodge, John W. Nevin, and Horace Bushnell* (Brooklyn: Carlson Publishing Co., 1991); Theodore Appel, *The Life and Work of John Williamson Nevin* (Philadelphia: Reformed Church Publishing House, 1889); James Hastings Nichols, *Romanticism in American Theology: Nevin and Schaff at Mercersburg* (Chicago: University of Chicago Press, 1961); and Sam Hamstra Jr. and Arie J. Griffioen, *Reformed Confessionalism in Nineteenth-Century America: Essays on the Thought of John Williamson Nevin* (Lanham, Md.: Scarecrow Press, 1995).

On the question of family and children in nineteenth-century America there is a burgeoning literature. Frances Trollope, *Domestic Manners of the Americans,* ed. Donald Smalley (New York: Alfred A. Knopf, 1949), provides some caustic comments. Harriet Martineau, *Society in America* (London: Saunders and Ottley, 1837), was kinder. See also (among many) Bernard Wishy, *The Child and the Republic: The Dawn of American Child Nurture* (Philadelphia: University of Pennsylvania Press, 1968); Arthur W. Calhoun, *A Social History of the American Family: From Colonial Times to the Present,* 3 vols. (Cleveland: The Arthur H. Clark Co., 1918); Colleen McDannell, *The Christian Home in Victorian America, 1840-1900* (Bloomington, Ind.: Indiana University Press, 1986); Sanford Fleming, *Children and Puritanism: The Place of Children in the Life and Thought of the New England Churches, 1620-1847* (New Haven: Yale University Press, 1933); Judith L. Newton et al., *Sex and Class in Women's History* (London: Routledge and Kegan Paul, 1983); Christopher Lasch, *Haven in a Heartless World: The Family Besieged* (New York: Basic Books, 1977); Stephanie Coontz, *The Social Origins of Private Life: A History of American Families, 1600-1900* (London: Routledge, Chapman and Hall, 1988); Karen Halttunen, *Confidence Men and Painted Women: A Study of Middle Class Culture in America* (New Haven: Yale University Press, 1982); Mary P. Ryan, *Cradle of the Middle Class: The Family in Oneida County, New York, 1790-1865* (Cambridge: Cambridge University Press, 1981); Ann Douglas, *The "Feminization" of American Culture* (New York: Alfred A. Knopf, 1977); and Philip Greven, *The Protestant Temperament: Patterns of Child-Rearing, Religious Experience, and the Self in Early America* (New York: Alfred A. Knopf, 1977).

On the question of the Puritans, much hung upon the relationship between the Great Awakening and the Puritan tradition. For three different interpretations of the meaning of the Great Awakening, see Jon Butler, "Enthusiasm Described and Decried: The Great Awakening as Interpretive Fiction," *Journal of American History* 69 (1982): 305-25; Joseph A. Conforti, "The Invention of the Great Awakening, 1795-1842," *Early American Literature* 26 (1991): 99-118; and Frank Lambert, *Inventing the "Great Awakening"* (Princeton: Princeton University Press, 1999). David Hall in his introduction to Jonathan Edwards, *Ecclesiastical Writings* (New Haven: Yale University Press, 1994), sides in large part with Bushnell's assessment of Edwards as an innovator in ecclesiastical practices.

On the memory of the Puritans in the nineteenth century, see Edward Arber, *The Story of the Pilgrim Fathers, 1606-1623, A.D., As Told by Themselves, Their Friends, and Their Enemies* (Boston: Houghton and Mifflin, 1897); Edwin Hall, *The Puritans and Their Principles,* 2nd ed. (New York: Baker and Scribner, 1846); Jan C. Dawson, *The Unusable Past: America's Puritan Tradition, 1830-1930* (Chico, Calif.: Scholars Press, 1984); Lawrence Buell, *New England Literary Culture: From Revolution Through Renaissance* (Cambridge: Cambridge University Press, 1986); Dixon Ryan Fox, *Yankees and Yorkers* (New York: University Press, 1940); Wesley Frank Craven, *The Legend of the Founding Fathers* (New York: New York University Press, 1956). Of critics of the Puritans, perhaps no one relished the task more so than James Fenimore Cooper. See Thomas R. Lounsbury, *American Men of Letters; James Fenimore Cooper* (Boston: Houghton Mifflin, 1882); John P. McWilliams Jr., *Political Justice in the Republic: James Fenimore Cooper's America* (Berkeley: University of California Press, 1972); and William M. Hogue, "The Novel as a Religious Tract: James Fenimore Cooper — Apologist for the Episcopal Church," *Historical Magazine of the Protestant Episcopal Church* 40 (1971): 5-26. For other contemporary accounts, see Philip Schaf[f], *The Principle of Protestantism as Related to the Present State of the Church . . .* (Chambersburg, Penn.: Printed at the Publication Office of the German Reformed Church, 1845); Henry Tuckerman, "New England Philosophy," *United States Magazine and Democratic Review* 16 (1845): 79-91; "New England Character," *North American Review* 44 (1837): 237-60; "New England Character," *Southern Literary Messenger* 3 (1837): 412-17; David M. Reese, *Quakerism vs. Calvinism: Being a Reply to "Quakerism Not Christianity" . . .* (New York: William A. Mercein, 1834); George Fitzhugh, *Sociology for the South, or the Failure of Free Society* (1854; reprint, New York: B. Franklin, 1965); *An Account of the Celebration by the New York Historical Society of Their Fortieth Anniversary* (New York: Press of the New York Historical Society, 1844); Thomas W. Coit, *Puritanism: or a Churchman's Defence Against Its Aspersions* (New York: D. Appleton and Co., 1845); Thomas C. Brownell, *Errors of the Times . . .* (Hartford: Case, Tiffany and Co., 1843); and Alonzo B. Chapin, *New-Englandism Not the Religion of the Bible . . .* (Hartford: Henry S. Parsons, 1844). For some background to this controversy see Robert Bruce Mullin, *Episcopal Vision/American Reality: High Church Theology and Social Thought in Evangelical America* (New Haven: Yale University Press, 1986).

Bushnell has probably been most discussed in relation to the question of Christian nurture. For a background to some of the theological issues, see H. Shelton Smith, *Changing Conceptions of Original Sin: A Study in American Theology Since 1750* (New York: Charles Scribner's Sons, 1958). Among the most important analyses of Bushnell written during his own era are [Charles Hodge], "Bushnell on Christian Nurture," *Biblical Repertory and Princeton Review*, n.s. 19 (1847): 502-39; the discussion by John W. Nevin in the *Weekly Messenger of the German Reformed Church* (n.s. 12 [23, 30 June; 7, 14 July; 1 September, 1847]); "Bushnell's Christian Nurture," *Church Review and Ecclesiastical Register* 1 (1848): 228-45; and two works by Bennet Tyler, *Dr. Tyler's Letter to Dr. Bushnell on Christian Nurture* (East Windsor Hill, Conn., [1847]); and *Letters to the Rev. Horace Bushnell, D.D., Containing Strictures on His Book Entitled 'Views of Christian Nurture'* (Hartford: Brown and Parsons, 1848). For other works on Bushnell and formation, see George Stewart Jr., *A History of Religious Education in Connecticut to the Middle of the Nineteenth Century* (New Haven: Yale University Press, 1924); H. Shelton Smith, *Faith and Nurture* (New York: Charles Scribner's Sons, 1941); Richard Rabinowitz, *The Spiritual Self in Everyday Life: The Transformation of Personal Religious Experience in Nineteenth-Century New England* (Boston: Northeastern University Press, 1989); David W. Haddorff, *Dependence and Freedom: The Moral Thought of Horace Bushnell* (Lanham, Md.: University Press of America, 1994); Lee J. Makowski, *Horace Bushnell on Christian Character Development* (Lanham, Md.: University Press of America, 1999); Amos S. Chesebrough, *The Theological Opinions of Horace Bushnell as Related to His Character and Christian Experience* (n.p., 1886); Luther A. Weigle, "The Christian Ideal of Family Life as Expounded in Horace Bushnell's 'Christian Nurture'," *Religious Education* 19 (1924): 47-57; Leander Samuel Harding, "Christian Nurture Revisited: A Theological and Psychological Exposition and Development of Horace Bushnell's Work on the Foundations of Christian Child-Rearing" (Ph.D. diss., Boston College, 1989); Paul H. Vieth, *The Church and Christian Education* (St. Louis: Bethany Press, 1947); and Jack L. Seymour, *From Sunday School to Church School: Continuities in Protestant Church Education in the United States, 1860-1929* (Washington D.C.: University Press of America, 1982).

CHAPTER SIX

The standard nineteenth-century American version of the life of Madame Guyon is Thomas C. Upham, *Life . . . of Madame de la Mothe Guyon . . .*, 2 vols. (New York: Harper and Bros., 1849). The most accessible and entertaining (but by no means the most objective) secondary literature in English on her and her movement is Ronald A. Knox, *Enthusiasm: A Chapter in the History of Religion . . .* (New York: Oxford University Press, 1950). On some of the various theological issues addressed in *God in Christ*, see Anselm of Canterbury, *Why God Became Man . . .*, with translation, introduction, and notes by Joseph M. Colleran (Albany, N.Y.: Magi Books, 1969); J. K. Mozley, *The Doctrine of the Atonement* (New York: Charles Scribner's Sons, 1916); J. N. D. Kelly, *Early Christian Doctrines*, 2nd ed. (London: Adam and Charles Black, 1960); Gustaf Aulén, *Christus Victor: An Historical Study of the Three Main Types of the Idea of the Atonement* (London: SPCK, 1931); R. L. Ottley, *The Doctrine of the Incarnation*, 2 vols. (London: Methuen, 1904); Bernhard Lohse, *A Short History of Christian Doctrine* (Philadelphia: Fortress Press, 1966); and C. C. Richardson, *The Doctrine of the Trinity* (New York: Abingdon, 1958). For particular discussions of Bushnell's theology, see Frank Hugh Foster, *A Genetic History of the New England Theology* (Chicago: University of Chicago Press, 1907); Fred Kirschenmann, "Horace Bushnell: Orthodox or Sabellian?" *Church History* 33 (1964): 49-59; Bruce M. Stephens, *God's Last Metaphor: The Doctrine of the Trinity in New England Theology* (Missoula, Mont.: Scholars Press, 1980); Bruce Kuklick, *Churchmen and Philosophers: From Jonathan Edwards to John Dewey* (New Haven: Yale University Press, 1985); and Claude Welch, *Protestant Thought in the Nineteenth Century*, Vol. 1: *1799-1870* (New Haven: Yale University Press, 1972). On Bushnell's invocation of Pastor John Robinson in his Andover discourse, see *The Works of John Robinson, Pastor of the Pilgrim Fathers, with a Memoir and Annotations by Robert Ashton*, 3 vols. (Boston: Doctrinal Tract and Book Society, 1851); and Alexander Young, *Chronicles of the Pilgrim Fathers of the Colony of Plymouth* (Boston: C. C. Little and J. Brown, 1841). On the vocation of the theologian in nineteenth-century America, see W. Clark Gilpin, *A Preface to Theology* (Chicago: University of Chicago Press, 1996).

Other scholars have offered a more exalted picture of Bushnell's theory of language. No one has done so more exhaustively than Donald A. Crosby, *Horace Bushnell's Theory of Language: In the Context of Other Nineteenth-Century Philosophies of Language* (The Hague: Mouton, 1975). Other studies include Harold A. Durfee, "Language and Religion: Horace Bushnell and Rowland G. Hazard," *American Quarterly* 5 (1953): 57-70; Michael P. Kramer, "Horace Bushnell's Philosophy of Language Considered as a Mode of Cultural Criticism," *American Quarterly* 38 (1986): 573-90; Philip F. Gura, *The Wisdom of Words: Language, Theology, and Literature in the New England Renaissance* (Middletown, Conn.: Wesleyan University Press, 1981); James O. Duke, *Horace Bushnell on the Vitality of Biblical Language* (Chico, Calif.: Scholars Press, 1984); David L. Smith, *Symbolism and Growth: The Religious Thought of Horace Bushnell* (Chico, Calif.: Scholars Press, 1981); and Michael P. Kramer, *Imagining Language in America from the Revolution to the Civil War* (Princeton, N.J.: Princeton University Press, 1991).

CHAPTER SEVEN

The debate over *God in Christ* was one of the great theological controversies in nineteenth-century America. Unfortunately, the primary materials are largely inaccessible to the general reader. Indeed, *Christ in Theology* was not republished until the late 1980s. It is the assertion of this volume that the standard account of the controversy is less than wholly impartial. The basic source other than Cheney's biography itself — Edwin P. Parker, *The Hartford Central Association and the Bushnell Controversy* (Hartford: Case, Lockwood, and Brainard, 1896) — is at key points both partisan and presentist. A far better account is Edward Robert Peterson, "The Horace Bushnell Controversy: A Study of Heresy in Nineteenth-Century America, 1828-1854" (Ph.D. diss., University of Iowa, 1984), although his and my interpretations differ on key points.

Part of the problem lies with the unavailability of the sources. Some of the most important discussion lies buried in mid-century church periodicals. *The Religious Herald* (Hartford), the *Puritan Recorder* (Boston), and the *New York Evangelist* (New York City) are all treasure troves for information on the controversy. In Britain, the *Westminster and Foreign Quarterly Review*, the *British Quarterly Review*, *The Inquirer* (London), and *The Witness* (London) provide important commentary.

Still another source is the *Minutes of the General Association of Connecticut* from the years between 1849 and 1853.

There are also the official protests of Fairfield West Association. See *Remonstrance and Complaint of the Association of Fairfield West to the Hartford Central Association together with the Reply of the Hartford Central Association* (New York: S. W. Benedict, 1850); *Appeal of the Association of Fairfield West to the Associated Ministers Connected with the General Association of Connecticut* (New York: Baker, Goodwin, and Co., 1852); and *A Protest of the Pastoral Union to the Pastors and Churches of Connecticut* (Wethersfield, [1854]).

Among the more significant theological responses the controversy evoked, see Orestes Brownson, "Bushnell's Discourses," in *The Works of Orestes Brownson*, ed. Henry F. Brownson, 20 vols. (New York: AMS Press, 1966), 7:1-116; [Charles Hodge], "Bushnell's Discourses: Review of *God in Christ*, by Horace Bushnell," *Biblical Repertory and Princeton Review*, n.s. 21 (1849): 259-98; "Bushnell's Discourses *[God in Christ]*," *Christian Examiner and Religious Miscellany* 46 4th s. 11 (1849): 453-84; "Replies to Horace Bushnell," *Christian Examiner and Religious Miscellany* 47 4th s. 12 (1849): 238-47; "Review of *God in Christ*," *The Christian Observatory* 3 (1849): 241-300; Henry Boynton Smith, "The Relation of Faith and Philosophy," reprinted in *Faith and Philosophy: Discourses and Essays by Henry B. Smith*, ed. George L. Prentiss (New York: Scribner, Armstrong and Co., 1877); David N. Lord, "Dr. Bushnell's 'Dissertation on Language,'" *Theological and Literary Journal* 2 (1849): 61-130; David N. Lord, "Dr. Bushnell's Discourses *[God in Christ]*," *Theological and Literary Journal* 2 (1849): 173-222; Robert Turnbull, *Review of Dr. Bushnell's Theories of the Incarnation and the Atonement* (Hartford: Brockett, Furner and Co., 1849); "The Position of Congregationalism," *Church Review and Ecclesiastical Register* 2 (1849-50): 559-72; [Amos S. Chesebrough], *Contributions of C.C.: Now Declared in Full as Criticus Criticorum* (Hartford: Brown and Parsons, 1849); Henry M. Goodwin, "Thoughts, Words, and Things," *Bibliotheca Sacra* 6 (1849): 271-300; and Enoch Pond, *Review of Dr. Bushnell's "God in Christ"* (Bangor: E. F. Duren, 1849).

Of those critics of Bushnell who were also his contemporaries, at present the best known is Charles Hodge. For an overview of his thought see Mark A. Noll, ed., *The Way of Life* (New York: Paulist Press, 1987); and Mark A. Noll, ed., *The Princeton Theology, 1812-1921* (Grand

Rapids: Baker Book House, 1983). For a discussion of the continuing significance of the Bushnell controversy, see D. G. Hart, "Divided Between Heart and Mind: The Critical Period for Protestant Thought in America," *Journal of Ecclesiastical History* 38 (1987): 254-70; and D. G. Hart, "Poems, Propositions, and Dogma: The Controversy over Religious Language and the Demise of Theology in American Learning," *Church History* 57 (1988): 310-21.

CHAPTER EIGHT

Two works that add some detail to the California world Bushnell visited are Lionel Utley Ridout, *Renegade, Outcast, and Maverick: Three Episcopal Clergymen in the California Gold Rush* (San Diego: University Press, San Diego State University, 1973); and William G. Chrystal, "'A Beautiful Aceldama': Horace Bushnell in California, 1856-1857," *New England Quarterly* 57 (1984): 384-402. Andrew Jackson Davis's critique of Bushnell was recorded in *The Approaching Crisis: Being a Review of Dr. Bushnell's Recent Lectures on Supernaturalism* (New York: Published by the Author, 1852). Ann Braude, *Radical Spirits: Spiritualism and Women's Rights in Nineteenth-Century America* (Boston: Beacon Press, 1989), offers insight into Davis and the larger appeal of spiritualism.

The interpretation here of Bushnell's *Nature and the Supernatural* is based on two earlier studies: Robert Bruce Mullin, "Horace Bushnell and the Question of Miracles," *Church History* 58 (1989): 460-73; and Robert Bruce Mullin, *Miracles and the Modern Religious Imagination* (New Haven: Yale University Press, 1996).

On the question of the miracles of the New Testament see R. H. Fuller, *Interpreting the Miracles* (Philadelphia: Westminster Press, 1963); Gerd Theissen, *The Miracle Stories of the Early Christian Tradition*, trans. Francis McDonagh (Edinburgh: T&T Clark, 1983); and for background, Howard Clark Kee, *Miracle in the Early Christian World: A Study in Sociohistorical Method* (New Haven: Yale University Press, 1983).

For a typical Catholic defense of modern miracles, see "De Notis Ecclesiae," in Roberti Cardinalis Bellarmini, *Opera Omnia . . .* , 6 vols. (Naples, 1856-62), 2:132ff. For Protestant ideas see Martin Luther, "Sermons on the Gospel of St. John: Chapters 14-16," in *Luther's Works*, ed.

Jaroslav Pelikan and Daniel E. Poellet, 55 vols. (St. Louis: Concordia Publishing House, 1958-86), 24:181. On John Calvin, see "Prefatory Address to King Francis," in *Institutes of the Christian Religion*, ed. John T. McNeill, trans. Ford Lewis Battles, 2 vols. (Philadelphia: Westminster Press, 1960), 1:16. For an extended discussion of Calvin's views see John Mark Ruthven, "On the Cessation of the Charismata: The Protestant Polemic of Benjamin B. Warfield" (Ph.D. diss., Marquette University, 1989), pp. 21-62. See, too, D. P. Walker, "The Cessation of Miracles," in *Hermeticism and the Renaissance: Intellectual History and the Occult in Early Modern Europe*, ed. Ingrid Merkel and Allen G. Debus (Washington: Folger Shakespeare Library, 1988), pp. 111-24; and D. P. Walker, *Unclean Spirits: Possession and Exorcism in France and England in the Late Sixteenth and Early Seventeenth Centuries* (Philadelphia: University of Pennsylvania Press, 1981), pp. 72-73.

For discussions of the idea of providence from the classic Reformed perspective, see Heinrich Heppe, *Reformed Dogmatics: Set Out and Illustrated from the Sources*, revised and ed. Ernst Bizer, trans. G. T. Thomson (Grand Rapids: Baker Book House, 1978), pp. 251-67. William Sherlock, *A Discourse Concerning the Divine Providence* (London: William Rogers, 1694), shows how the subject was interpreted by late-seventeenth-century Anglicans. For an analysis of the implications of providence see Perry Miller, *The New England Mind: The Seventeenth Century* (Boston: Beacon Press, 1961), pp. 227-31. For a discussion of its role in popular religious thought see Keith Thomas, *Religion and the Decline of Magic: Studies in Popular Beliefs in Sixteenth- and Seventeenth-Century England* (London: Weidenfield and Nicolson, 1971).

On the interest in signs and wonders in Puritan New England see Increase Mather, *An Essay for Recording of Illustrious Providences . . . Especially in New-England* (Boston: Samuel Green, 1684); and for a discussion of the phenomenon see David D. Hall, *Worlds of Wonder, Days of Judgment: Popular Religious Belief in Early New England* (Cambridge, Mass.: Harvard University Press, 1990); and Jon Butler, *Awash in a Sea of Faith: Christianizing the American People* (Cambridge, Mass.: Harvard University Press, 1990).

David Hume made his famous critique of the miraculous in *An Inquiry Concerning Human Understanding;* an easily accessible edition is the one edited and with an introduction by Charles W. Hendel (Indianapolis: Bobbs-Merrill, 1955). On Hume's argument, see R. M. Burns,

The Great Debate on Miracles: From Joseph Glanvill to David Hume (Lewisburg, Pa.: Bucknell University Press, 1981).

The standard account of the nineteenth-century antebellum American Protestant view of the relation between science and religion is Theodore Dwight Bozeman, *Protestants in an Age of Science: The Baconian Ideal and Ante-Bellum American Religious Thought* (Chapel Hill, N.C.: University of North Carolina Press, 1977). See, too, Walter H. Conser Jr., *God and the Natural World: Religion and Science in Antebellum America* (Columbia, S.C.: University of South Carolina Press, 1993). On counter-themes, see Conrad Cherry, *Nature and Religious Imagination: From Edwards to Bushnell* (Philadelphia: Fortress Press, 1980). The literature on Transcendentalist critiques of this compromise between science and religion is enormous, but among the best general surveys are Octavius Brooks Frothingham, *Transcendentalism in New England: A History* (1876; reprint, New York: Harper, 1959); William R. Hutchison, *The Transcendentalist Ministers: Church Reform in the New England Renaissance* (New Haven: Yale University Press, 1959); Paul F. Boller Jr., *American Transcendentalism, 1830-1860: An Intellectual Inquiry* (New York: Putnam, 1974); and Catherine L. Albanese, *Corresponding Motion: Transcendental Religion and the New America* (Philadelphia: Temple University Press, 1977). The classic account of the dispute over miracles is Hutchison, *The Transcendentalist Ministers*, pp. 52-137. Many of the documents of the debate can be found in Perry Miller, ed., *The Transcendentalists: An Anthology* (Cambridge, Mass.: Harvard University Press, 1950).

Bushnell used Louis Agassiz as his scientific authority. He quoted from Agassiz's *An Essay on Classification*, which was originally published as the introduction to *Contributions to the Natural History of the United States* (Boston: Little, Brown and Co., 1857). On Agassiz's view of evolution, see Edward Lurie, *Louis Agassiz: A Life in Science* (Chicago: University of Chicago Press, 1960), pp. 252-303; and Peter J. Bowler, *Evolution: The History of an Idea*, rev. ed. (Berkeley: University of California Press, 1989), pp. 126-29. On Bushnell and evolution, see Thomas Paul Thigpen, "On the Origin of Theses: An Exploration of Horace Bushnell's Rejection of Darwinism," *Church History* 57 (1988): 499-513.

The Scottish miracles involving the brothers James and George MacDonald and a "Miss Fancourt" were a great issue of debate within evangelical circles in the early 1830s. Their integrity was upheld by the Irvingite *Morning Watch or Quarterly Journal on Prophecy, and Theological Review* (which was Bushnell's source). The criticism of them was led by the *Christian Observer,* which was the source Bushnell alluded to in the text. See (American edition) 41 (1831): 99 ff. This is based on John Howie, *Biographia Scoticana: or A Brief Historical Account of . . . Scots Worthies,* 2nd ed. (Glasgow: W. R. M'Phun, 1827).

The controversial nature of Bushnell's "solution" is discussed in Robert Bruce Mullin, "Horace Bushnell and the Question of Miracles," *Church History* 58 (1989): 468-71. For a classic later liberal appropriation of some of the elements of *Nature and the Supernatural,* see George A. Gordon, *Religion and Miracle* (London: James Clark, 1910). For an appeal to Bushnell by an early proponent of faith healing, see A. J. Gordon, *The Ministry of Healing, or Miracle Cures in All Ages* (Boston: F. H. Revell, 1882). On the widespread interest in the experience of religious reality among both liberal and proto-Pentecostals see Grant Wacker, "The Holy Spirit and the Spirit of the Age in American Protestantism, 1880-1910," *Journal of American History* 72 (1985): 45-62.

CHAPTER NINE

Each of Bushnell's Civil War essays is most easily available in volumes of his collected works. "Reverses Needed" is republished in *The Spirit in Man: Sermons and Selections* (New York: Charles Scribner's Sons, 1903). "The Doctrine of Loyalty" is found in *Work and Play; or Literary Varieties,* rev. ed. (New York: Charles Scribner's Sons, 1881). "Popular Government by Divine Right" is reprinted in *Building Eras in Religion* (New York: Charles Scribner's Sons, 1881). And "Our Obligation to the Dead" is also found in *Building Eras in Religion.* This last address is also abridged and reprinted in Conrad Cherry, ed., *God's New Israel: Religious Interpretations of American Destiny,* rev. ed. (Chapel Hill, N.C.: University of North Carolina Press, 1998).

The question of the churches, slavery, and the crisis of Union has been approached in so many ways that any suggestion for sources must be in part serendipitous. On the broader question of slavery, see C. Duncan Rice, *The Rise and Fall of Black Slavery* (New York: Harper and Row, 1975); John Hope Franklin and Alfred A. Moss Jr., *From Slav-*

ery to Freedom, 8th ed. (New York: Alfred A. Knopf, 2000); and Eric Foner, *Slavery and Freedom in Nineteenth-Century America* (New York: Oxford University Press, 1994). On the Christian response to slavery, see James D. Essig, *The Bonds of Wickedness: American Evangelicals Against Slavery, 1770-1808* (Philadelphia: Temple University Press, 1982); C. C. Goen, *Broken Churches, Broken Nation: Denominational Schisms and the Coming of the American Civil War* (Macon, Ga.: Mercer University Press, 1985); and John R. McKivigan and Mitchell Snay, eds., *Religion and the Antebellum Debate Over Slavery* (Athens: University of Georgia Press, 1998). Kenneth M. Stampp, *And the War Came: The North and the Secession Crisis, 1860-61* ([Baton Rouge]: Louisiana State University Press, 1950), is still the masterful account of the twilight period between Southern secession and the firing upon Fort Sumter. George M. Fredrickson, *The Inner Civil War: Northern Intellectuals and the Crisis of Union* (New York: Harper Torch Books, 1968), offers insights into Northern intellectuals (including Bushnell); and James H. Moorhead, *American Apocalypse: Yankee Protestants and the Civil War, 1860-1869* (New Haven: Yale University Press, 1978), acutely describes Northern clerical attitudes toward the war.

William A. Clebsch, "Baptism of Blood: A Study of Christian Contributions to the Interpretation of the Civil War in American History" (Th.D. diss., Union Theological Seminary, 1957), is still the best analysis of Bushnell's wartime writings. Of similar quality is the discussion in Sydney E. Ahlstrom, *A Religious History of the American People* (New Haven: Yale University Press, 1972), and Ahlstrom's essay "Comment on the Essay of Professor Clebsch: History, Bushnell, and Lincoln," *Church History* 30 (1961): 223-30. For other aspects of Bushnell and the crisis of union, see Howard A. Barnes, *Horace Bushnell and the Virtuous Republic* (Metuchen, N.J.: Scarecrow Press, 1991); as well as his earlier essay, "The Idea That Caused a War: Horace Bushnell versus Thomas Jefferson," *Journal of Church and State* 16 (1974): 73-83. A thorny question for historians has been Bushnell's attitudes concerning race. For different interpretations see Charles C. Cole, "Horace Bushnell and the Slavery Question," *New England Quarterly* 23 (1950): 19-30; Ralph E. Luker, "Bushnell in Black and White: Evidence of the 'Racism' of Horace Bushnell," *New England Quarterly* 45 (1972): 408-16; and Louis Weeks, "Horace Bushnell on Black America," *Religious Education* 68 (1973): 28-41. For some broader considerations of race theory at the time, see George M. Fredrickson, *The Black Image in the White Mind: The Debate on Afro-American Character and Destiny, 1817-1914* (New York: Harper and Row, 1971); and Curtis R. Grant, "The Social Gospel and Race" (Ph.D. diss., Stanford University, 1968).

Bushnell's theory of atonement elicited discussion both at the time of its publication and since. For very different contemporary interpretations, see W. W. Andrews, *Remarks on Dr. Bushnell's 'Vicarious Sacrifice'* (Hartford: Case, Lockwood and Co., 1866); Oliver S. Taylor, *Dr. Bushnell's Orthodoxy, or an Inquiry Whether the Factors of the Atonement Are Recognized in His 'Vicarious Atonement'* (New Haven: E. Hayes, 1867); James Freeman Clarke, "Bushnell on Vicarious Sacrifice," *Christian Examiner* 80, n.s. 1 (1866): 360-77; and Henry James Sr., "Review of *The Vicarious Sacrifice*," *North American Review* 102 (1866): 556-71. For later assessments see F. W. Dillistone, *The Christian Understanding of the Atonement* (Philadelphia: Westminster Press, 1968); H. R. Mackintosh, *The Christian Experience of Forgiveness* (London: Nisbet and Co., 1927); L. W. Grensted, ed., *The Atonement in History and Life* (New York: Macmillan Publishing Co., 1929); and R. W. Dale, *The Atonement*, 23rd ed. (London: Congregational Union of England and Wales, 1904).

CHAPTER TEN

"Inspiration by the Holy Spirit" is found in *The Spirit in Man: Sermons and Selections* (New York: Charles Scribner's Sons, 1903).

On the new social milieu of postbellum America, see John Tomsich, *A Genteel Endeavor: American Culture and Politics in the Gilded Age* (Stanford: Stanford University Press, 1971); Lewis O. Saum, *The Popular Mood of America, 1860-1890* (Lincoln: University of Nebraska Press, 1990); Ellsworth Strong Grant and Marion Hepburn, *The City of Hartford, 1784-1984: An Illustrated History* ([Hartford]: Connecticut Historical Society, 1986); Burton J. Bledstein, *The Culture of Professionalism: The Middle Class and the Development of Higher Education in America* (New York: W. W. Norton and Co., 1976); and Mark Twain and Charles Dudley Warner, *The Gilded Age: A Tale of To-day* (New York: Penguin, 1994).

Of the new scientific trends none was more far-reaching than

Darwinism, and on this topic the literature is legion. The best, and most provocative, biography is Adrian Desmond and James Moore, *Darwin* (New York: Warner Books, 1991). Still one of the most thoughtful studies is Gertrude Himmelfarb, *Darwin and the Darwinian Revolution* (London: Chatto and Windus, 1959). On the religious impact, James R. Moore, *The Post-Darwinian Controversies: A Study of the Protestant Struggle to Come to Terms with Darwin in Great Britain and America* (Cambridge: Cambridge University Press, 1979), is the best general study, while Jon H. Roberts, *Darwinism and the Divine in America: Protestant Intellectuals and Organic Evolution, 1859-1900* (Madison: University of Wisconsin Press, 1988), and Ronald Numbers, *Darwinism Comes to America* (Cambridge, Mass.: Harvard University Press, 1998), are the most complete accounts of the American debate. On the movement toward "free religion" among Unitarians, see Sydney E. Ahlstrom and Robert Bruce Mullin, *The Scientific Theist: A Life of Francis Ellingwood Abbot* (Macon, Ga.: Mercer University Press, 1987); and Stow Persons, *Free Religion: An American Faith* (New Haven: Yale University Press, 1948).

The literature on gender, feminism and suffrage is impressive both in size and quality. On gender and feminism, see Rosalind Rosenberg, *Beyond Separate Spheres: Intellectual Roots of Modern Feminism* (New Haven: Yale University Press, 1982); Mary P. Ryan, *Womanhood in America: From Colonial Times to the Present*, 3rd ed. (New York: Franklin Watts, 1983); Linda K. Kerber and Jane Sherron De Hart, eds., *Women's America: Refocusing the Past*, 5th ed. (New York: Oxford University Press, 2000); and Amanda Porterfield, *Feminine Spirituality in America: From Sarah Edwards to Martha Graham* (Philadelphia: Temple University Press, 1980). On suffrage, see Anne Firor Scott and Andrew MacKay Scott, *One Half the People: The Fight for Woman Suffrage* (Urbana: University of Illinois Press, 1982); Mari Jo and Paul Buhle, eds., *The Concise History of Woman Suffrage: Selections from the Classic Work of Stanton, Anthony, Gage and Harper* (Urbana: University of Illinois Press, 1978); and Keith E. Melder, *Beginnings of Sisterhood: The American Woman's Rights Movement, 1800-1850* (New York: Schocken Books, 1977).

The movement of Protestant theology in the decades after the death of Bushnell is recorded in John W. Buckham, *Progressive Religious Thought in America: A Survey of the Enlarging Pilgrim Faith* (Boston:

Houghton Mifflin, 1919); Alexander Viets Griswold Allen, *The Continuity of Christian Thought* (Boston: Houghton Mifflin, 1884); Frank Hugh Foster, *The Modern Movement in American Theology: Sketches in the History of American Protestant Thought from the Civil War to the World War* (New York: Fleming H. Revell, 1939); Daniel Day Williams, *The Andover Liberals* (New York: Kings Crown Press, 1941); Washington Gladden, *Recollections* (Boston: Houghton Mifflin, 1909); and Benjamin W. Bacon, *Theodore Thornton Munger: New England Minister* (New Haven: Yale University Press, 1913). For contrasting claims over whether Bushnell was Ritschlian or Schleiermachian in his theology, see George B. Stevens, "Horace Bushnell and Albrecht Ritschl: A Comparison," *American Journal of Theology* 6 (1902): 35-56; and Walter M. Horton, *Realistic Theology* (New York: Harper and Bros., 1934).

Philosophical developments are traced in Woodbridge Riley, *American Thought: From Puritanism to Pragmatism and Beyond* (1915; reprint, New York: Peter Smith, 1941); Barbara MacKinnon, ed., *American Philosophy: An Historical Anthology* (Albany: State University of New York Press, 1985); Paul W. Kurtz, ed., *American Thought Before 1900: A Sourcebook from Puritanism to Darwinism* (New York: Macmillan Publishing Co., 1966); Herbert W. Schneider, *A History of American Philosophy*, 2nd ed. (New York: Columbia University Press, 1963); and Elizabeth Flower and Murray Murphey, *A History of Philosophy in America*, 2 vols. (New York: Putnam, 1977); and none of these studies mention Bushnell. For the interest in Bushnell's theory of language among students of general semantics in the late 1940s, see Wayne C. Minnick, "Horace Bushnell: Precursor of General Semantics," *ETC.: A Review of General Semantics* 5 (1948): 246-51; and Sherman Paul, "Horace Bushnell Reconsidered," *ETC.: A Review of General Semantics* 6 (1949): 255-59. In the field of literary criticism Bushnell does play a key role in Charles Feidelson, *Symbolism and American Literature* (Chicago: University of Chicago Press, 1953). See, too, Philip F. Gura, *The Wisdom of Words: Language, Theology, and Literature in the New England Renaissance* (Middletown, Conn.: Wesleyan University Press, 1981). For background to Literary Symbolism, see Edmund Wilson, *Axel's Castle: A Study of the Imaginative Literature of 1870-1930* (1931; New York: Charles Scribner's Sons, 1947).

Index